Dysfunctional Culture

The Inadequacy of
Cultural Liberalism as a
Guide to Major Challenges
of the 21st Century

Sigurd N. Skirbekk

UNIVERSITY PRESS OF AMERICA,® INC.
Lanham • Boulder • New York • Toronto • Oxford

Copyright © 2005 by
University Press of America,® Inc.
4501 Forbes Boulevard
Suite 200
Lanham, Maryland 20706
UPA Acquisitions Department (301) 459-3366

PO Box 317
Oxford
OX2 9RU, UK

Library of Congress Control Number: 2005924199
ISBN 0-7618-3060-X (clothbound : alk. ppr.)
ISBN 0-7618-3061-8 (paperback : alk. ppr.)

Contents

Foreword

Dysfunctional Culture is a new book, even though some chapters have been extracted from a book published in 1999 in Norwegian under the title *Ideologi, myte og tro ved slutten av et arhundre. Sosiologisk kulturteori og funksjonsanalyse.* It received favorable reviews in Norway and in other Nordic Countries.

Several people have asked me to write an English version of the book in order to reach a wider audience. The original text has been abridged and new chapters have been added. The original book's underlying theme, which discusses the functional adequacy or inadequacy of contemporary liberal culture and morality, has by no means lost its relevance during the last few years.

Many colleagues have provided both constructive criticism and inspiration. I would like to thank them all.

This publication has being supported by a program at the University of Oslo for research and actualization of ethical issues.

Oslo, Christmas 2004
Sigurd Skirbekk

Preface

The title of this book is "Dysfunctional Culture." The manuscript was originally written to demonstrate how studies of contemporary culture can be based on analytical concepts derived from recycled sociological theory. Culture is not just another name for social life or esthetic experiences. Culture is the way we collectively structure our concepts of reality and of moral judgments. If we have no analytical concepts for recognizing our culture, we will be incapable of correcting our outlook when necessary. Cultural correction may be necessary when new social and environmental challenges manifest themselves, or when we encounter other civilizations with patterns of collective understanding far removed from ours.

Cultural studies have always contained hermeneutic traditions that focus on entity study, such as "ideology" and "myth" in certain texts and from certain spokesmen, to clarify the topic of discussion. However, developing universal theories on how these entities function in modern society without providing any analytical definitions has been no easy task, nor has knowing how to allow positive and negative ideological references to safeguard our points of reference.

For almost two generations, the liberal West was able to regard the ideology of the socialist East as the primary counterforce to its own cultural point of reference. After the West had been declared the winner of this contest, the natural reaction of many westerners was to regard their own culture as superior in every respect, and to assume that prevailing liberal ideas would serve as the crucial framework in future adjustments. However, climatic changes, indicating a conflict between ecological systems and an anthropocentric morale, and signs of inadequate biological and cultural reproductive systems suggest that liberal ideas are indeed limited. The same could be said of the threat from terrorists who, besides their own personal fanaticism, often share references to non-western cultures.

Experts within the cultural and social sciences will benefit from an analytical discussion of the concept of ideology. These discussions could boost shared knowledge of the functional potential as well as limitations of contemporary liberalism—which is often assumed to be the modernist culture. Even though this book is written primarily with students of the social sciences in mind, others should find it interesting as well.

Our discussion of new liberalism as an ideology is based partly on a critical reading of literature on ideologies and partly on research carried out by the author and others. Admittedly, a certain amount of personal experience has also played a role. For several decades, the author has personally lived through a traditional conservative society, a national-socialist society, a social democratic society (interrupted by brief stays in European and Asian countries with Marxist governments), and then the new liberal society. For those of us with this kind of experience under our belts, it seems obvious that the validity of most political ideologies is historically relative, and that this also conforms to contemporary anti-authoritarian ideas of individual rights. It might be hard for people who lived through a Nazi occupation to fully accept the popular notion that the spirit of individual liberty was the force that decisively defeated the Nazi regime. Societies following lop-sided principles of liberal rule were at that time easily overcome. Ultimately, it became obvious that even democracy needed moral discipline and a collective orientation in order to survive. However, even the principle of historic relativity of ideas has its limitations. Functional measurements for collective survival do not have to be so relativistic.

This book consists of two parts: a theoretical section, in which certain key concepts of cultural analysis are discussed, and a second section, in which these concepts are employed to analyze recent moral challenges concerning family formation and reproduction. A more detailed presentation of the intentions and organization of the book can be found under the heading "Approach" at the end of Chapter one.

This book was published with funding from NORLA non-fiction.

Chapter One

From 11/9 to 9/11

11/9: THE NOTION OF WESTERN VICTORY

November 9, 1989 will go down as one of the most memorable days in western history. On this day, the Berlin Wall was torn down, which was such an earth-shattering event in terms of political development that it led to the fall of the so-called Iron Curtain between the Eastern Block and the West. There was no turning back after this. The move toward German reunification was inexorable; the dissolution of the Warsaw Pact was just around the corner; the fragmentation of the Soviet Union was well underway, ultimately leading to an elected government and market economy in Russia. And it wasn't long before a number of former East Bloc countries were clamoring to join NATO and the EU.

In 1989, western politicians had every reason to celebrate. 1989 saw the end of the Cold War; it spelt victory for the dominant political agenda of the West. The critics of this policy, who had maintained the necessity of military intervention also in central Europe, championing the need to give up capitalism and western democracy and pass legislation to accommodate a socialist takeover, had been proven wrong. The West had won by the sheer virtue of its inner strength.

The West won not only because of its unrivalled technology and vast economic and military resources, but because it encompassed some of the most open, democratic, and humanistic societies on Earth. "Good" had conquered "Evil." The victory of the West was deemed just.

Furthermore, 1989 would be remembered not only as the year of western liberal democracy's victory over the Warsaw Pact, but also as the final victory

1

in a series of struggles against various kinds of autocratic societies: traditional right-wing societies, fascist societies, totalitarian Nazi societies, minor Marxist societies, and finally the superpower of the Soviet Union. Those who regarded the West as the epitome of strength and contemporaneity found much to support their view.

1989 was a year of victory for the liberal cultural of the West, even from a broad historical perspective. It was the bicentenary of the beginning of the French Revolution, which saw the birth of the political manifesto: *Liberté, egalité, fraternité.* This was the year when human rights were touted as part of the heritage of the French Revolution and the American Declaration of Independence. A common feature of the heritage of the French and American revolutions was the belief that different sets of benefits would exert a similar kind of influence. Enlightenment and liberty, democracy and economic prosperity, peace and tolerance were all regarded as values that would reinforce each other and thus make progress a known quantity. Even though this notion has been criticized by many over the past 200 years, it took on an air of reality in 1989—in the West, at any rate.

But in eastern Europe, developments during the years that followed were nowhere near as rosy. Russia experienced severe economic and political problems, and people's standard of living plunged during the 1990s. Crime soared, and many mafia organizations became entrenched. As the central government grew weaker, uprisings occurred in several of the former Soviet republics as they made a grab at independence.

But if things were going badly in Russia, they were going even worse in Yugoslavia, the country which, in Tito's heyday, sought to carry the banner for a third way between East and West. Yugoslavia staggered under the burden of political disintegration, civil war and military intervention. The 1990s were a time of war in other parts of the world, as well. There were armed conflicts in the Caucasus, the Middle East, Africa, and southern Asia.

In spite of all the frustration that followed in the wake of these conflicts, the conflicts themselves were not considered a challenge to the West's firm belief that it had discovered the road to progress. It was fairly easy to interpret these wars as manifestations of the policies of evil men and outmoded social systems. In the former Soviet Union, wars were often regarded as a revolt against an autocratic political system; in Yugoslavia, as a manifestation of ethnic nationalism; in the Middle East, as a manifestation of religious fanaticism; in Asia, as a manifestation of feudal traditions; in Africa, as a manifestation of post-colonial aggression and political immaturity. In other words, wars could be explained as the absence of modern liberal culture and forms of democratic government. Viewed in this light, such conflicts tended to confirm, rather than call into question, the accepted view that liberal culture was somehow superior.

The cultural aspect of the West's sense of superiority expressed itself in a variety of ways. The media began to harp on the individual's right to choose, as opposed to a nation's right to develop particular forms of culture. Major political projects, such as the EU, were viewed as something more than mere economic cooperation across national borders. Undermining national sovereignty and expanding the supranational market were said to promote peace and strengthen the individual's freedom of choice—a key liberal goal. Membership in the EU was made contingent on candidates having a market economy, on democracy, and on respect for human rights as defined by international government agencies.

The 1990s bore the marks of the liberal culture not just in the tales of politicians and the media. Philosophers and scientists, who are usually quite critical of prevailing power structures, added their voices as well. Social scientists could now confidently say that never before in history had democracy been as entrenched worldwide as it was at the end of the 20th century. Even those who had once distrusted the purported benefits of a multi-party system began to write about the advance of democracy in countries with a history of strong authoritarian traditions. As early as 1987, the sociologist Peter Berger became a pioneer in his field when he wrote that capitalism was superior to its competitors.[1] Not only was it an economic powerhouse, it was also superior in terms of political freedom and social equality, and was even an agent in mitigating environmental disasters.

Later, David Conway, a professor of philosophy, described classical western liberalism as "the unvanquished ideal."[2] The philosopher Richard Rorty, who was often critical on general principles, claimed that contemporary liberal society possessed the institutions for its own betterment and that western social and political thought had already undergone the last of the conceptual revolutions that were a prerequisite for continued development.[3]

One could almost say that Arnold Toynbee was right when, in the middle of the 20th century, he wrote that western European civilization was the only surviving civilization of our times with a modern development potential.[4]

So overwhelming did the victory of the West appear to be, that some saw it as the realization of the goal of history. The American historian Frances Fukuyama wrote: "What we may be witnessing is not just the end of the Cold War or the passing of a particular period of post-war history, but the end of history as such: that is, the end point of mankind's ideological evolution and the universalization of western liberal democracy as a final form of human government."[5]

9/11: THE NOTION OF THREAT

What happened on September 11, 2001 was a profound shock, not just to the United States but to the entire western World. This initial reaction was understandable. The fact that one country's key military and financial centers had become the target of unprovoked attacks in peacetime was bound to provoke a strong reaction. What is less obvious is the nature of those reactions.

Since the attack could be traced back to a handful of terrorists connected to the al-Qaida organization, it was only reasonable that an attempt should be made to disarm them. The war against the Taliban regime in Afghanistan, where al Qaida had training camps, can be defended as a fitting reaction to this challenge. The same can be said about the various security measures designed to keep terrorists from entering the US and other western countries and prevent them from committing further terrorist acts. But this doesn't tell the whole story.

The American assessments of the terror attacks on the Pentagon and the World Trade Center cannot be explained in terms of the attacks themselves. There is a background of a century of history here. It has been estimated that approx. 170 million people have been killed as a result of political decisions in addition to casualties of war on the battlefield. So a terrorist act that costs a few thousand people their lives is not all that conspicuous when viewed in this light.

Many Europeans, as well as people of other nationalities who have experienced war and terror at close quarters, have said they felt the Americans overreacted to the events of September 11. Americans, to some extent, have been accused of being spoiled, since there has not been a war on US territory for quite some time.

Accusations like these are not necessarily fair. Rather than overreacting, Americans might just as well be accused of not having taken terrorism seriously enough. Nor do we get a true picture of the facts when we are told that Americans are unfamiliar with violence and war. Americans have participated in wars and suffered casualties in different parts of the world in every decade of the last century. The entire period of the Cold War was, in fact, a preparation for the worst. Nevertheless, the site of the Twin Towers was called Ground Zero, as though we were dealing with a unique event that marked the emergence of a new era.

Nor does the internal criticism directed toward the national government in Washington seem to cover the whole perspective. After President Bush had established the Department of Homeland Security to coordinate security measures against new terrorist attacks, and following his declaration of "either you are for us or against us," an organized outcry arose against this policy, particularly from 67 well-known and lesser-known Americans. In this outcry, the so-called Patriot Act and other aspects of the new official policy were decried as suppression of the rights of the opposition. "We will not exchange our consciences for empty promises about security," they said. They quoted many examples from American history, where people had pitted their consciences against official policy—from those who had fought against slavery to those who had opposed the Vietnam War by refusing military service or by taking sides with conscientious objectors.

American officialdom exploited its tradition for patriotic mobilization against the forces that represented a threat to the country. For its part, the opposition exploited a tradition of moral protest based on the principle that a free country had to offer its citizens the right to follow their consciences. In addition, a number of people said that the US would have to expect to make enemies among Muslims on account of its support for Israel, and among poor countries on account of its one-sided capitalistic globalization policies.

More could be said about this criticism. But no matter what kind of negative picture we may care to paint, this hardly constitute a convincing diagnosis of the events of September 11. It is just as hard to find logical, unambiguous financial or political explanations for the attacks on New York and Washington as it is to find explanations based on the same premises for the suicide attacks in Israel.

The United States, and the West in general, were unquestionably faced with enemies bent on committing acts of destruction. But the enemy was invisible, not the kind of opponent you could square off with in a standard war. Nor was it the kind of opponent that would tolerate neutralization by an inner moral criticism of American politics, not even perhaps by reference to dubious aspects of American foreign policy.

The enemy could perhaps be called extremist or fanatical. In recent years, the term fundamentalist has enjoyed popularity. But this term doesn't tell us all that much, except for the fact that the West was being confronted by people who did not share the liberal orientation that the West had just finished celebrating as the victorious form of culture. The enemy was not merely invisible; it also came across as incomprehensible—and thus all the more threatening.

A CULTURAL CHALLENGE

The shock resonating from the events of September 11 can be understood as a contrast to the cockiness and optimism in the wake of November 9. Up to a point, these reactions can be compared with the British reaction after the tragic sinking of the Titanic. The Titanic represented state-of-the-art technology in her day; she was supposed to be unsinkable, but the contrary proved true. Likewise America, assumed to be the best-protected country in the world, proved to be more vulnerable than anyone had previously imagined.

But the subsequent shock expressed more than just a rude awakening from a pleasant dream to a brutal reality. The terrorists were not only a reminder that America had enemies, or that these enemies had succeeded in mounting a terrorist attack on American soil. The menacing image was so powerful and effective because it seemed so inconceivable, in spite of all its diagnostic characteristics.

Terrorist acts had been committed by people who didn't think and feel the way Americans did. And when people think, feel and make assessments in line with specific collective patterns, we are dealing with some kind of cultural difference. Once we realize this, it should be obvious that American, or western, culture is not universal, since not everyone shares it. People in different parts of the world have unique cultural frames of references, even though they may share the technological know-how behind airplanes and explosives.

This means that trying to provide explanations for the events of September 11 without taking these cultural differences into account is unrealistic.[6] We are not merely dealing with social differences and disparities on a national level, but rather differences in civilizations. National sovereignty has assumed less importance, and increased contact with various parts of the world has not automatically led to fewer world conflicts. On the contrary; it might seem that we are experiencing a "clash of civilizations."

Islamic civilization is not the only civilization that can conflict with current western ideals. The potential for conflict with the West is also present in the Indian and East-Asian civilizations, as well as in several features of Latin American and African culture. In many parts of the world there are people who react strongly to what they perceive as imperialism, economic exploitation, or cultural and moral subversion. Even though most of these people are unlikely to act on their thoughts or impulses, some might do so.

Leading western countries can also expect to encounter opposition and strong reactions from others besides those groups that are not oriented toward western civilization. Many western groups, for instance, find "Americanization" provocative. The most conspicuous opposition comes from various left-wing groups, which view American-dominated liberal principles as an ideology that secretly harbors both economic self-interests and social oppression, especially in countries and regions with a scarcity of resources. But even from conservative quarters, protests can be heard—and not just "right-wing" conservatism, either. One could say that liberalism that is adapted to a market-governed economy is certainly not adapted to all key institutions in differentiated societies, such as religious opinions, moral socialization, family formation, and reproduction over a period of generations.

CHALLENGED BY FOREIGN TERRORISTS
OR BY OUR OWN CULTURE

Ground Zero is a symbol not only of American technological vulnerability, but of cultural vulnerability as well. A country with no elite that can explain why America's politics, its economy and media-promoted lifestyle triggers unintended reactions in other parts of the world is a country lacking in cultural preparedness.

Public reaction in the wake of September 11 tells us not just about a warning system against potential assassins that had failed. What we are dealing with here is a striking lack of understanding as to why America is the object of so much hatred, in view of the fact that Americans themselves feel they represent universal values of welfare and peace, democracy and tolerance.

A fundamental rule in the study of culturally initiated conflicts is that we must be able to distinguish between intentions, which may be good in one culture, and interpretations, which may be less favorably regarded by people with different cultural points of reference. We find the most systematic differences between cultural references among civilizations based on different religious and social outlooks. Civilizationist Samuel Huntington foresaw the lines of conflict that would emerge after the Cold War; he said they would follow, not national boundaries, but the boundaries of civilization.[7] The greater the civilization gap, the greater the chance for conflict the parties cannot resolve by simple political means.

Civilizational boundaries have followed hot on the heels of almost all serious international conflicts that have arisen after the fall of the Berlin Wall—between Muslim and the eastern Russia civilization; between Muslim and the western Afghan civilization; between Muslim and western-Jewish civilization in the Middle East; between Hindu and Muslim civilizations in Sri Lanka and in Kashmir; and between Muslim, eastern and western civilizations in Yugoslavia. Culture-based civilizational explanations are more help to us than those based solely on economic differences, or on the political contrasts between autocratic and liberal societies.

Even people residing in European countries might take a dim view of the American way of defending liberal principles on behalf of western civilization. Liberal spokesmen, who may try to legitimize their endeavor by resorting to slogans about democratic openness and multicultural ideals, often

seem to have difficulty accepting the limitations of their own hidebound orientation. These limitations apply not only to people suspected of harboring
economic or social interests, which could be legitimated by a new liberal social philosophy. Apparently we are dealing with well-established conceptions,
or a culture-based mind-set to which many are endeavoring to adapt.

More detailed studies of cultural forms and their limitations could help us understand why people in different cultural circles and civilizations develop situational understandings that give rise to a consuming hatred of the West. Studies
like these could also help explain why western leaders seem to understand so little about why their policies have unintended consequences for people with other
interpretive frames of reference. Cultural studies might also help explain the
premises for some of the mental blocks raised by western interpreters when they
refuse to contemplate the detrimental effects of their communications.

This suggests that we ought to take a closer look at cultural studies that promote better understanding of civilizations and ideological interpretive frameworks. We should ask whether the interpretations considered victorious after
November 11, 1989 have anything in common with those constrained ideologies that were once considered passé.

We could ask whether western reactions after 9/11 and 11/9 rest on ideological interpretations of world events, and whether a more satisfactory understanding would have to rise above the most typical ideologies of the times.

A THREAT TO A COUNTRY
OR A CHALLENGE TO A CIVILIZATION

We have just passed the threshold of a new century—not to mention a new
millennium—which will provide us with countless challenges that cannot be
satisfactorily met with the aid of culturally determined reactions handed
down from previous centuries.

In a sense, this goes without saying. No one expects the generation that is
alive at the start of a new century to have developed all the insight needed to
tackle the challenges that will arise later that century. But what many *do* believe, which is also reflected in people's reactions after November 9, is that
the new liberal culture in the West is inherently qualified to provide renewal
and adjustment. This is what Fukyama and others meant when they said that
history had come to an end—that is, that it would no longer be necessary to
develop new ideological frameworks for understanding future challenges ad-
equately. Merely subscribing to transparency, rationality, and democracy
would be enough to ensure the necessary cultural creativity and make sure
that the best is sorted out from the bad and that the best will carry the day.

We should question this smugness. If the new liberal culture can be shown to be encumbered by the same kind of mind-set as that of the older ideologies, then it is hard to see how an ideological renewal can emerge—much less win the day. Ideologies have self-immunizing characteristics that impede ideological excess, unless we can see through the relativity of ideologies.

All ideologies tend to focus attention on challenges that can be addressed within an ideological framework. A liberal ideology will attach particular emphasis to challenges associated with the circumstances of freedom, just as a conservative ideology will emphasize the conditions for order and hierarchy. Despite these limitations in the general political debate, it is possible, on an independent scientific basis, to arrive at certain challenges that cannot be avoided, whether they can be resolved within specific ideological frameworks or not.

This applies to a number of ecological challenges facing us in the new century. In the not-too-distant future we will witness a distinct clash of interests between a liberal culture on the one hand, with its praise for anthropocentric values, and natural resourses on the other. We can also foresee clashes between political ideas about our right to realize individual liberty, as long as one individual does not violate the rights of other individuals, and social entities that are dependent on a supraindividual morality that is obliged to limit the individual's freedom. We can also predict that coming generations will face demographic challenges unforeseen by those who formulated the articles on human rights. The imbalance in population growth between different peoples, and the relationship between the form of the family and reproduction, is bound to challenge a liberal culture that is partly responsible for defining family formation and reproduction in terms of individual rights.

It is not just that we have no pat answers to long-term ecological, moral, demographic and reproductive challenges. We could also say, with some justification, that it is going to be hard to find realistic solutions to these challenges within the framework of a liberal culture. Worse still, there is evidence that a liberal culture could wind up exacerbating these challenges, making them harder to resolve than necessary.

We are now approaching a critical perspective. Even though the culture and social philosophy that won the day in the wake of the Cold War can be viewed as superior in relation to Soviet-dominated forms of socialism—indeed, superior even to previous traditionalistic and radical right-wing challengers— this does not imply that it is equal to the task of coping with challenges that will arise later this century. The liberal culture's superiority could well prove to be a very relative thing indeed.

As to whether dominant forms of culture are adequate to enable people to see, structure and find satisfactory solutions to unavoidable challenges, we have already said that our focus must be on the consequences and ramifications, rather than the motives of various players. There are countless theories as to what constitutes a good society. But this doesn't mean that we have to start by trying to find some universal ideas about what kind of life is best. Not only will people from different civilizations have opposing views on this issue, but proving that a contemporary goal of one civilization is a common denominator for all human endeavors would be nigh well impossible. It can also be argued that every known form of culture is encumbered by so many serious limitations that maintaining a civilizational variation could prove crucial.

This also means there are limits as to how far we can apply a declaration on human rights as a general rule of thumb in bringing about an acceptable culture. For that matter, liberal interpretation of these rights is fraught with self-contradictions, including the declaration of equal rights for everyone, while all cultures are declared equal—or at least only judged on their own terms. If all cultures were morally equal, then all human beings, as individuals, would not have the same rights, because some cultures grant some men with more rights than other men and women. If, on the other hand, all men and women were granted equal human rights, all cultures could not then be regarded as equal, since cultures that acknowledge the equality of men must then be regarded as superior to those that do not.

The most serious objection to the liberal culture, however, is not about such ill-thought-out self-contradictions. To be more precise, it is the fact that liberal principles, in terms of their impact, are unsuitable for use in eco-systems or for promoting conditions for productive moral regulation.

An analysis of consequence, which involves determining whether a given culture tends to promote or to militate against vital systems, can be called a functional analysis. We should hasten to add that functional analyses do not rest on some precondition which states that societies or cultures are self-regulating systems. Most varieties of culture can be said to have both functional and dysfunctional effects. The question of whether specific forms of culture contribute to lasting forms of adjustment within ecological frameworks is more important than the question of whether a given form of culture commands majority support at any given time. This would suggest that a discussion on functionality must take center stage.

APPROACH

We intend to proceed step-by-step. In the next chapter, we will discuss several features of the sociological approach to cultural analysis, compared with cultural interpretations adapted to a natural science framework and to the more humanistic sciences. We will start with Edward Tylor's definition. Although it was written as early as in 1871, it might still prove useful.

We will discuss the difference between studying cultural structures and cultural systems. In a differentiated society, culture may consist of different structures and systems. If we can define parts of a culture as a system, we can also make explanatory use of that part. Some patterns of thought and some patterns of interest can confine ideologies as systems. Such ideologies can have a socially unifying and politically activating effect. But these ideologies are unlikely to be widely accepted unless they are supported by a broader and deeper system of trust. In this connection, systems of belief, associated with mythical narratives, may constitute key elements for cultural analysis. We will argue that sociology makes possible a functional analysis of the consequences of ideologies, over and beyond the intentions and considerations of their proponents.

In the next chapter, "Cultural Systems and Functionality," we will discuss our experiences with ideologies that lost ground during the last century. This includes *laissez faire* liberalism, or "the old liberalism"; fascism and National Socialism; authoritarian conservatism, and Marxist Socialism. Although all these ideologies arose in distinctly different ways and offered different sets of programs for their particular social philosophy, it is still possible to apply certain analytical criteria to them, enabling us to compare them. We would suggest that what might appear to be the greatest strength of an ideology—an uncomplicated conception of reality, with an appeal to the interests of activist groups, and an attendant self-immunizing neutralization of threatening criticism—is also its biggest weakness, not just because no ideology has accounted for all aspects of reality, but also because ideologies set the stage for their own downfall by opposing essential correctives in the face of external challenges.

We will ask whether our experience with the fall of ideologies is due to their innate characteristics. This would mean that classifying a commonplace world view as an ideology would also suggest an insight into the weakness of this particular mind-set. If so, we might even make some prediction about the kinds of challenges to which a system of thought and a complex of interests could be expected to find suitable solutions, and the kind of answers that are incompatible with this ideology and thus most likely to be avoided.

After the more theoretical and historically-oriented first section, the second section of the book deals with what some contemporary critics have gone on record as saying about the social trends of our time. We ask whether this can be explained as system-governed error adjustment or, more precisely, whether there is a relationship between new liberal premises for understanding society and various forms of dysfunctional adaptation. From the vantage point of general sociological theory, the claim can be made that modern societies need institutional guidelines in order to retain meaning and morality. There will be built-in limitations here, in a culture governed by ideology where the relationship between the individual and society is perceived in terms of "external relations."

In layman's terms, morality is usually associated with sexual morality and the formation of families. There are several reasons why such an association should be explored. The issue of whether a given society is capable of generating a family-oriented morality leads us directly to the matter of whether we are preserving family structures functional for that particular society's continued survival. The question of what constitutes functional or dysfunctional family forms can be analyzed in relation to what appears to promote moral solidarity, to what will ensure adequate reproduction, and to what benefits a primary socialization and the introduction of new families in a common culture. If family formation is perceived solely in terms of providing as much happiness as possible to as many individuals as possible in a contemporary generation, this must somehow relate to the inherent nature of a specific interpretation of modernity, rather than to modernity per se.

Since western families no longer reproduce their population at a rate that will ensure the continuation of our society for future generations, we look for explanations in the social structure to which people adapt, and in the cultural patterns that serve as their frame of reference. But not even the shocking statistics on the breakdown of the family and falling birth rates automatically led to a radical soul-searching as to whether there is something inherently wrong with the new liberal framework in contemporary western culture. One reason for this is that many see widespread immigration as a solution to a dwindling work force in future generations.

Many countries in the West have sought to compensate for falling birth rates with increased immigration from the South and East. But this approach is fraught with problems—partly because of conflicts between the native population and immigrants, and partly because of conflicts among different groups of immigrants. The notion that migration is justified as a means of improving living standards in the rich countries, and that poor countries do not have to work with determination to lower the rise in population, soon runs up against an ecological wall.

In light of this fact, we devote an entire chapter to familiar arguments in the so-called immigration debate. The pervasive focus on "racism" in this debate is no mere coincidence. The status of anti-racism in contemporary western culture can tell us a great deal about contemporary forms of cultural domination. Common forms of argumentation in a dominant anti-racist front can illustrate both the interdependence of and the differences between arguments based on research, those based on ideology, and those based on myths and beliefs.

Functional analyses often do little more than analyze the benefits of a given social system over a limited period of time. Nevertheless, in rounding off our functional analysis of contemporary liberal culture, we can also apply it to western societies at the civilizational level, and for a longer period of time. Analysis at the civilizational level can help us determine whether an ideological guide to cultural orientation will lead societies in a functional or a dysfunctional direction. Despite everything that western writers have written about the superiority of their civilization, there are clear indications that, relatively speaking, western civilization will ultimately lose out during the course of this century. In terms of ecology, the current world-wide population explosion, coupled with increased consumption and pollution levels in the wealthiest part of the world, all point to a critical situation in an absolute sense. This suggests that, instead of asking whether the rest of the world can come to grips with the western response to modernity, we should ask whether these answers will be considered modern for very long. If they are found to be dysfunctional with respect to vital challenges, the answer is "no."

NOTES

1. Peter Berger, *The Capitalist Revolution. Fifty Propositions about Prosperity, Equality and Liberty* (Aldershot: Gover, 1987).

2. David Conway, *Classical Liberalism. The Unvanquished Ideal* (New York: St. Martin Press, 1995).

3. Richard Rorty, *Contingency, Irony, and Solidarity* (Cambridge University Press., 1989), p. 63.

4. Arnold Toynbee, *A Study of History* (Oxford University Press, 1935).

5. Francis Fukuyama, *The End of History and the Last Man* (London: Hamilton, 1992), chp. 4: The Worldwide Liberal Revolution.

6. Amy Chua, *World on Fire. How Exporting Free Market Democracy Breeds Hatred and Global Inststability* (London: Random House, 2003).

7. Samuel P. Huntington, *The Clash of Civilizations and the Remaking of World Order* (New York: Simon & Schuster, 1996).

Chapter Two

Cultural Systems and Functionality

SOCIOLOGY AND THE CONCEPT OF CULTURE

The main subject of this book is whether dominant forms of contemporary culture are adequate for understanding and responding to the challenges of the 21st Century. This question calls for a general discussion of the concept of culture before we move on to examine the explanatory power of cultural systems, such as ideologies.

Even though all scholars agree on the basic meaning of the word "culture," which comes from the Latin verb *colere* and the noun *cultura*, the word is still versatile. In the natural sciences, culture might be construed in a very broad sense as everything formed by man in contrast to nature. In the humanistic sciences, or *Geisteswissenschaften,* culture has a more limited and qualitative meaning, often centered around art and philosophy.

The conception of culture within the social sciences has centered on definitions somewhere between these two extremes. Culture has been regarded as guiding symbols in social settings. In sociology, the term has usually been distinguished from social activity, and has therefore not encompassed everything man-made. The common approach to culture in the social sciences is Edward Burnett Tylor's descriptive definition from 1871: "Culture, or civilization, is that complex whole which includes knowledge, belief, art, morals, law, custom, and any other capabilities and habits acquired by man as a member of society."[1]

This definition focuses on rules for social actions rather than on concrete behavior itself. It encompasses more than what is qualitatively good, but is also more circumscribed than a cultural perception based on the distinction between nature and culture. It emphasizes the collective aspect of culture as something the individual learns as a member of a society. The reference to a complex "whole" can lead to a focus on the inner cohesiveness of culture in a given society.

In spite of this heritage, culture is defined in a variety of ways in the social sciences literature. Even within the confines of English literature, the authors Kroeber and Kluckhohn found 164 partly different definitions of the word as early as in 1952.[2] By the same token, not all these definitions are useful for systematic research—nor are all equally clear on philosophical problems relating to the ostensibly scientific nature of cultural studies.

Some researchers have restricted their study to that part of society which artists and politicians have dubbed the "cultural sector." Others have depicted culture as a virtual "life form." A life form is usually something learned, something acquired, something collective—something that characterizes a collective or specific social category of human beings, e.g. agrarian culture, youth culture or immigrant culture. Descriptions of these life forms can be employed to interpret specific traditions, in contrast to urban culture, class culture and national culture. In sociology, the study of identity markers can also serve as an operational approach to the study of culture as life forms.

However, the most common approach in the field of sociology involves analyzing culture as a collective system of symbols. Ideas, norms and emotional ideals are crucial to the way in which members of a given society perceive things and how they are collectively prone to react to their perceptions.

An analytical cultural concept, adapted to a model for differentiated societies, enables us to distinguish between different levels of explanations of human attitudes and actions. From an analytical point of view, culture serves as a collective framework for cognitive and moral orientation. In the theories of Talcott Parsons, cultural systems are distinguished from social systems, from personality, and from biological organisms. Where Freud had posited a simple three-part division between the id, the ego and the superego, with culture reduced to mere memories of paternal suppression, Parson's model opened the way for studies of cultural systems in their own right. And he did so in such a way that cultural systems could be broken down into differentiated subsystems.[3]

Sociological models are often built upon presuppositions of a necessary institutional differentiation in society. Such models can show that different institutions must be regulated by different sets of norms. It could be argued that all societies need cultural norms linked to the resolution of a set of important and recurring tasks. Furthermore, there are sound sociological reasons for why modernization has made these institutions more differentiated. It became important to distinguish between norms that are adapted to an economic institution, those adapted to a family situation, those adapted to political rule, and those adapted to religion and science. If a single institutionally-oriented type of norm were to dominate all aspects of society, this would create certain forms of anomaly. Modern societies cannot automatically be perceived as cohesive units with a single set of norms valid for all aspects of life.

In sociological theory, a given culture can be deconstructed in a variety of ways. Further on in the chapter, we will argue that ideologies, myths and systems of belief are meaningful units for understanding how culture functions in a social context. These units will prove useful, not only in providing a systematic overview of recurring means of orientation, but also in helping us determine whether a particular cultural pattern will be adequate in the long term. This means that functionality becomes a key indicator in the study of cultural systems.

Before more is said on culture and functionality, we ought to ask ourselves what potential sociologists have for analyzing cultural patterns in their own day and age. Many are doubtful about whether sociology can function as a discipline uniquely qualified to analyze culture. Even sociologists are a part of society and the culture of their time, and thus never completely free from cultural bias in their interpretations of culture.

This is actually a long-standing dilemma. The early sociologists of the 18th Century reacted to the sheer idealistic meaning of culture, which had dominated a number of humanistic disciplines. Philosophers and lawyers had been agents for this kind of philosophy in the processes leading up to the Great Revolution, which had in many ways failed—not in the sense that the revolutionaries had lacked motivation to destroy the old regime, but in the sense that the outcome of the revolution differed considerably from their program. Instead of a great society dominated by brotherhood and a social order based upon freedom and equality, the revolution had led to social chaos, despotic rule and imperialistic wars—and to a France that never managed to regain its status as Europe's leading nation.

The irrationality of the idealistic revolutionary thinking was one of the reasons that Auguste Comte and Emile Durkheim developed a new social discipline, one that would promote a more realistic understanding of culture and social processes. To do this, they needed a social physics or a science of morality based upon objective experiences, but they ran into new problems here.

Both Comte and Durkheim were originally thinking in terms of examples from natural science when they tried to make sociology a scientific discipline, even though Durkheim later underwent a radical change in his fundamental professional views, from the time he wrote his book on the division of labor to the time he wrote a book on the elementary form of religious life. Durkheim envisaged a rise in occupational differentiation, combined with greater social cohesion, as factors that would undermine "the mechanical solidarity" in society but also lay the foundation for a new morality, one based on insight into increased dependence among different groups—an "organic solidarity."

In hindsight, it is not difficult to see that far more is needed to ensure the integration of morality within modern societies. Durkheim's weakness in this instance was not merely that he operated with too few factors in his attempt to clarify these integration conditions; even his attitude toward these factors left something to be desired. The classification of reality in terms of factors (Latin: *facere* = what is done) is a fundamental methodological prerequisite for research that studies objects and seeks to determine the correspondence between theory and objective reality. For natural scientists, whose task is to study the laws governing a given external reality, this could represent a possible ideal. But for a discipline whose task was to study such phenomena as integration and society, morality and marriage, all talk of a correspondence between theories and external factors became problematic. This is because social reality does not exist solely as an external factor in relation to people's orientation. One of the reasons institutions and societies are the way they are, is because people understand and relate to them in specific ways. Institutions and societies are culturally constituted. This makes objective studies of culture quite problematic.

German dictionaries define objectivity in two ways: as *gegenständlich*— that is, as something that exists independently of the recognizing subjects. What is objective, in this sense, can be categorized in terms of factors and studied from the vantage point of a correspondence between theory and fact. The second definition of objectivity involves making the term a synonym of *sachlich*—that is, something that is balanced, neutral or close to reality, without presuming that our understanding of reality is independent of culture.

A hermeneutic method might be appropriate here, i.e. a doctrine concerning understanding based on correspondence between the whole and the part of what is being studied. A comprehensive or factual representation will rely on the inclusion of many different perspectives, so that culturally constituted phenomena can only be studied in contrasting perspectives to the object with a selected background. In theory, the number of these perspectives is infinite; but in practice, we will say that a description is objective, or *"sachlich,"* when new perspectives do not lead to significant shifts in the conclusions.

The discipline of sociology is doubly dependent on culture. What it studies is, in part, culturally dependent. And in part, sociologists will depend upon perspectives, models and terminology, all of which are in turn dependent on cultures.

This dependence on cultural traditions and sociological ways of studying culture makes finding a common point of departure, one that everyone agrees is the most *sachlich* or scientific, very difficult indeed. But, even if cultural sociologists are unable to find a common reference for terms and perspectives, it should be possible to demonstrate relations between certain cultural premises and consequences of these premises in order to understand society.

A lot of socio-cultural research has involved attempts to discover structures in people's behavior within specific societies. These structures can lead to something interesting. But before we can present anything cohesive with real explanatory power, we must first discover cultural *systems*, not just structures.

CULTURAL STRUCTURES AND SYSTEMS

In the anthology "Culture Matters," we find an article by Orlando Patterson, who describes contemporary cultural research as follows: "In the humanities and liberal circles generally, a rigid orthodoxy now prevails that can be summarized as follows: Culture is a symbolic system to be interpreted, understood, discussed, delineated, respected, and celebrated as the distinctive product of a particular group of people, of equal worth with all other such products. But it should never be used to explain anything about the people who produced it."[4]

If this is representative, then the significance of cultural variation is disallowed. Such interpretations do not defend culture as an explanatory principle. The understanding of society has far too often been left to people who want to provide an overall explanation of human behavior on the basis of material conditions and individual decisions.

Even though the leading structural functionalist Talcott Parson spoke in terms of cultural systems, social systems and personality systems, in addition to the biological organism, the physical environment and an ultimate reality, much of his theoretical constructs were ultimately based on observed structures rather than on systematic theory in the strictest sense. In hindsight, his theories have been criticized for being too abstract and too general, ill-suited to prediction and falsification, and for not being open to conflict analyses. But whatever may be said about Parson's form of structural functionalism, there are other options for studying culture in the context of a system.

A guiding principle for such studies is that they must not assume that every cultural form of daily life necessarily constitutes a coherent system. On the other hand, on an analytical level, cultural forms can be analyzed as several systems, which in part complement and balance one another, provided they are not in direct conflict. Here it is important to emphasize what we mean by "system," as opposed to "structure."

Axiomatic researchers have defined several notions of system. The criteria for a mathematical system cannot be fully applied to the study of living beings. The notion of system as employed in biology is necessarily different than that which is employed in the social sciences and in disciplines that study thinking human beings. Before anything can be analyzed as a system in sociology, it must meet four criteria:

1. The elements being studied must be mutually dependent on, or formative for, one another.
2. The elements being studied must be a part of a whole, which is delimited by the world around them.
3. This whole must relate to external entities; we will usually find mutual dependence between related systems.
4. The studied whole must contain self-maintaining or reproductive characteristics.

Language, for example, can be analyzed in such a light from a systematic perspective. So can ethics and legal regulations. Theology and various philosophical outlooks on life can also be made amenable to systematic analysis. The common denominator for all these systems is that they share an inner logic.

In the discipline of sociology, there are a number of classic works that have dealt with cultural phenomena from a systematic perspective and have accordingly been able to point up consequences over time, consequences that might have been unintended by the social players. Most familiar is perhaps Max Weber's study of how the Protestant Ethic facilitated the spread of materialistic capitalism. These studies display a cultural dynamic associated with identifiable systems, while the consequences, over time, cannot be adapted to the interests or goals of the players in the system. The studies also show interaction between cultural and economic systems, although the one should not be determined by the other.

Not all cultural system building is compatible with sociological models for relationships between cultural and social forms. The semiotics of the linguistic disciplines can become so fixated on texts that references to an external—and potentially falsifiable—reality are weakened. This is particularly the case in a number of postmodern textual analyses, based on the assumption that meaning lies in linguistic distinctions and is unrelated to the orientation and external challenges of individuals. Such studies can help sociologists understand why many groups become lost in a world of interpretations and perceptions of reality, even when a change in course would have been prudent in view of the external reality. On the other hand, these studies will fall short if what we are looking for is an explanation of why some groups and societies manage to find functional answers to their challenges, while others become increasingly bogged down in dysfunctional forms of adjustment.

There are several aspects of a dominant culture that could be studied from a systematic perspective. Our point of departure in this study was whether western interpretive culture provides satisfactory answers to the challenges confronting us on the threshold of the 21st Century. Or, to be more specific: whether new liberal attitudes, which have predominated in modern societies since 1989, represent the ultimate answer to the challenge of modernity, or whether new liberalism itself is an ideology with the same set of seductive characteristics as ideologies.

Before we take a closer look at this question, we would like to comment on how ideologies can be understood as cultural systems.

STUDIES OF IDEOLOGIES

The concept of ideology is over 200 years old. And though, from a purely etymological point of view, it has always meant the study of ideas (from *idea* and *logos*), the political meaning of the word has undergone considerable change over the years. Destutt de Tracy, a theoretician living during the French Revolution, used the term to denote a program for the scientific study of the spread of ideas. Napoleon used it as a term of derision for impractical and far-fetched ideas. For others, the term has been a badge of honor, meaning something along the lines of a captivating, idealistic unified view. Karl Marx regarded ideologies as social deceptions ruled by social agents.[5]

Many have wanted to build further on Marxist assumptions on how ideologies primarily promote the interests of an economic upper class, and on presuppositions about how Marxist principles, properly understood, could be regarded as a means of liberating themselves from ideological constraints.[6] A number of social scientists have taken the Marxist assumptions about class positions as a key to understanding what constitutes social interests and the basis for people's choice of ideological interpretation. Even non-Marxist writers have often regarded ideologies as socially determined perceptions of reality, shaped more by social interests than by epistemology.[7]

Ultimately, more and more scholars have come to regard Marxism not just as one ideology among many others, nor even as an archetypal ideology. Karl Mannheim, preeminent sociologist of knowledge, was the first person to make systematic comparisons of the world views of the various political parties of his day and age as variations on an ideological concept. His analysis is contained in *Ideology and Utopia*, written in the late 1920s and based primarily on his German experiences.

Mannheim's comprehensive concept of ideology could have led to social relativization of the understanding of ideologies, which would then have helped ward off single-minded fanaticism. But it also spawned epistemological problems concerning the status of his ideological analysis. If all political theories were understood as ideological and interest-governed, then even Mannheim's analyses would have attained the status of something relative and interest-governed. It was not easy to define all political views as ideologies, which meant perceptions were determined by specific social interests. And defining some views as ideological, but not others, proved problematic, at least in the absence of concrete evidence to substantiate intellectual superiority of the latter.[8] References to judgments by "free-floating intellectuals" were an unsatisfactory solution to that problem.

The main problem with studying ideologies after that time has been finding a common platform that is universal enough to serve as a springboard for comparative studies. In one sense, an analytical platform set at an abstract level had to be constructed in order to observe the striking similarities and contrasts between social perceptions that could be termed ideological. On the other hand, analytical substance in a formal context should not be so abstract that any contact with the concrete political struggle becomes too remote.

In practice, determining the typical characteristics of political ideologies will depend on a hermeneutical approach to the ideologies. This approach could be met with counter-ideologies and critique. Even if this does not result in permanently valid ideological determination, our claim here proves that it is possible to list several common traits of all the major ideologies that have had an impact on political life in our part of the world over the past two centuries.

It is important to analyze these ideologies—and, to a certain extent, debunk them—not just because they were key elements in modern political society. Societies based on mass mobilization in support of political decisions are indebted to a set of simplistic and appealing notions regarding the tasks and potential of society. Ideologies should be recognized and possibly risen above, primarily because the simplifications following in their wake tend to lead to a social distortion of reality and irrational forms of adjustment.

It can be difficult indeed for social scientists to maintain neutrality in such analyses. On the other hand, not all analyses of ideology will hinge on their determining the truest and most rational social interpretation. Researchers are also useful when they can submit convincing arguments for what is clearly not rational, or for what lies beyond the scope of that which is rational and acceptable, leaving it up to others to choose a political course within the framework of the "acceptable." This kind of falsifying, or negative goal, often seems more realistic than a positive one.

Although discovering the hallmark categories of ideology so that comparative studies can be performed is both possible and important, this does not mean that every aspect of the major ideologies matches a system's criteria. Even ideologies with the same political orientation can, in practice, appear both varied and vague at the same time. The use of ideologies like these is often fraught with opportunism.

Nevertheless, it is possible to list a number of recurring hallmarks of ideologies that enable us to compare systems.

ANALYTICAL HALLMARKS OF IDEOLOGIES

In Marxist and anti-Marxist literature alike, we find at least five formal criteria for ideologies: system context, interest-dependency, reality distortion, the adversely affected party, and self-immunization.[9] Let's take a closer look at each of these hallmarks:

1. *System context*: For thoughts or interpretations to be categorized as ideologies, they must comprise a continuous flow of perceptions in which one claim enhances the reliability of the other. An ideology used by many as a point of reference must contain a number of mutually dependent principles for social analysis. Its systematic character will thus be recognizable, because it is not possible to eliminate one part without affecting the other parts of the social interpretation. Before we characterize something as ideology, the interpretations concerned should also have been applied by many, and over a period of time. Situation-governed devices for justifying a particular standpoint do not qualify as ideological analyses.
2. *Interest-dependency*: The appeal and spread of ideologies is to a large extent based on social interests rather than on the weight of superior arguments. Suggesting some form of dependency between interests and perspectives does not, however, justify the claim that what we are dealing with is an ideology. Most perceptions have some sort of affinity for personal motivation or social interest. To prevent everything from being grouped together under an umbrella of ideological determination, the term should be reserved for interests that are particularistic while pretending to be universalistic or serving a general purpose.
3. *Distortion of reality*: Ideologies should be exposed and recognized as such because, in one way or other, they represent a distorted perception of reality, usually a kind of "false consciousness." To claim that something is false and not merely at odds with our own perceptions and interests, we must be able to show that a stated claim is clearly inconsistent with expe-

rience or with a logical way of thinking, or that the interpretations in question are clearly less functional than plausible alternative interpretations. Demonstrating that we are up against arguments with non-falsifiable metaphysical and axiomatic principles does not, in itself, qualify as ideological determination. No interpretations lack presuppositions. Nor should all types of human assessment error and maladjustments be traced back to ideologies. False assessments that originate from the personality traits of a given player, or from coincidental situation-governed circumstances, lie beyond the scope of the present discussion.

4. *The adversely affected party*: In the literature on ideologies, the notion that some people will be suppressed or adversely affected if a reigning ideology remains predominant is a recurring theme. There are often several reasons why reality-distorted notions, defended by people with vested interests, will ultimately cause people to lose touch with reality and also lead to an increasing number of maladjustments, which are bound to affect something or somebody. This "something or somebody" need not consist of social categories such as class or gender. The fact that the ideology-exposing literature still suffers from a lopsided emphasis on major—and potentially strong—groups as those most adversely affected is undoubtedly due to a hope that these very groups will be motivated enough to break free from the dominant ideology. This is understood clearest when a person develops a rebellious and vengeful streak as they learn to view themselves as one of "the suppressed." Nevertheless, we must take into consideration how an adversely affected party in a reality-distorted ideology might in fact be Mother Nature herself, future generations, a specific civilization or society on a grand scale, for that matter.

5. *Self-immunization*: Since, analytically speaking, ideologies enjoy an intellectual status other than the one they invoke, it is only reasonable to expect that people who have benefited from a specific ideology will do their utmost to ward off close scrutiny and criticism. Individual defenders of an ideology are not the only ones with such needs. We can expect to find immanent interpretations built into the ideological system for the purpose of defending social groups against intimidating arguments. Systems of self-immunization, closely related to the general system of political interpretation, often have easily recognizable structures. Arguments threatening the credibility of an ideology are not always met with superior intellectual arguments. Such arguments are more often generally interpreted as expressions of particular interest on the part of hostile persons, groups, classes or nations. More to the point, an ideology may present itself as indisputable, as representing reason, science, history, modernity or progress.

This list could undoubtedly have been extended, but then the categorization would have excluded a number of social interpretations that should be included in comparisons to enhance our insight into ideologies. The goal here was not to maximize precision, but rather to highlight certain key contexts.

These five hallmarks should be sufficient for recognizing ideologies, even in the face of social interpretations that are not presented as ideological. This list should also help us focus on the search for ideologies' system characteristics. It applies, first and foremost, to a way of thinking, the system characteristics of a society or the relationship between society and the individual. An ideology that offers a simplistic and appealing interpretation of this relationship can be expected to support mutually supportive interpretations. Not only will an ideology accentuate key elements, but, based on earlier comments on self-immunization, we can safely assume that an ideology will also reject interpretations dependent on ideologically inconsistent premises. And in view of the social sciences' quest for perspectives, we might expect to discover considerable disparity here between ideological and research-oriented attitudes.

In addition to the systems of thought, we could probably detect system characteristics in the social utilization of ideologies as well. The interaction between specific interests and the choice of ideological interpretation is hardly coincidental.

An ideology depends on credibility. All ideologies represent interpretations that put competing ideologies in a bad light. Nevertheless, the most substantive references for credibility are on a different level than mutual competition among ideologies. We need to distinguish between ideologies, myths and beliefs.

THE DEPENDENCE OF IDEOLOGIES ON MYTH

A recurring theme of ideologies is that they are designed to unite and stimulate collective action. Their credibility is often closely tied to the traits of specific leaders or parties, which are perceived as representing specific groups or life forms that are distinctive from other leaders, groups and life forms. An ideology is often skewed toward an antagonistic relationship to conflicting ideologies. This implies that an ideology's credibility depends on an overarching justification of its attempt to express what is rational, good or just.

Social myths enter the picture at this point, and not only those with a clear political imprint. Nowadays, myths, from the Greek word *mythos*, are spread and interpreted in variety of ways.[10] By no means can it be taken for granted that the most important myths in contemporary society are labeled and recognized as myths. As a rule, myths are perceived as concrete, often personified, accounts that provide us with dramatic pictures and explanations of the world order. Myths may be used to spread a religious message and to make the substance of politicized ideologies believable.[11] But myths are primarily tall tales, not ideological programs or religious beliefs.

Myths are often reminiscent of the sagas. A saga usually tells the story of a specific historical character, e.g. a central figure in a heroic battle. As opposed to fairy-tales, sagas purport to relate actual historic events. We should guard against a hasty dichotomizing of the antithetical terms mythos/logos.

The question as to how true or false myths really are does not necessarily enter into an analytical delimitization of myths. If "myths" are automatically assumed to represent what is false—as is often the case—then an anti-myth can easily attain a status of being true because it is in opposition to the myth in question, which leads to an oversimplification. We expose a myth the same way that we expose an ideology—by using analytical criteria. As a working breakdown of myths, the following five hallmarks are typical for what are called myths:

1. Myths refer to familiar notions that purport to say something important about our lives.
2. Myths give shape to a universal struggle by reducing it to a conflict between two forces.
3. Myths incite our involvement by dramatizing these two forces as expressions of good and evil. There need not be equilibrium in the presentation of the two. As long as the one has been determined to be unequivocally good or bad, the other has thereby been defined.
4. Myths are archetypal or repetitive in character. It is up to alert guardians to remind us of their presence in shifting guises in ever changing situations. People can be taught to recognize the mythical drama in a given situation through specific codes or symbols.
5. Myths are usually geared more toward mobilizing the individual mind than toward inciting collective political action. They can be directed toward the cultural sphere rather than the political arena.

We have only to look at political history to find examples of contemporary tales that fit better in a framework of myths than in a rational analytical framework. This holds true even for frequently told stories of how enlightenment and rational democracy appeared on the historical scene just in the nick of time.

In the handed-down accounts of the French Revolution, the decisive, but relatively non-dramatic weapon thefts from the Invalide are played down in favor of the events surrounding the subsequent gunpowder theft from the Bastille prison on July 14. This was an event with all the ingredients of battle and blood, since the forces assigned to defend the fortress shot about 100 people before they surrendered and were massacred by their captors. What clinched the fortress' fall, however, were the canons from a deserting military unit that joined forces with the rebels. In the mythical recounting of events, those who rammed the barricades were spoken of as "the people." This wasn't just because women and children took part in the battles, but because through the destruction of an opponent symbolizing the old regime the people were able to become bearers of their own sovereignty, while the concept of popular sovereignty was embellished. Soon "the people" became synonymous with "the nation." Previously, the people (*le peuple*) in the French state had meant all Frenchmen, or that part of the population not belonging to the nobility, whereas *la nation* was represented by the politically privileged: the authoritative elite. Now the nation was perceived as a society of justice comprised of citizens of equal rank and rights. Those who voluntarily embraced the law, i.e. those who relinquished their privileges, were permitted to be part of the nation. Those who were more inclined to fight for their privileges became enemies of the nation.

In this new picture of the people's battle with their enemies, it became necessary to elaborate on those circumstances that could specifically make it clear that the old regime had kept the people in bondage. The popular attack on the Bastille, which from the rebels' viewpoint was mainly because they wanted to get its hands on some gunpowder, was mythically presented as a battle to liberate the people from the yoke of bondage. At the outset, this motive was hardly more than a secondary consideration. Even in hindsight this explanation seems strained, since at the time of the attack, the Bastille was only holding seven prisoners: two were mentally ill, one was a forger, and one was an aristocrat!

Mythological stories about July 14 convey one interpretation that is presented as politically correct: the one about the people's righteous battle against tyranny, and about a victory that must be won, over and over again, in order to secure the people's freedom and sovereignty. The violent events of that day were an outgrowth of the suppression under the old regime. The overthrow of the old regime's representatives marked a violent but necessary transition to a new and more liberated order.

There is more than one reason for calling this mythical: not just because this type of story represents only one particular version of events or simply because many of the details and facts that did not tally with the story were either hushed up or distorted. Basically, what makes it mythical is the fact that its presentation has a typical form, one that is intended to say something important about many later political events. This story dramatizes a complex conflict—a battle between the suppressed and their suppressers, a fight between good and evil, and does so in such a way that key interpreters can later use symbols from the story in order to get people to relive a drama that presumably provides an explanatory basic pattern for "correct" orientation even in our time.

Both short-term and long-term historical interpretations have their own mythical elements.[12] Where interpretations refer to such a basic mythical pattern, we can expect even the ideologies and political discourse to be cast in a special mold to which they must adapt.

THE DEPENDENCE OF MYTHS ON BELIEF

A certain story about The Great Revolution as the victory of freedom over the suppressors and the victory of reason over superstition fits the mythical pattern. So could a story from the opposite viewpoint, which describes the defeat of a civilized order and the disorder of rabble-rousers. Myths are not designed as analytical presentations of the kinds of social factors most likely to ensure a reasonable balance between individual liberty and supraindividual order and the kinds of cultural circumstances that could lead to social upheaval and arbitrary abuse of power, or to a calcified order that benefits only the few. In mythical accounts, there is conflict between good and evil—either freedom versus constraint or order versus chaos.

Traditionally, liberal groups have rallied around myths of the former type, whereas conservative groups tend to prefer myths of the latter type. It is easy to see that these preferences are not coincidental and that they are geared to a variety of social interests. All the same, the potential power of ideologies and myths is not explained. To gain acceptance, a myth must be compatible with deep-seated notions in a given culture; it is not enough that it is compatible with certain ideologies.

The notion that all we have to do is fight for freedom is closely linked to the belief that human beings are inherently good and that, given half a chance, they will behave with integrity. The notion that morality depends on a certain cultural order stems largely from the belief that human beings are egotistical and anarchistic, that they can behave decently only within a civilizational or religious framework.

Faith in the noble savage can be regarded as a counter-faith to the doctrine of original sin. If two or more forms of faith can be pitted against each other, liberal spokesmen tend to view this as an incentive to individual choice. But this is by no means a foregone conclusion. Truth and credibility are not necessarily synonymous with popularity.

Several controversial questions concerning belief and morality can be answered by referring to logic or to a systematic empiricism. But this does not

answer all our questions. Reason and research are not necessarily unambiguous, since arguments depend on premises and categories that are often culturally dependent. When reason and research arbitrate and resolve ideological controversies, this tends to lead to a negative culling process—that is, it
points to what is not credible, rather than aiding the formation of a comprehensive world view. This kind of negatively charged research can also be
provocative, particularly among those who invoke humanity and research
when justifying their views. This applies to a number of interpretations of
people's natural morality and innate reason.[13]

Even though a certain program of modernity implies that reason and
research should enjoy an overarching ontological status, the experimental research method implies that reality, *an sich,* isn't unambiguously accessible to
the senses. Nor can logic encompass everything. The program for explaining
everything with the help of rational, causal analyses leads us to conclude that
it is impossible. Rationally speaking, causal analyses lead to the concept of the
initial cause, which must be its own cause and thus must be categorically different from what follows. Logic leads us to a starting point that cannot be
grasped logically, one that argumentation nevertheless must presuppose. This,
then, is a rationalistic basis for rejecting deterministic categories as exhaustive.

This type of reasoning can lead to the conclusion that acknowledgment involves an element of faith and that culture is dependent on collective beliefs.
In this context, faith means axiomatic choices of categories of understanding
in relation to the acknowledgment that such categories provide.

In light of the above, an approach to "systems of belief" will only be able
to capture certain aspects of the collective faith that religion typifies. Without
trying to list all the reasons why we can expect to find religion as a hallmark
of human cultures, we will mention two of them.

One of these has to do with people's need to feel a sense of security. From
an emotional, ethical and even cognitive standpoint, people depend on mutual
structure and on certainty. Ludwig Wittgenstein wrote at length about how
certainty presupposes trust, without our being able—strictly speaking—to
prove what we take for granted.[14] But for such a perception of reality to be
meaningful and functional, there must first be a cultural institutionalization
based on premises other than the strictly rationalistic.

By extending this type of reasoning, we can claim that no unified perception of reality can be established apart from hypothetical premises, which in
a certain sense contain an element of faith. Strictly speaking, the existence or
non-existence of God can no more be proved or disproved than historic determinism or indeterminism.

Dissimilar cultures are constructed around different but specific answers to
these questions. Christian culture has maintained the existence of both a di-

vine order and an individual accountability—that is, indeterminism in an essential field of reality. Islamic culture, by and large, has regarded the social sector as being determined by Allah's will. Buddhist culture has basically perceived reality as being determined by major repetitions, but without a personal God being behind the determinism. Humanists have usually taken a non-deistic view of reality, in which natural explanations are perceived as an adjustment to deterministic laws, while human values and individual freedom have been linked to an extreme emphasis on indeterminism.

The sociologist and moral philosopher Zygmunt Bauman has given an account of different cultures in relation to their choice of "life strategy" with respect to death and a consciousness of the risk of death.[15] The religious response has consisted of identifying true life with the soul and immortality. What he calls "the modern strategy" has consisted of identifying with social groups and politico-cultural movements and fighting for their supraindividual survival. Furthermore, it consisted of an attempt to deconstruct the insolubility of death into specific problems that can be resolved at the individual level, such as health and accident insurance. Different life strategies predispose people to a predilection for widely different institutions and orientations.

A "meaningful life" usually means one with purpose, a life where sorrows are counterbalanced by pleasures, a life where the overall goal gives direction to minor goals and purpose to major sacrifices. When people write and speak at length about a "cry for meaning," they are thinking about something more than finding explanations for what is happening in people's surroundings and for the need to have order in their daily lives.[16] In this context, "meaning" denotes something qualitatively important, something not necessarily found through mundane social interaction.

Meaning in this last sense of the word has to do with the human longing to find an explanation and a justification for the most difficult and critical challenges of life. It is meaning at this level that can inspire efforts beyond egocentric calculation and can get people to want to control their impulsive actions in favor of more exalted goals. Our development as moral beings is closely related to the question of whether we can succeed in adapting our lives to this kind of framework of meaning.

Even though the acquisition and development of meaning have important personal aspects, no civilization can relegate meaning to the status of a strictly private matter, with important social tasks reduced to supplying the necessities of life and maintaining a modicum of law and order. Communicative social bonds presuppose a common culture, also in the sense of common frameworks of meaning. Without these frameworks, society's social bonds would ultimately disintegrate. From such a viewpoint, development and the maintenance of an adequate framework of meaning is imperative to ensure long-term viability of any society.

Deductively, this can lead to the conclusion that in all cultures we can expect to find, not only a collective faith in axiomatic values, but an institutionalized religion as well. This jibes with Berelson and Steiner's empirical inventory, that "all societies have religion(s)."[17] In cases where the socially supported religion is not transcendental in nature, we can expect political ideas to have a religious hue. This applies not just to ideologies in totalitarian societies. Even a belief in liberal humanity can assume religious forms. We will return later to the subject of the cult of human rights in our kind of society.

FUNCTIONAL ANALYSIS

Based on this type of reasoning, religion in a social context can be regarded as a conglomeration of sacrosanct rites which revolve around axiomatic values that involve an element of faith. Moreover, we can conclude that ideologies, myths and beliefs can all be analyzed in terms of systems within a cultural context.

The significance of being able to define ideologies, myths and beliefs as systems lies in the fact that they can figure in cultural explanations. This, in turn, means that such systems can figure in functional analyses.

Essentially, a functional analysis is a study of how structures contribute to the adaptation of units larger than the structure being studied. Such contributions may be positive or negative in nature, and can then either promote or hamper long-term adjustment. Since functional analyses relate to the adaptation of larger systems, they are not identical to general consequential analyses, or analyses of the extent to which players are able to realize their intentions. Nor are functional analyses automatically identical to "functionalistic" theories of explanation. Much confusion has reigned in this area in the social disciplines. Thus a brief rundown could prove useful.

"Functional analysis is at once the most promising and possibly the least codified of contemporary orientations to problems of sociological interpretation," wrote Robert Merton in the middle of the 20th century, at a time when functional analyses were being used rather uncritically in much of the social science literature.[18] To bring some order to the use of terminology, he compiled a list of principles for such analyses. Among other things, he stressed that social functional analyses would be analyses of how structural elements contributed to the survival of a given society. At the same time, he maintained that there was no reason to assume that all customs and ideas necessarily promoted vital functions. Like his mentor, Talcott Parsons, Robert Merton was aware that society's ability to survive could not be taken for granted. It was Merton who introduced the term "dysfunctions" as a means of characterizing consequences that weakened a system's ability to regulate and adapt. In other words, a certain form of society could give rise to positive functions, sometimes called eufunctions, and negative or dysfunctional forms of adjustment.

By emphasizing that structural social conditions could give rise to both eufunctions and dysfunctions, Merton distanced himself from a form of naive functionalism which assumed that whatever wins acceptance or becomes predominant for a time must necessarily benefit society or people the most. The latter assumed that a society was a kind of self-regulating organism, or that evolution would guarantee that the latest development is always the most forward-looking.

The term "function" has a long history in academic circles, from the time Leibniz used the expression in mathematics to its subsequent use as a common term in biology. Later it was also embraced by sociologists and anthropologists. A general definition of function might be the following: A function is the contribution of a given element to the maintenance or survival of the unit of which that element is a part.

As already mentioned, Robert Merton distinguished between positive functions and negative dysfunctions. Each represents processes that were intended or unintended by those who set them in motion. Finally, the consequences of such a major adjustment could be recognized by those actively involved. The latter option must mean that processes set in motion, based on certain intentions on the part of the players, would not necessarily be recognized as consequences of these processes. One plausible example of non-observed consequences of intended actions would involve some of the negative trends in social development that caught many by surprise as the 1990s wore on. Criminality and asocial behavior were no doubt observed, but little understood as possible unforeseen consequences of a predominant liberal ideology. Instead, they might be regarded as individual deviations from a liberal culture.

Since functional analyses exceed intentional analyses, they are prone to stir up antagonism. One form of criticism claims that functional analyses belong to the sphere of biology and not to the study of intentional human beings. But this rests on a series of misunderstandings. Sociologists speak of social structures and cultural systems without having to resort to a biological theory of organisms as a model for social analysis.

Clearly, Charles Darwin's studies from the middle of the 19th century have occupied a central place in the development of theories on the adaptation and non-adaptation of living systems. But the same can be said of an older historical school of thought that can be traced to Edward Gibbons' studies from the end of the 18th century on the decline and fall of the Roman Empire.[19]

An up-to-date functional analysis cannot be presented as a mere extension of an earlier form of social Darwinism. The former social Darwinism was not sufficiently critical of the limitations of the categories for "natural selection" in explaining cultural conditions and social development. Darwin's categories of mutations and selection were based on an assumption of nature as a more or less static framework for selecting species and forms of adjustment. Human beings, however, seldom adjust directly to natural frameworks, but rather to culturally-formed societies. Culture is not nature. Cultural frameworks might change according to human understanding. This calls for explanatory steps other than "natural selection."

In human societies, individuals or groups might appear to be well-adapted with respect to a predominant culture, a culture they in turn might help to maintain. Nonetheless, such an adjustment can only appear to be successful in the short term, since the cultural framework can shift unexpectedly—partly for reasons beyond the orientation of the players, and partly as a result of unforeseen consequences of what the players are clearly oriented toward.

A classical sociological example of this relationship is Max Weber's study of how the Protestant Ethic helped foster an expansive capitalism. In practice, a religion-based quest for an awareness of salvation fostered a strict work ethic, coupled with frugality and a rational eagerness to invest, which in turn led to the accumulation of capital and the rise of new economic living conditions.

The question of whether this should be regarded as a functional or a dysfunctional form of adjustment depends in part on the time perspective and on what overarching systems we choose to emphasize. We can certainly call into question modern capitalism's functionality for capitalism as a system. One perspective in this regard is particularly relevant, and this is what Daniel Bell points to when he said that modern capitalism depends on a mass consumption which can only be maintained by means of an intense flurry of advertising that links buying and consumption to people's sense of identity. This promotes a form of self-indulgent hedonism, which will be increasingly at odds with the puritan ethic of unselfish initiative, hard work and manufacturing effort.[20] What might appear to be functional for an economic institution will only apply insofar as the old cultural framework is preserved.

In analyzing such processes it is helpful to have a perspective on systems beyond the perspective of the individual player. It can also be helpful to possess models for the kinds of cultural solutions a given society must preserve in order to maintain long-term viability.

During the 1940s and '50s, a wide-ranging debate raged among sociologists about what kinds of functional tasks every society had to find the answer for in order to survive. This became known as the debate on "the functional requisites." Inherent in this expression was the concept that socio-cultural systems could not automatically be assumed to function in favor of their own preservation, or for the continuation of life. To function over time, every cultural system and every society would depend on a number of prerequisites of a structural nature. These structural prerequisites had to be institutionalized. Their distinguishing characteristics had to be safeguarded by norms and by viable social rules. In undifferentiated societies, authority, tradition and a common world view suffice as a frame of reference. In differentiated societies, different institutions would be required to safeguard the crucial functions of those societies. John Bennet and Melvin Tumin formulated the following requirements for the institutional prerequisites of those functions: Regulations governing the preservation of the biological conditions of life for society's members, regulations governing the production and distribution of goods and services, regulations governing the reproduction of new members, regulations governing the socialization of new members, the preservation of internal and external order of society, and the cultural preservation of meaning and motivation.[21]

This practical discussion was an extension of Talcott Parsons' more abstract arguments that societies could be analyzed as systems and that all systems had to satisfy certain structural conditions in order to be preserved. As all sociologists know, Parsons spoke of adoption, goal-attainment, integration, and latency as tasks that every society was obliged to find structural solutions to. These "requisites" were later supplemented with four structural "prerequisites": (1) communication based on symbolic language, (2) organization of kinship based on the taboo of incest, (3) a rudimentary technology at the very least, and (4) religion and a fundamental community of values.[22]

General models of functional and non-functional societies can serve as useful rules of thumb in determining how a specific society is adapting. They can provide social researchers with guidelines for functional analyses. In addition, an understanding of ideology as a cultural system—and of myth and belief, as well—could help determine whether or not a given culture is developing in the direction of a functional adjustment.

Before we begin to ask whether predominant forms of culture in the West after 1989 have ideological hallmarks, and how these affect our functional adjustment, we must first take a closer look at those ideologies that lost out in the 20th century. Are there grounds for claiming that *laissez-faire* liberalism, National Socialism, classical conservatism and Marxist Socialism lost because of internal characteristics that their ideological supporters failed to detect and transcend? If so, we might have a good reason for comparing the previously dominant ideologies with the one predominating in our own day and age.

NOTES

1. Edward B. Tylor, *Primitive Culture* (1871) (London: Murray, 1920).
2. A. L. Kroeber and Clyde Kluckhohn, *Culture. A Critical Review of Concepts and Definitions* (London: Vintage, 1952).
3. Talcott Parsons, *The Social System* (Glencoe: Free Press, 1951).
4. Orlando Patterson: "Taking Culture Seriously: A Framework and an Afro-American Illustration" in: *Culture Matters*, eds. Lawrence Henderson and Samuel P. Huntington (New York: Basic Books, 2000), 202–218.
5. Karl Marx and Friedrich Engels, *The German ideology*, (London: Electric Book Co, 2001).
6. Georg Lukacs, *Geschicte und Klassenbewusstein* (Berlin: H. Luchterhand, 1968). Cf. also the anthology *On Ideology*, published by the Centre for Contemporary Cultural Studies, (Birmingham: Hutchinson, 1978) and Robin Blackburn, ed., *Ideology in Social Science. Readings in Critical Social Theory* (London: Fontana, 1972).
7. Jorge Larrain, Jorge, *The Concept of Ideology* (London: Hutchinson, 1984)—John B. Thompson, *Studies in the Theory of Ideology* (Cambridge: Polity Press, 1984).
8. Karl Mannheim, *Ideology and Utopia* (London: Routledge & Kegan Paul, 1936).
9. Sigurd Skirbekk, *Ideologianalyse som ideologi. En argumentasjonsanalyse av norsk moraldebatt. (An analysis of ideological definitions of ideologies)* (Oslo: The University Press, 1986), 38f.
10. Victor Turner, "Myth and Symbol," in vol. 10 of *International Encyclopedia of the Social Sciences* (New York: Collier & McMillan, 1968): 576–582—Edith Hamilton, *Mythology* (New York: Mentor, 1940)—David Adams Perowne, *The World of Myths* (New York: Oxford University Press, 1990)—Cf. also Claude Lévi-Strauss, *Myth and meaning,* (London: Routledge classics, 2001).
11. Colette Beaune: *The Birth of an Ideology: Myth and Symbol of Nation in Late-medieval France* (Berkeley: Univ. of California Press, 1991).
12. Carl Lotus Becker, *Heavenly City of the Eighteenth Century Philosphers* (New Haven, 1932) (London: Yale, 1968).
13. Carl N. Degeler, *In Search of Human Nature: the Decline and Revival of Darwinism in American Social Thought* (New York: Oxford University Press, 1991)—Robert B. Edgerton, *Sick Societies. Challenging the Myth of Primitive Harmon* (Glencoe: Free Press,1992).
14. Ludwig Wittgenstein, *On Certainty (Über Gewissheit),* (London: Blackwell, 1962).
15. Zygmunt Bauman, *Morality, Immorality and Other Life Strategie* (Cambridge: Polity Press,1992).
16. Viktor E. Frankl, *The unheard cry for meaning, psychotherapy and humanism.* (London: Hodder and Stoughton, 1978).
17. Bernard Berelson, and Gary A. Steiner, *Human Behavior. An Inventory of Scientific Findings* (New York: Harcourt, Brace & World, 1964).

18. Cp. the introduction "Manifest and Latent Functions" in Robert Merton, *Social Theory and Social Structure* (Glencoe: Free Press, 1949).

19. Edward Gibbons, *The History of the Decline and Fall of the Roman Empire* (1776–88) (London: Methuen, 1902).

20. Daniel Bell, *The Cultural Contradictions of Capitalism* (New York: Basic Books, 1976).

21. John W. Bennet and Melvin M. Tumin, *Social Life, Structure and Function,* (New York: Knopf, 1948).—Cf also Donald E. Brown, *Human Universals* (New York: McGraw Hill, 1991).

22 Talcott Parsons, "Evolutionary Universals in Society," *American Sociological Review,* Vol. 29 (June 1964):339–57.

Chapter Three

The Internal Causes of Ideological Demise

UNTENABLE EXPLANATIONS FOR IDEOLOGICAL DEMISE

In around 1930, Karl Mannheim published his book *Ideology and Utopia* in both German and English. This is a classical textbook on the sociology of knowledge and also includes a key study of the similarities and differences between what would be referred to later as the "loser ideologies" of the twentieth century. At that time, however, these ideologies were all still very much "alive," in the sense that there were political spokesmen fighting for their party's cause.

Mannheim not only presented theories on interaction between dominant ideas and the interests of select professions and social classes; he also provided an overview of world views on the ideologies current in Germany at that time. Mannheim called these ideologies bureaucratic conservatism, conservative historicism, liberal-democratic thought, socialist-communist ideas, and Fascism.

Of these ideologies, bureaucratic conservatism fell outside the scope of what Mannheim referred to as world views, since this type of politics was determined by the tendency of bureaucrats to transmute political problems into administrative ones. Conservative historicism, on the other hand, could be termed a world view and was firmly entrenched among German historians. The same applied to liberal-democratic thought with bourgeois foundations, to socialistic and communistic notions with roots in the working class, and to fascist views originating in vulnerable and socially deprived groups.

The form of liberalism prevalent in Europe during the 1920s had as many similarities with 19th century *laissez faire* liberalism as it did with late 20th century socio-liberal welfare policies. Many believe this older form of liberalism was dealt a mortal blow by the stock market crash of 1929, with Fascism and National Socialism suffering defeat in 1945. Conservatism lost much of its traditional authority in 1968, and Marxist Socialism collapsed in 1989.

The years between 1929 and 1989 can be described as the age of the rival ideologies' demise until a new socio-liberal philosophy emerged as a unifying ideal for surviving ideologies. Before taking a closer look at the ideological implications of contemporary social thinking, we ought to see whether we can learn something from older ideologies. Even though these could be described as losers, at least when viewed in relation to their original programs, we might stand to glean some general information as to why ideologies wane. This information might be central in judging contemporary views on society and history.

We could start by asking whether there are any collective explanations for the loser ideologies' demise. Some would say they lost simply because they were wrong, whereas the winners survived because they stood for the truth. This is too simplistic. Although we can rank ideologies according to their degree of logical consistency and social realism, it is difficult to dismiss some as utterly wrong and then herald others as entirely true—particularly in view of attitudes that have gained acceptance through the structuring and legitimizing of social interests. Some ideologies are purportedly more prone to morality and truthfulness in certain situations than others, but this does not explain why some prevailed while others fell from favor, or even why critical processes came to a head during the dramatic events that occurred at specific times.

Nor is it tenable to regard the ideologies' strength and viability as merely a phenomenon corresponding to the strengths and weaknesses of specific classes or occupational groups that have exploited these ideologies in order to legitimize their own social interests. Socialism made a political breakthrough long after our kind of society had developed a vast industrial working class, which continued its political dominance after the working class had shrunk in many countries. The liberal ideologies, for their part, have been drawn on as a point of reference by many different professions for over two hundred years.

Explaining the demise of ideologies as merely the result of overwhelming challenges is also untenable, as this is impossible for an ideologist to foresee. If ideologists had not had notions about how to handle all potential challenges facing them, they would not have claimed total control of political reality. Besides, challenges from the opposition were indirectly triggered by the dominant ideology in many cases.

Ideologies certainly do not act like automatons, permitting only one kind of strategy and adaptation. For example, the reputations of both National

Socialism and Marxist Socialism might have fared better had it not been for the despotic regimes of Hitler and Stalin. On the other hand, the ideologies used by these tyrants to legitimize themselves were of such a nature that control of power became more difficult for the opposition and the abuse of power that much easier.

Nor can the ebb and floe of ideologies simply be explained away as a consequence of immutable historical laws that are designed to keep development moving in an unswerving direction to the right, granting more power to new elitist groups; or the complete opposite, steering a course to the left, granting more power to the people; or steering a course toward the center, toward a more pragmatic liberalism; or to a social view perceived as non-ideological.

Attempts to pit various ideologies against each other in a kind of one-dimensional left-wing/right-wing axis are ideological in themselves. If we persevere with the original distinction between a political left and right wing — between a monarchy and republic, hierarchy or egalitarianism — some aristocratic conservatives will wind up further to the right, followed by liberals and mass-oriented fascists, with the socialists left standing on the left. If we rank ideological parties according to their attitude toward a strong state authority, fascists will wind up at the one extreme, followed by communists, socialists, conservatives and liberals. If we were to say that the left favors a state-run economy and the right favors a private economy, we get yet another breakdown. Various socialist groups will then end up on the left, with communists out on the extreme wing in relation to western socialism. At one time, these would have been followed by fascists, then by conservatives, and finally by those with a traditional liberalist view bringing up the rear on the extreme right. We ought to point out here that the term "liberal" differs slightly in meaning for Americans and Europeans. In the United States, proponents and adherents of political liberalism, combined with the Protestant Ethic, would be classified as "conservatives." American history shows how a liberal economy was part of the Founding Fathers' agenda and absorbed into the nation's historical constitution.

If we introduce more dimensions to our ranking, different pictures will emerge. A religious-secular axis can rank the parties according to their stand on economic materialism, in which socialism and early liberalism have something in common. According to their position on Darwinian biological materialism, some early liberals and Nazis shared a number of presuppositions. The "tough and tender" principle introduces yet another ranking as intersecting dimensions on a left-wing/right-wing scale.[1]

From a liberal perspective, liberalism will appear as an open, liberating and progressive philosophy, while all other ideologies will be portrayed as examples of dogmatic rigidity, doomed at some point to clash with reality. From a conservative point of view, conservatism will represent a balanced and sensible approach to a multifarious reality, while all other ideologies will be portrayed as an unrealistic set of ideas, construed to make sense of the world using simplistic theories. From a socialist perspective, socialism will represent universal democracy in a progressive society, while conservatism will be portrayed as an ideology for old-fashioned people. Liberalism will appear as an ideology for resourceful groups with limited social loyalty, while extreme right-wing attitudes will come across as an expression of threatening, violent trends supported by desperados. People with fascist views might view liberals as irresponsible, conservatives as naive, socialists as dangerous, and might feel justified in ranking them on a par with someone committing treason.

Attempts have also been made to place ideologies in historic order. Liberalism has been regarded as the unifying ideology of the bourgeoisie after the French political revolution and the British industrial revolution. Conservatism, as a distinct ideology, came about as a direct response to liberalism—partly to overthrow it and partly to correct it. Socialism arose in order to counter both liberalism and conservatism, but also, in part, as a synthesis of liberalism's demand for freedom and conservatism's demand for law and order. National Socialism, the doctrine of national unity with different foundations than those based in democratic interests, can be perceived as the antithesis of all the other ideologies and an attempt to create a unifying synthesis of particularist bourgeois and socialist interests. In this perspective, the new liberal doctrine from the end of the 19th century can be seen as the antithesis of Fascism and as a synthesis of liberal and social democratic thought.

However, the way these ideologies should be described in relation to each other remains a matter of dispute. Hardly any generally accepted framework exists for describing all ideologies in relation to each other. This may be an argument for considering the older ideologies one by one. The focus for such a description should be such questions as to whether systems of thinking, related to a certain ideology, will lead to inadequate or dysfunctional response to unavoidable challenges. And, if ways of correcting the ideologies were at hand, why did its central spokesmen not use them to save themselves and their world view? If we can say something about the fall of ideologies in these terms, then we are perhaps dealing with some kind of general insight that can also be applied to analyze contemporary political thought.

THE OLD LIBERALISM

As a unifying political program, liberalism is the oldest ideology of modern times. Depending on whether we take Adam Smith's principles of economic liberalism or John Locke's principles of political liberalism as a starting point, we can trace liberal heritage back two or three hundred years. Characteristic for Locke was his pre-political concept of an individual's distinctiveness and his notion that society is based on contracts. We may feel that the crux of liberalism is a human perception that attaches special value to individual freedom, even when this conflicts with collective demands and the management of society, but we can trace historical roots in European civilization that go back much farther.[2] For that matter, there is justification in claiming that the history of individualism is at the heart of the liberal philosophy.[3] If we regard liberalism as an ideology competing with other ideologies, we need only take 19th century political thought as our point of departure.

In the United Kingdom, the leading European country during the 19th century, liberalism gradually became the predominant ideology in both commerce and social management. The Enlightenment principles for the modern distribution of power had proven to have conspicuous shortcomings during the French Revolution. Despite this, it was felt that these principles could be preserved through the institutionalization of parliamentary law and by an independent judiciary. Citizens' moral obligations were emphasized and defined as a prerequisite for individual liberty. In a word, freedom was understood as the individual's freedom of action in a multiplicity of markets. The categories of the individual and the state were fundamental, recurring features of social thought on the part of liberal economic theoreticians such as Adam Smith and David Ricardo, and on the part of political liberals such as John Stuart Mill and Herbert Spencer. Spencer, a social Darwinist, stressed the use of science as a reference for the truth. Mill championed democratic debate and claimed that we could not know whether a fact was true before allowing our viewpoint to be challenged by opposing arguments. John Stuart Mill can also be regarded as a pioneer of social liberalism, of political guarantees for social rights, a hallmark of what could be called "new liberalism." But in terms of viewing the individual as the goal and the unit of social development, the old and the new liberalism have much in common.[4]

Liberalism was originally conceived as a social philosophy for the promotion of liberation—first and foremost of the individual, but also of political, economic and cultural entities upon which the individual depended. Since individuals and supraindividual entities do not have the same qualifications for being liberated, this provoked further antagonism. Liberal theoreticians have generally played down these differences. Either they have suggested that the liberation of society is a prerequisite for the liberation of its citizens or, more often, that society may be understood as the sum total of individuals in society, so that their liberation becomes a prerequisite for a free society. This led to an attempt to make individual morality the overarching moral dimension, even with social systems in focus.

If our aim is to maximize the liberty and happiness of the individual, as long as that person does not hurt others, we might give minimal attention to the cultural implication of this orientation. Relations between individuals and between individuals and society will then usually be viewed and described in terms of "external relations" only.

This way of thinking may fit the criteria for an ideology. There can be a link between systematic traits in liberal thought, based on terms determined by the individual and the state, and a distortion of reality in relation to conceded cultural structures. We can also find links between these principles and an outlook among people who try to maximize their own liberty, while at the same time regarding it as the manifestation of good and universal principles. The liberal way of understanding the relationship between the individual and society can prompt us to overlook processes with a harmful effect on collective cultural consciousness. Interpretations of social winners in terms of natural selection easily lead to a notion that political opponents of the game are losers. This mentality leads easily to an immunization of liberal philosophy.

The general acceptance of selection as part of progressive processes may be seen both as a strength and as a weakness of classical liberalism. It paves the way for principles of competition, which can prove to be effective, despite their harshness. The tragedy of differentiation and selection might, however, have been easier to bear in strictly religious societies than in the more secular ones. But even if liberalism has depended upon religious surveys, liberalism has been one of the forces undermining these views.

When a principle of selection becomes associated with specific economic interests instead of general models of functioning societies, it is likely to lead to "false consciousness" and to a distortion of the perception of social reality.

The old liberalism, because it legitimized capitalistic interests, has been accused of turning a blind eye to the economic and social processes it promoted. But the most hotly debated failures of the old liberal philosophy are closely linked to those groups that have exploited it. What emerged was a dubious combination of special economic interests on the part of a capitalistic class of owners and a liberal ideology that could be legitimized as progressive. Society's economic progress was explained as a positive by-product of profit-making interests on the competitive playing field. There is little doubt that this ideology gave many an all too clear conscience toward groups that were unable to appropriate resources at the individual level. When liberalism was challenged politically, many of her advocates sought comfort in the notion that they were championing reason over irresponsibility, which led to a political polarization. Indirectly, the old liberalism contributed to the spread of a radicalized socialism.

In the 1920s, a liberalistic monetary policy, with its emphasis on the gold standard, led to a divergence between the nominal and the real value of

money. This ended in a stock market crash and led to widespread mass unemployment, to social disintegration and to an increase in support for both
National and Marxist Socialism—even to some collaboration between the
two.[5] This, in turn, ended in a war and a subsequent period of reconstruction,
during which management by the state assumed greater importance and the
old liberalism went out of fashion, at least in the West.[6]

The fall of the old liberalism cannot be divorced from its imminent characteristics as an ideology.[7] The ideology created a propensity for a certain
mind-set, and argued in favor of insulating itself from criticism that could
have challenged the premises of a liberal social philosophy, even though just
such a corrective criticism was made to order for preserving certain liberal
values. In other words, it will not do to interpret this ideology merely as an
instrument for promoting an economy that would serve a specific social class.

Nor would it be reasonable to declare all liberal values null and void because a liberal-oriented policy, with inadequate reservations, had triggered
economic and political crises that could have been avoided with more realistic policies.

CLASSICAL CONSERVATISM

We can apply the same reasoning to ideologies classified in western political
thought as classically conservative. But first we must define what we mean
by the phrase "classically conservative ideologies." The legitimizing ideologies did not evolve into a dominant political factor until after the French Revolution. Hardly anyone had thought in terms of an ideological legitimizing of
tradition. It was not until liberal groups had banded together under the slogan
liberté, egalité, fraternité that conservative circles developed conservatism as
a counter-ideology. Classical conservatism has taken aim at liberalism. Alliances with liberal players in forming a united front against various forms of
socialism came later, and even then in a rather diffuse form.

Conservatism, distracted by the urge to preserve, has otherwise assumed
different forms in different societies, although there have been a number of
features in common.[8] In the United Kingdom, it is customary to speak of Ed-
mund Burke as the key theoretician for conservative opposition to liberal social philosophy. In the United States, Alexander Hamilton is considered to be
an early spokesman on behalf of conservative principles. In Germany, the
philosopher Friedrich Hegel was invoked as an opponent of liberalism and in
France, Joseph de Maistre is a key name here. At the beginning of the 1800s,
conservative politicians adopted terms such as faith, authority and order in
opposition to *liberté, egalité, fraternité*.

For conservative thinkers, tradition has always been a term of endearment. This is reflected in the programs of movements whose overriding goal has been to preserve something of historical importance. Unlike liberal and socialist thinkers, conservatives have not perceived history as an inevitable march of progress, with each successive stage more developed than the one before. Nor, for this reason, do conservatives regard old traditions and beliefs as something to be relentlessly exposed and thrown away. It has been regarded as naive and irresponsible to suppose that society can be reconstructed according to principles within the grasp of popular reason. Traditions should be regarded as footprints from previous generations' filtering of experiences. These often encompass more wisdom than what one-dimensional, rationalistic constructions are able to pick up on. This skepticism toward theories of a certain period suggests a cautious, step-by-step approach to social and cultural change.

The cultivation of tradition can assume forms that are quite down-to-earth. Conservative ideology can also be rather elitist. Certain elites are presumed to be better qualified than the majority to speak on behalf of a culture with many important, but not entirely transparent, contexts.[9] The reason for this is that conservative theoreticians, like many social scientists, have seen that culture consists of more than the sum of individual perceptions. They have also seen that culture has structures and functions that neither the general public nor eccentric specialists can be expected to have enough insight into. Interestingly enough, Jürgen Habermas, among others, has pointed out that sociology is a discipline in which conservative opinions should have potential in a modern context.[10] The functionality of societies depends upon more than politico-administrative and techno-economical achievements. The sociocultural sphere is vital for cohesion in all societies.

Religious faith should be respected not merely as an integral aspect of the public psyche. Religion is usually socially important, both in terms of value integration in a culture and of popular loyalty. Interpretations of collective culture as being dependent on supraindividual values, myths and perceptions of reality suit a conservative framework much better than most other forms of political philosophy.

The fact that conservatives have tended to support specific elites, are suspicious of rationalism, and have loathed rapid change has branded many as old-fashioned, undemocratic and even socially repressive. The conservatives' conviction that they belonged to the elite party with the right to hold power has driven some to identify with groups that actually do hold power. In some cases, this involved being connected to the pre-modern aristocracy; in others it meant a strong connection with the wealthy upper classes in industrial societies.

The fact that conservatism can be regarded as an ideology with the hallmarks of a system, and not merely as a collection of pragmatic principles for legitimization, is due to its inherent mentality and to social practice. Its mentality tends to direct its attention toward certain types of challenges while neglecting others. The legitimization of elites leads them to overlook the fact that these favored groups can represent very special interests, though they many appear ordinary and universal to those in established positions. The conservative mind-set, and the way conservatives tend to focus their attention in certain directions, can lead to distorted perceptions and to political misjudgments. Conservatives haven't always been amenable to giving individuals from all groups a chance to develop and gain influence. They haven't always appreciated the need to maintain a critical attitude toward traditions, including those that awarded privileges to the elite.

The ways that conservatives have failed in attempting to govern society have varied from one country to another and from one era to another. We have only to mention the aristocratic resistance to democratization in 1848, the feudal social philosophy that prevailed before World War I, and the Russian Revolution—not to mention countless other examples of a poor appreciation of historical challenges. It is odd that a political persuasion based on elitism— where it is assumed that society should be governed by the best, and not by the majority—should have such a major dispute with new elitists on the subject of knowledge and competence rather than heritage and tradition. A key reason for this is the fact that conservatives couldn't adapt their elitism to arguments that were acceptable to rationally oriented liberals. Many arguments against liberalism, such as it being socially disintegrative, contained features of particularized interest binding, but this was not a good enough reason for excluding liberal spokesmen.

Nor would conservatives succeed in regaining their former status after organized socialists became their most important opponents. While the most conspicuous weakness of conservatives in the 19th century was their inability to include the liberal opposition, their greatest weakness in the 20th century was their eagerness to forge uncritical alliances with liberal groups.

A typical feature of conservative parties, especially after World War II, has been their habit of striking up pragmatic alliances with erstwhile liberal opponents—internally as a front against the socialists, and externally as a front against totalitarian movements. Despite the apparent good reasons for these alliances, the effect has been to dilute conservatism as an independent cultural front. Conservatives have been notoriously apathetic in realizing that their support of liberalism has also led to the legitimizing of commercial culture. With their elitist mentality, they have been prone to brand rebellious groups as ignorant and vulgar—both rightly and wrongly. But even when they could be said to be in the right, any satisfactory, modern argument would have to be based on superior argumentation and not just to references to tradition, bureaucratic practice and fear of irresponsible extremists.

A number of events that took place in 1968 illustrate how modern conservative attitudes played some role in undermining the conservative cultural tradition. The data suggests that an anti-conservative cultural shift took place in the 1960s.[11] Less certain is the reliability of the reasons subsequently given for this shift. "The '60s generation" is widely regarded as having been responsible for a rebellion against the conservative and authoritarian repression of young people and sex, of women and equal opportunity, of underdeveloped countries and development, of peace and love. Opponents of the Vietnam War popularized the slogan "make love, not war." Among young people, opposition to the war was equated with opposition to political imperialism and economic capitalism, opposition to the traditional authority of the family, opposition to companies and educational institutions, and opposition to authoritarian, handed-down culture. For this reason, the hippie movement, with its blaring music and an explosive surge in the use of drugs, all became part and parcel of a collective, anti-conservative rebellion, which reached its peak in the landmark year of 1968.

According to liberal interpretation of events, these changes were a manifestation of an inevitable modernization, or of a youthful rebellion against suppression as one aspect of a general liberation. Conservative spokesmen had come to oppose these interpretations, but for the most part they held their peace. Culturally and historically, 1968 came to mark liberalism's victory over conservatism, and not just that it was an example of liberal mendacity.

At first glance, it should not have inspired much confidence that the very generation that was history's best fed, best educated young people, born in peace-time in egalitarian consumer-oriented societies, came across as revolutionary rebels in the cause of liberation. It has never been systematically documented that the individual urge to rebel was a special hallmark of this generation of young people.[12] Moreover, such an interpretation fits poorly with other research findings on youthful conduct. Previous studies of young people suggest that deviant behavior in these age groups generally occurs in the context of a social collective, and not as the sum total of individual rebellions.[13] Many young people also excelled by quickly joining politically totalitarian movements, or by championing collective views that were rapidly becoming politically correct.[14] However, there are alternative theories which suggest that a better job could have been done of interpreting these events.

The 1960s was a prosperous decade; it witnessed an explosion in education and consumer spending, as well as a plethora of leisure activities. But the '60s are perhaps noted most for the emergence of television as a part of people's day-to-day lives. Internationally, the period is remembered for the Vietnam War, but even more for the freedom movements against former colonial powers. Small businesses, traditional communities and moral attitudes all came under attack by the commercial media and culturally radical journalists. Those who could see these events in context were able to form highly influential fronts. At the same time, groups of young people were being exploited; radical cultural interpreters needed players willing to be identified as rebels in the campaign against repression. Backers of a liberal cultural industry needed young people who epitomize a liberated lifestyle, with international appeal. A new generation of young people needed role models to help them create their own identity.[15] Everyone needed "conservatism" as a counter-force to their own self-legitimization.

The fact that conservative spokesmen were unable to take the offensive in this conflict was not due to the strength of the liberals' arguments. Rather, the conservatives had become bogged down in their own ideology. Many had entered into a lop-sided alliance with liberal spokesmen who tried to explain all cultural changes in terms of liberation, without taking note of intellectual socialists' criticism of commercial culture as a system-governed phenomenon. Moreover, they had begun to support a foreign policy perspective that viewed the conflict between East and West as a struggle between democratic freedoms on the one hand and totalitarian coercion on the other. As a result, they were in a weak position when it came time for them, on the basis of their historical mission, to show that much that purported to represent freedom hardly deserved to be called that, and that liberation itself was a value that had to be weighed against social order and cultural meaning in order not to become destructive.

What happened during this period cannot be explained as historically inevitable, or as the result of the players' strategic interests. To understand this development, and why the liberals encountered so little real opposition, we need to examine the inner logic of what had become the conservative ideology.

MARXIST SOCIALISM

Socialism entered the political arena after liberalism and conservatism had come on the scene. In part, it appeared as a protest against the once predominant ideologies, which were considered to be bourgeois interests serving the affluent classes.

Even socialism appears in many national guises and represents several periods, ranging from utopian socialism to branches of socialism based on a specific perception of scientific materialism, from Marxist-Leninist one-party systems to pluralistic social democracies—which bears more resemblance to social liberalism than Marxism. Nevertheless, socialism was regarded as a universal, world-wide ideology, with ties to Marxist Socialism. The dissolution of Marxist Socialism in major countries around 1989 sped the weakening of the position of socialist parties the world over. This also partly explains why new liberalism has encountered little systematic opposition.

The Marxist version of socialist theory was intended to be scientific and at odds with ideology and false awareness. In Marx's day, the scientific approach was understood in terms of its relationship with materialistic interpretation and not, as in modern scientific philosophy, in terms of whether the principles of a given theory had passed a falsification test. True, the Marxist brand of materialism contrasted with the mechanical version of materialism. The economic division of labor became the foundation of Marxist theory. According to Marx, the resurgence of technical, economic and productive forces limited people's ability to systematize society. With bourgeois capitalism came the chance to mobilize the proletariat to build a society in accordance with its own interests. At the same time, the interests of the proletariat were regarded as most universal and democratic for a progressive socialist government, as opposed to policies initiated by the bourgeoisie, even though the latter attempted to use economics and other disciplines to legitimize their special interests as universal. Marx saw the basis of society from this double perspective, with an emphasis on a dialectical relationship between economic and material productive forces and class-governed production methods. Ideology acquired the status of a secondary superstructure.[16]

The acclimatization of politics and culture with economic circumstances pointed up a potential overlooked by many liberal social theoreticians. It could now be argued that political ideas were not the total equation of separate, independent evaluations. To be more precise, they were structured by social class distinctions. Culture and social life were seen as having sprung from economic conditions—the less acknowledged and managed, the more pervasive and irrational. This perspective offered a number of promising approaches for sociological thinking.

Adapting all political thought to socio-economic interests might appear both a strength and a weakness—a strength in the sense of immunity: hunkered down with explanations placing history, science and democratic liberation on one side; and a weakness in the sense that opponents could be summarily dismissed as historically outdistanced, socially repressive, or scientifically idealizing. Marxism had a far greater appeal in most modern societies.[17]

Intellectual critics had long seen weaknesses and contradictions in the Marxist interpretation of society. However, this criticism was most apparent in the context of certain philosophical contradictions: If all consciousness were assumed to be a product of a social sense of belonging, then even the status of this interpretation would have to be regarded as a social product. The claim of social reductionism could not justify itself from a universally accepted point of view without contradicting itself at the same time. In other words, the claim was not self-referentially consistent. It was a demand that had to be met to command authority on logical and scientific grounds.

Another type of criticism dealt with the scientific aspect of historical laws and predictions. Karl Popper argued logically and scientifically that contemporary players were incapable of predicting future attitudes, unless they were already a part of that future.[18] Jaques Monod claimed that the statement on historical dialectics clashed with empirical science.[19]

In time, it became abundantly clear that the apparent invulnerability of Marxist social thought was a weakness that gave rise to self-destructive processes. Marxist Socialism rests on the assumption that all human consciousness and intellectual argumentation, in one way or another, has a socio-materialistic origin, understood in terms of economic categories. It was hard to take conflicting arguments seriously, in view of how this kind of materialism was linked with a historical view which holds that development always moves toward the ever-increasing liberation of social classes and the previously repressed, and when socialistic parties and groups regarded themselves as representative of the latest stage in this development. Arguments that ran counter to what was presumably the most historically progressive would be interpreted as an expression of historical reaction. Thus, fundamental criticism could be dismissed on historical grounds, without the need to examine the truth content of the criticism.[20] In many countries socialism, which was intended to expose all ideologies, itself became a self-immunizing ideology for the political oligarchy.[21]

As long as socialist countries were in transition from an agrarian to an industrial society, Marxism was useful for controlling and managing this development. The system was less capable of developing a satisfactory decentralized service community, and even less capable of rising to the challenge of what was termed a knowledge society.

Predictions proved to be wrong. Marxist Socialist countries did not surpass capitalist countries' living standards and technological development, and neither did capitalism crush the middle class and usher in a pointed two-class social distinction. The prediction that religion and nationalism would one day be perceived as outmoded agents for individual and political identity was equally misguided.[22] The leaders of the Soviet Union grew progressively less capable of acknowledging their own weaknesses and responding to them satisfactorily.

The Soviet period culminated in tragedy; we could look upon it as a well-meant, albeit ill-fated interlude.[23] We cannot explain this development by assigning all blame to external circumstances, even though civil war, the two world wars and the Cold War clearly made huge demands on resources. External circumstances are certainly partly to blame for the failure of the Soviet experiment; but they also account for much of its success as well. The weakness of the West after the two world wars, the popularity of socialism in parts of the Third World, and the coinciding of socialist and nationalist revolutions are all external causes in relation to Marxist doctrine. It could even be said that had the external system not contained these weaknesses, or lacked stamina derived from national revolutions, the various socialist revolutions would probably never have succeeded.

Marxism as a philosophy cannot be faulted for the rise to power of people like Stalin, although Marxist thought enabled Stalin to find grounds relatively easily for neutralizing his opponents and becoming an absolute ruler. There are several reasons why Marxism came to have so many enemies, besides its class opponents: for example, the widespread abhorrence of terror that followed in the wake of the new regime, along with a fear that the Red army would be used for imperialistic expansion under the guise of progressive programs.

In short, Marxist Socialism became an ideology, forcing its agents to believe they represented history and a universal progressive movement, while suppressing all hostile criticism as reactionary. This became a reason for not taking criticism seriously and why necessary adjustments were not made to the system in time. Despite the many positive values of social solidarity, Marxist ideology failed as an agent for turning these values into political reality.

NATIONAL SOCIALISM

The first half of the last century saw the advent of a number of ideologies that opposed classical conservatism and liberalism on the one hand, and Marxist-inspired socialism on the other. These ideologies were blamed for dividing society into special pressure groups for the bourgeoisie and workers, and for demoralizing society with their decadent culture and opportunistic party politics. To resolve these crises, national programs were set up with unification under strong leadership as the goal.

Some of these movements were extremist, aristocratic and elitist, and justifiably termed radical right-wing, with terms traceable to the French Revolution. Other movements favored mobilization of the masses and formed a united front against what they perceived to be degenerate elitists. Italian Fascism and German National Socialism slotted into this latter category.[24] If the term "radical right-wing" applies to the latter, it is because it rested on a hierarchical party structure with one leader at the top, and because different races were ranked according to a hierarchy.

National Socialist parties sprang up in a number of countries during the 1930s, representing a significant degree of variation. The Nazis, as they were called by their opponents, ran a variety of political election programs throughout Europe. Nevertheless, all these programs bore a similarity to the German variant, led by Adolf Hitler, which was indisputably the strongest among them. While focusing on German National Socialism, we could ask ourselves whether the fall of the right-wing radicals can be ascribed to specific aspects of their ideology.

This ideology originated from the Twenty-Five Points, delivered by Hitler on February 24, 1920, which was proclaimed the day after as the goal of the National Socialist German Workers' Party. It could also be read in several publications written over the following years. Much of this literature appears oversimplified, as an extreme manifestation of the kind of thinking then current in many European circles with crisis experience from the years between the wars. Even so, a couple of features are undeniably unique to German National Socialism. The first concerns the perception of people and leaders, and the second explores the link between Arian mythology and racial research.

The concepts of *volk* and *nation* had been a widely discussed topic after the French Revolution, as this was of vital importance in determining a national democracy's scope and function, with "the people" ruling the nation. A distinction has to be made between nationalism based on the democratic idea of the suzerainty of the people and older notions of dynastic nationalism. The German version did not quite match either of these, being modern and mass-oriented, and definitely not democratic. *Der Führer* was seen as an exponent of the German *volk*, which was understood as a combination of spirit and race. This notion made it difficult to define limits for *der Führer's* authority and to establish legislation when the political leadership had to be dismissed.

Another specific trait of German National Socialism was its racial belief. Racism, and the notion that people of Nordic descent were superior, were widespread in many circles. The inimitability of Nazi racism is found in the myth of the superior Aryan race. Aryan, originally a term for the language of the ancient conquerors of northern India, was the name given to people with a homeland around the Baltic Sea, whose ethnic traits supposedly made them invincible warriors.

This notion of belonging to a superior race, determined by fate to be *Herrenvolk*, could certainly serve as military inspiration in conquering new pastures green. But it could also lead to fatal miscalculations and uncritical political behavior.

These ideas became key ideological features of National Socialism. One idea supported the other. They appealed to the special interests of a humiliated people. These ideas caused a sense of distorted reality and legitimized suppression of others. The notion of belonging to a superior race, with a superior leader, served as immunization against criticism and correction, and the political organizations built on these foundations.

However, it's one thing to say that German National Socialism met the criteria for an ideology and that this ideology led to political illusions and ill-fated destruction. But it's quite another thing to say that this was a decisive factor in the fall of Nazism. We are not attempting to analyze the truly appalling events of World War II here, nor criticize Nazi ideology on moral grounds, but rather elaborate on the cause of its demise. To blame the authoritarian military discipline or the brutal treatment of prisoners for the fall of Nazism is hardly convincing.

Full mobilization of the Soviet Union and the democratic West came a bit too late in the game, primarily as a reaction to war atrocities. By 1939, circumstances could have paved the way for Germany's victory. On the other hand, Germany was ruled by an unpredictable *Führer* churning out inflammatory, intolerable decisions that were beyond repair by the political opposition or by military means. One unforeseen result was the war on two fronts. Another was the notion of "Bolshevism," which posed a threat to civilization, and the racist beliefs intended to legitimize launching an attack on the Soviet Union. These proved singularly destructive for the German forces, as Germany's inhumane treatment of Ukrainian and other Slavic nations in the East turned potential allies into bitter enemies. The notion of Aryan superiority led to the issuing of military orders to German soldiers that were impossible to carry out.

But the blame cannot be laid solely at the door of a mad leader for all the political and military mistakes that ultimately led to the German defeat and the subsequent widespread aversion not only to National Socialism, but to right-wing conservative politics in general. The German *Führer* made depraved decisions because of his belief in the ideology. When Hitler finally became impossible to correct, this demonstrated how the political system was built on the foundations of dictatorial ideology. The history of German National Socialism tells the tale of ideologies in political development, regardless of any objective interests canvassed by ideological agents.

THE RELATIVITY OF IDEOLOGIES

The foregoing ought to convince us that important European ideologies of the past share a number of traits. Being uncomplicated social models with strong moral appeal, they often had a politically unifying and rallying effect. At the same time, they fostered oversimplification and a distorted reality. These ideologies gave many people an insight into certain social contexts, but they also provided blinders. The self-immunizing explanations, which could appear to be a defense against system-threatening criticism, have hampered genuine dialogue with and correction from other approaches and traditions. This was a key factor in a series of flawed conclusions that resulted in the loss of credibility and influence on the part of once dominant ideologies.

Ideologies not only contain legitimate interests of a personal and political nature; they also represent interpretive approaches with an inner logic, whose end results are at odds with the interests of the spokesmen for these same ideologies.

Perception after the fact is always easier. It is, however, far more difficult to decide whether contemporary cultural life and politics are also characterized by a pervasive mentality associated with an overarching ideology. Nor is it all that easy to see what kinds of challenges are destined to collide with the logic of such an ideology. This is discussed in later chapters.

Despite everything that would seem to suggest that relativization of once predominant ideologies is permissible, widespread bias exists in our day and age to label these ideologies as either good or evil, in keeping with a specific moral standard for democratic freedom. The liberal tradition is usually categorized as "good," even though the old liberalism fell short in terms of legislative frameworks and social policies. Socialism can be said to have good intentions, and can be called "righteous" as far as keeping democratic traditions is concerned, but dangerous when it led to too much power for a political party. Generally speaking, conservatism is seen as historically outmoded. To the extent that traditions need defending, they must be justified in terms of modern values. National Socialism and Fascism are altogether regarded as "evil," as deviations from a mainline historical tradition that pointed in the direction of humanitarianism and more freedom for the individual.

Based on such perceptions, it might seem reasonable and impartial to build further on the liberal tradition of individual freedom, combining this with a select socialism-inspired social policy in order to safeguard citizens' rights and ensure that no one becomes a social pariah. We have seen relatively little in conservative political debate that argues for how the formation of modern states presupposes a civil union of beliefs and tradition, of culture and cult. Similarly, little has emerged in the way of radical right-wing arguments in favor of cultural elitism or conscious selection in order to keep culture on an even keel.

The reasons for this taboo label are clearly related to the genocide that took place during World War II. We should by no means underestimate these dastardly crimes, although we cannot sum it all up in one statement. In view of the relativity of all previous prevalent ideologies, there are grounds for taking a closer look even at the spread of genocide in the last century and to ask ourselves whether this was typical only of regimes with a marked radical right-wing ideology, and whether it is reasonable to regard genocide as a direct diversion on the part of political ideologies of a certain stripe. This is not a search for arguments in favor of rehabilitating some form of Nazism, but a desire to make democracy more open to pertinent criticism, which will in turn boost its resistance in the face of inevitable challenges.

It is easy to find examples that demonstrate how all previously dominant ideologies were manipulated to legitimize social conditions which in some way or another were contributing factors to civilian mass murder—from the British concentration camps during the Boer War, to Belgian colonial policies, to the Soviet Gulag, the German Holocaust, the starvation policies under the Chinese Great Leap Forward, and the systematic executions in the former Cambodia. Literature is rife with examples, although estimates of the scope of the genocide remain, for obvious reasons, a matter of opinion.

R. J. Rummel, an American professor of political science at the University of Hawaii, is among those who tried to survey serious literature on genocide during the 20th century. After comparing the work of scientists in the field, he arrived at average figures for civilian genocide committed by governments. He concluded that the death of between 160 and 170 million non-combatants resulted from political decisions made during the 20th century. Stalin and his fellow party members are believed to be responsible for around 40 million of these deaths, Mao for 30–40 million, Hitler for about 20 million, and Chiang Kai-Shek for about 10 million.[25] Although some of these figures are in dispute—the total number of Stalin's victims was probably an overestimation by professor Rummel's referees, while the number of Mao's murders an underestimation—the scale of these tragedies simply cannot be justified.

Rummel's figures seem to suggest that left-wing ideologies have tended to be more dangerous than those on the right, with a key exception for the years of Nazi dominance. Rummel argues, however, that we will miss the mark if we attempt to explain monumental genocide on the basis of specific ideologies. The unbridled power of totalitarian regimes is the lethal element in this instance, rather than ideologies—which, after all, make room for opponents and allow them to serve as correctives. This conclusion tells us something about the characteristics of totalitarian regimes that are typically associated with mass murderers during the 20th century.[26] Totalitarian regimes of sundry ideological flavors were always more brutal than authoritarian regimes, which in turn were more bloodthirsty than democratic regimes. The annual average statistics for executions given by Professor Rummel were 0.40% for totalitarian regimes (0.52% for totalitarian communist regimes), 0.21% for authoritarian regimes and 0.01% for democratic regimes.[27]

These comparative figures indicate more than the notion that genocide is primarily associated with radical right-wing movements, which spokesmen for left-wing radicals have often taken for granted. This comparison could have been interpreted by liberal spokesmen as proof that extremism in itself is dangerous. But even when ideologies are categorized into moderate and extreme forms, this expresses how something relative is transformed into something absolute. Some will argue that even liberal ideology can be exploited to legitimize social conditions that might trigger discrimination and even murder.

Here we should stress that all ideologies can have inadvertent repercussions, and that external circumstances often determine the potential realization of a given ideology. It's one thing to show that political structures that lead to genocide can be legitimized on the basis of specific ideologies, but quite another thing to claim that certain ideologies are bound to lead to genocide. As a rule, it is the fatal combination of ideological and external circumstances that makes these genocides possible. Nor can the most notorious link between ideology and genocide—between German National Socialism and the extermination of European Jews—be explained solely on the basis of ideology. In the original 25-point program for NSDAP, one of the points stated, admittedly, that Jews could not be citizens of the Third Reich; but no mention was made as to how Jews were to be excluded. Later, a number of proposals were put forth, mostly involving banishment, until the political events at the end of 1941 gave rise to a plan for the Final Solution—*ein Endlösung*.[28]

Based on Rummel's reasoning, it is not ideologies of a certain stripe that are dangerous—provided they tolerate opposition. Rather, it is power with no corrective counterforce that sooner or later leads to abuse of power and to murder. One of Rummel's books is entitled, quite simply, *Power Kills*.[29]

Thus, the best institutional guarantee against genocide should be pluralistic democracies, which grant the opposition the right to voice its opinion, where power shifts are possible on the basis of public debate and elections. Even though this is hardly a satisfactory recipe for a functional democracy, and even though democracy cannot guarantee that the best side will always win, this should nevertheless prove to be a good defense in hindering the worst elements from assuming absolute power.

NOTES

1. Hans J. Eysenck and Glenn D. Wilson, *The Psychological Basis of Ideology* (Lancaster: MTB, 1978), 210–222.

2. Harold Laski., *The Rise of European Liberalism* (New Brunswick and London: Transaction Publications, 1997).

3. Steven Lukes, *Individualism.* (Oxford: Basil Blackwell, 1973).

4. The expressions "old liberalism" and "new liberalism" in this context correspond roughly to the terms "classical liberalism" and "modern liberalism" as used by David Conway, *Classical Liberalism* (New York: St. Martin's Press, 1995). Conway claims that in the US, "classical liberalism" has often been called "conservatism." The latter does not, however, apply to all conservative theoreticians in America; for example, it does not apply to Irving Kristol, *Reflections of a Neo-Conservative* (New York: Basic Books, 1983).

5. Geoffrey Roberts, *The Soviet Union and the Second World War. Russian-German Relations and the Road to War, 1933–1941* (Basington: Macmillan, 1995).—Cf. also "Communism, Fascism and National Socialism," in *The formation of the Soviet Union: communism and nationalism 1917–1923*, ed. Richard Pipes (Boston: Harvard University Press, 1964).

6. Cf. chpt. 4, "The Fallacy of Liberalism," in Eric Hobsbawn, *The Age of Extremes. The Short Twentieth Century 1914–1991* (London: Michael Joseph, 1994).

7. Anthony Arblaster, *The Rise and fall of western Liberalism.* (Oxford: Blackwell, 1984).

8. Russel Kirk, *The Conservative Mind: From Burke to Eliot* (Chicago: Regnery Books, 1986)—Clinton Rossiter, *Conservatism in America* (New York: Vintage, 1955)—Irving Kristol, *Reflections of a Neo-Conservative* (New York: Basic Books, 1983)—Jenzy Z. Muller, ed., *Conservatism. An Anthology of Social and Political Thought from David Hume to the Present* (Princeton University Press, 1997)—Bruce Frohnen, *Law, Virtue and the Promise of Conservatism. The Legacy of Burke and Tocqueville* (University of Kansas. 1993).

9. T. S. Eliot, *Notes toward the Definition of Culture* (London: Faber & Faber, 1948).

10. Jürgen Habermas, *The New Conservatism: Cultural Criticism and the Historian Debate* (Cambridge: Polity Press, 1989). Cf. also Robert A. Nisbet, *The Sociological Tradition* (New York: Basic Books, 1966), Amitai Etzioni, *The Spirit of Community: Rights, Responsibilities and the Communitarian Agenda* (New York: Crown Publishers, 1993) and Anthony Giddens, *Beyond Left and Right: the Future of Radical Politics* (Cambridge: Polity Press, 1994).

11. In 1957, *Ifop,* the official French polling institute, carried out a study of attitudes among young people between the ages of 15 and 29. In reply to the question: "Is your generation becoming quite different from that of your parents?" 16% answered "yes" and 76% "no." A similar poll taken in 1968 produced a 92% "yes" rate, with only 5% responding "no."

12. On October 16, 1978, the French weekly *Novel Observateur* made public an opinion poll from SOFRES that uncovered more revolutionary attitudes among 13–20-year-olds in 1978. These findings ran directly counter to all interpretations that pointed to a younger generation more radical than that of their elders: 13% of both older and younger people felt that French society should be radically changed; 19% of the young people and 26% of the older ones wanted meaningful reforms; 34% of the younger and 46% of the older wanted reform in certain areas; 16% of the younger and 7% of the older wanted to keep society unchanged; the rest replied "don't know."

13. Clifford Shaw and Henry McKay, *Social Factors in Juvenile Delinquency* (Washington: Reports on the causes of crime, 1931).

14. Bernt Vestre, *Den totalitare lengsel (The totalitarian longing),* (Oslo: Tanum-Nordli, 1981).

15. Bernice Martin, *A Sociology of Contemporary Cultural Change* (Oxford: Blackwell, 1981)—Christopher Lasch, *The Culture of Narcissism,* (New York: Warner Books, 1979).

16. Karl Marx and Friedrich Engels *The German Ideology,* Part 1, plus *Introduction to a critique of political economy* (New York: International Publishers, C. J. Arthur, 1970).

17. David Caute, *The Fellow-Travellers* (London: Weidefeld and Nicholson, 1973) —Raymond Aron, *The Opium of the Intellectuals* (West Point: Greenwood Press, 1977).

18. Karl R. Popper, *The Poverty of Historicism* (London: Beacon Press, 1958).

19. Jaques Monod, *Le hasard et la nécessité* (*Chance and necessity*) (Paris: Seuil, 1970).

20. André Glucksmann, *Les maîtres penseurs (The master thinkers)* (Paris: Grasset 1977).

21. John Plamenatz, *Ideology* (London: Pall Mall Press 1970).

22. Ephram Nimni, *Marxism and Nationalism: Theoretical Origins of a Political Crisis* (London: Pluto Press, 1994).

23. Martin Malia, *The Soviet Tragedy: A History of Socialism in Russia 1917–1991* (New York: Free Press, 1994)—Adam B. Ulam, *The Communist. The Story of Power and Lost Illusions 1948–1991* (New York: Charles Schribner's sons, 1992).

24. Reinhard Heyrich described the tasks of the *Einsatzgruppen* in Poland to be a fundamental cleansing of Jews, the intelligentsia, clerics and nobles. ("*Flurbereinigung: Judentums, Intelligenz, Geistlichkeit, Adel*")—hardly an aristocratic program. Cf. also Christopher R. Brownin: *Nazi policy, Jewish workers, German killers* (Cambridge University Press, 2000), p. 3

25. R. J. Rumel, *Death by Government* (New York: Transaction Publications, 1994), p. 8.—Other discussions on the number of victims are found in Stéphane Courtois et. al.: *The Black Book of Communism: Crimes, Terror, Repression* (Harvard University Press, 1999) and in Getty Arch and Roberta T. Manning, eds., *Stalinist Terror. New Perspectives* (Cambridge University Press, 1994).

26. R. J. Rummel, *Power Kills: Democracy as a Method of Nonviolence* (New Brunswick: Transaction publishers, 1997).

27. R.J. Rummel, *Power Kills,* Table 1.6.

28. The gradual shift in the Third Reich's policy toward the Jews, from one of expulsion to one of genocide, is described in detail in Christopher Browning: *Nazi Policy, Jewish workers, German killers.*

29. R. J. Rummel, *Power Kills.*

Chapter Four

New Liberalism as an Ideology Related to Myth and Belief

"NEW LIBERALISM"—THE TERM AND ITS LIMITATIONS

It is easy to see how idealized individual freedom, combined with political assertions of social security, dominates contemporary western culture. And tracing these ideas back to liberal traditions is just as easy, as is tracing some claims associated with Democratic Socialism. However, the fact that these ideas constitute a new ideology, albeit similar to earlier ideologies, is a bit more difficult to demonstrate.

It is, of course, futile to propose that all dominant ideas in certain societies at any given time should be interpreted as ideological. We are not suggesting that all features of contemporary culture can be linked to a new version of the liberal tradition; rather, we assume that important aspects of contemporary ideas appear in an ideological system, and that by recognizing this connection, we stand better equipped to understand and control contemporary cultural development.

The new liberalism can be regarded as a modern variant of the theories of John Stuart Mill, Thomas Hill Green and L. T. Hobhouse.[1] It might also have much in common with what Jürgen Habermas termed "late capitalism," which he found to resemble an interplay between the state, public administration and markets, as opposed to "liberal capitalism," which was more unduly market-based. All the same, there is a limit to how far a term developed within one specific theoretical framework can be applied to another.

Contemporary mainstream liberalism has learned from the mistakes of old liberalism and its *laissez faire* philosophy, based on the ideal of the minimal state. In the trade-off between individual liberty and state control, the latter was regarded as an evil—albeit an unavoidable evil—in an ordered society, but one that should nevertheless be severely restricted. Morality was closely associated with individual liberty. Such liberty was only possible when the governing authorities allowed individuals to take responsibility for their own choices, without undue interference designed to rectify the consequences of poor choices. What this social philosophy overlooked was the fact that not everyone had the means or the opportunity to make important life decisions. Many tragic fates were the result of others' choices, not one's own. Furthermore, the choices that had brought happiness to the fortunate were not always moral ones. Old liberals had been naive in their belief that social prosperity was merely the result of many individuals' quest for their own prosperity and well-being.

The new liberalism is not hostile to the state, as the old liberalism was.[2] Government programs for guaranteeing decent income levels and social security benefits are no longer regarded as restricting individual liberty—in many cases, quite the opposite. A welfare state regulated by legislation is an intrinsic element in new liberalism's doctrine of individual liberty and rights. Just how far we should go in legislating welfare is a topic that is much discussed. In most cases, the answer will depend on national income levels and tax policies that take into consideration industry's ability to compete. A competitive economy is not only a prerequisite for generating government revenue, but also for safeguarding jobs. Full employment is an ideal, though an elusive one, in an ever-changing, technologically-specialized workplace with relatively high wage levels.

In addition to safeguarding its citizens' living standards, the modern state is also assigned other tasks whose goal is to preserve individual liberty. Through education and recreational programs, the authorities try to promote self-development adapted to an individual's abilities and aspirations. State and local laws and regulations prevent church leaders, schools, organizations and families from imposing sanctions that might unduly restrict the rights of individuals. Far from being a typical government of cohesion, the modern liberal state has championed the rights and realization of individuals.

This kind of social philosophy has not been fully implemented anywhere. It does, however, serve as a cultural reference for how modern societies should be developed, especially in western Europe. People in most democratic countries disagree on the scope of the public sector and the appropriate level of legislation in different fields. But the general pattern remains the same for most major parties, and is in no way limited to parties explicitly calling themselves liberal.[3] Modern Social Democrats do not wish to be perceived as a left-wing alternative to these ideals, but rather as a party with greater emphasis on the ideals of social equality and state management.

Because parties in democratic countries compete for votes and also need to stake out a position, there is a tendency to resort to terms such as "radical" and "conservative," "socialist" and "liberal" to describe parties that may well differ quite a bit in their views on state obligations and the scope of individual liberty. But viewed in relation to older ideologies, the political references are remarkably similar for all major contemporary political parties in our part of the world. It is in relation to the older and loser ideologies that the prevailing social philosophy of our day deserves an inclusive name.

It is a paradox in the development of the political culture of new liberalism that political parties which have traditionally stood for social liberalism have had trouble keeping the allegiance of their voters. After all, exclusively socio-liberal political parties tend to lose focus when viewed against a socio-liberal backdrop. Parties whose arsenals contain a few contrasting causes have the easiest time attracting attention. This is true even when their views on most issues are well within the bounds of the new liberal repertoire.

A SYSTEM OF THOUGHT—THE LIBERAL DILEMMA

We will be arguing that liberal thought, both in its traditional and modern forms, has all the earmarks of a system. In liberal philosophy, the following characteristics are mutually dependent: The relationship between the individual and society is taken to mean "external" relationships. Individual freedom is understood to mean freedom "from society." This implies certain limitations as to the interpretation of culture. Culture can be perceived as art, a way of life, a mark of identity, or entertainment—but not as something constituting a community as well as consciousness of the individual. This mentality is a prerequisite for understanding the privatization of cultural issues as a neutral policy

One epitome of liberal thought has been the notion of individual freedom as an overriding aim, together with a grasp of the correlation between the individual and society as an external relation. These seem to be the prevailing arguments for social interpretation in many fields.

We should clarify what we mean by an "external" understanding of the relationship between the individual and society. No enlightened liberal would deny that there are many forms of mutual influence in the interaction between the individual and society. When this influence is seen as external, it means that both can be determined independent of each other, and that the relationships between them in principle can be studied as relationships between external factors. This framework for understanding the relationship between the individual and society downplays the significance of a collective culture. Culture may be viewed as something individuals can choose to relate to as they please, for their own development or just for fun. The opposite, the "internal" understanding of this relationship, suggests that both the individual and society become what they are because of the way they relate to a common culture.

Both old liberals and new liberals would categorize "society" either as an entity that springs from the Government, or as a set of conventions, habits and agreements that spring from individuals who make choices. Once freedom is perceived as an individual right in relation to state power and tradition, it is tempting to regard "society" as an external factor in relation to the individual. The more positive attitude of new liberals to public involvement does not contradict this perception—that is, as long as it is emphasized that the state exists for the individual, and not vice versa. This external kind of thinking contrasts with the premises in classical conservative opinion about people in a binding union, as well as with socialist philosophy about the individual's dependence on the class system, and on Fascist philosophy about the constitutional significance of collective inheritance.

When the relationship between the individual and society is seen as external, we must consider what the individual is, quite apart from how it is constituted by culture. The individual can be seen as being governed by its reason or its nature, its will or its needs, and by its right to exploit its inherent potential. By thinking in terms of individuality apart from specific cultures, one can even theorize that the essential characteristics of a social collectivity of individuals is not dependent on religion, language, history and cultural setting. As we will show later, there is a clear link between the liberal notion of individualism and modern interpretations of universal human rights. This same perspective predisposes us to regard culture as a set of goods or benefits —benefits that people from all four corners of the globe are entitled to experience and enjoy.[4]

Liberal philosophy has always been prone to criticism, with some critics pointing out the dubious assumptions and debatable consequences of an individual-centered social philosophy. In recent years, various "communitarians" have criticized the notion of individual choice as a fundamental ethical objective.[5] More pointed criticism can be found, for example, in Hegel's philosophy of rights—where he examines the relationship between religion, the state and the individual. According to liberal thought, a neutral policy for this relationship would be to leave the matter of religious conviction to individual choice. This was considered a program with no great demands, intended to promote rationality and freedom. But Hegel maintained that the program contained veiled dogma. For the program to cohere, religion had to be recognized as largely a private matter, regardless of the doctrine or the way believers felt; or, for that matter, regardless of the opinions of social scientists on collective religious functions. The principle of privatization thus became a major demand rather than a topic of discussion or a matter of personal conviction.

What Hegel wrote about a liberal understanding of religion, others could write about the liberal understanding of culture in general. A criticism here could be formulated as follows: *Either* a liberal, to be consistently free on behalf of the individual, must subscribe to the idea that only formal, non-substantive rules should be binding for everyone. Thus freedom could be negatively defended as an absence of constraint. But then a liberal would at the same time have to interpret society's authority within a special framework and define culture as a matter of personal taste. But this would be an enforced order for those who felt justified in regarding culture as a social issue, since culture is a vital constituent of collective communities. Furthermore, ensuing privatization could lead to a steady large-scale trans-formation of all society in a non-functional direction, thus destabilizing so-cial conditions which brought about liberal freedom in the first place. *Or*, a liberal must subscribe to a specific substantive perception of freedom, a positively defined restriction of what free people ought to realize; but in doing so, he or she could no longer be termed a liberal in the original sense.[6] Notions of the neutral liberal state, based solely on formal rules, seemed an illusion.

This was later termed "the liberal dilemma": No matter which choice lib-erals make, they run afoul of their own doctrine of a society based solely on formal liberty. This system of thought rests on an inherent contradiction, one that cannot be resolved practically by means of social liberal correction or by advocating tolerance. If a philosophical model with built-in contradictions is to maintain credibility as being rational and universally adaptable, this dilemma will have to be forced into the background in some way or other.

OTHER HALLMARKS OF AN IDEOLOGY

We must be able to detect four other hallmarks of thought concerning social conditions before we can say we are dealing with an ideology.

One of these hallmarks is reality distortion, associated with systematic thought and not just actions. A philosophy that structures the relationship be-tween the individual and society in external relations, one that conceals the constituting nature of culture and that sees freedom in terms of an individual breaking free from the shackles of society, leads to all kinds of peculiar no-tions. Clearly there are fields in which this kind of philosophy restricts a so-cial understanding of reality.

If culture is reduced to mere entertainment and symbols for identification, this will most certainly have consequences for our collective orientation. Po-litical principles of individual freedom and philosophical doctrines of natural

rights do not provide an adequate background for understanding our dependence on cultural structures and social functions.

Liberal ideology has implications for our understanding of public duties as
well as individual freedom. The emphasis on individual freedom and rights
must, on liberal terms, assume that "good societies" are directly derived from
the well-being and self-realization of the individuals in a society—in other
words, an underestimation of the structural and supraindividual prerequisites
for a functional society.

We will return to these subjects in later chapters. At this stage, we will simply make our point that the new liberal philosophy, even in its new welfare
version, is not just formal and open, but also substantial, with dispositions for
certain ways of understanding culture and society.

Some interpretations concerning morality might have been more consistent
with ideologies other than new liberalism. One type of context that is hard to
defend from the vantage point of new liberal philosophy is the internal relationship between an individual morality—culturally based on conscience and
guilt, on the one hand—and political principles of freedom and responsibility
on the other. A discussion of these issues is more compatible with classical
conservative principles than with new liberal thought. Even a socialist philosophy might be more open to the study of internal relations between economics and social structures and individual dispositions for thinking and acting.

Another issue that is rarely brought up in new liberal circles is the relationship between morality and selection. Old liberals might once have been
more open than new liberals to discussions on the relationship between moral
responsibility and the obligation of individuals to accept the consequence of
their choices. An uncritical acceptance of those whose lifestyles are immoral
could promote moral decay. Moreover, those with radical right-wing tendencies could maintain that a selection principle should also apply for collective
units, that society's well-being depends in part on people refusing to support
decadence.

Malevolent people are not alone in their desire to champion detrimental social adjustment. Predominant ideologies can act as specially-built rooms in
which those inside might well regard long-term maladjustment as a reasonable, moral right. This means that we should not just be looking at specific
occupational groups in an attempt to determine the degree of popular interest
in new liberalism. Once a particular lifestyle has become established, many
will want to live up to its norms, in confirmation of their acceptance and position "on the inside."

Nevertheless, some occupational groups stand out with special interests
geared to the new liberal ideology. Traditionally, those profiting from free
trade and the manufacturing sector have always been seen as key supporters of

liberalism. But liberalism can also be in the self-interest of cultural workers, if they see culture as primarily a commodity for consumption; and for lawyers, if they see the defense of individual rights as the key moral of society.

New liberalism comes across as a philosophy for a social order in which the individual is given as many choices as possible from which to chose, and a social order in which society bears responsibility when individuals get into trouble. Such a program can appear to be the exact opposite of suppression. All the same, many would say that new liberal societies are indirectly suppressive in a number of ways—partly because freedom for market forces tends to legitimize processes that exacerbate social differences, both within, between and among nations. Among the wealthy, free trade can mean unfettered freedom to exploit manipulative impulses, where the victims are most often those with far more limited resources.

Liberal freedom in our kind of society has many contemporary victims. Nevertheless, the major victims will be future generations, which also risk losing valuable cultural traditions as well as natural resources vital to the realization of a satisfactory life. The fact that our generation uses new liberalism to legitimize ecologically unsound adjustment is bound to adversely affect future generations. And the fact that new liberalism can be presented as a combination of liberal and democratic socialist traditions will not help. Neither liberal nor Marxist socialistic ideology has included environmental limits in their theories on people's rights to exploit modern technology to serve their own interests.

There is little to suggest that new liberalism will go down in history as the framework that made it possible to master the challenges of modernity with rational discussion. Despite its limitations, new liberalism, like many ideologies that went before it, is encumbered by many self-immunizing traits. One in particular is the fact that it is less prone to direct censorship and more likely to promote freedom for all kinds of noisy escapism, which indirectly encourages people to think in terms other than rational criticism. But it has a built-in self-defense mechanism on an argumentative level as well.

Not only are democracy and welfare often presented as aspects of the new liberal social philosophy, but new liberalism can also be regarded as a modern backdrop for staging universal social development—in other words, as something it is foolish to resist.

We are faced with a defense with several bastions and battle lines. When, for instance, radical criticism of liberal culture is dismissed as "authoritarian" and "non-democratic," this should not only be regarded as a random attempt to cast suspicion on the critique itself. Compared with the situation for old liberalism, recent history has imbued new liberalism with new myths and new belief systems to fulfill a need for ideological self-immunization.

THE COLD WAR AS
REFERENCE FOR A POLITICAL DICHOTOMY

This is not the place for an in-depth description of cultural shifts throughout the latter half of the 20th century. Suffice it to say that liberal culture has manifested itself in various contexts during this period. But to understand the depth of this cultural shift, we should take a look at some of the cultural systems that have supported liberalism and lent historic legitimacy. We are referring here to some of the dichotomies that gained ascendancy during the Cold War period, including a certain approach to human rights.

A myth is based on the concept of two parties with opposing moral values, good versus evil. No particular myth would be required to react with moral repugnance against those who had run death camps and used political coercion as a weapon of their own. All the same, there is something contrived about the way liberals view the Allies' wartime efforts as a battle for freedom against cohesion. The war was eventually won when the western democracies had become hardened and more disciplined and, in a certain sense, less liberal than before. Moreover, Stalin's clearly anti-liberal Soviet Union had played a vital role in the Allies' victory.

During the immediate post-war years, the idea of raising liberalism as a common standard under which the victorious democracies could unite was bizarre. On the contrary, the old liberalism could be deemed a backdrop for the crises that brought Hitler to power. Nationalism, and the will to resist foreign occupation, enjoyed a broader appeal at that time. Alongside nationalism, democracy also enjoyed considerable appeal in the 1940s. These two monoliths were usually perceived as more or less synonymous, even if communism also had considerable appeal at that time, even in the West. Furthermore, Christian standards were of overriding importance to many.[7] Faced with Nazi brutality, a number of humane principles became key motivating forces. Nevertheless, the kind of humanitarianism referred to during the War differed from the philosophy of human rights laid down in the Declaration of Human Rights in 1948.

Many conservatives of the time stated that the causes and reality of the War had merely confirmed their warnings of incitement to rebellion against religious and moral principles. For instance, French Catholics viewed Nazism and anti-democratization in Europe as a betrayal of Christian culture.[8] Traditional authority was not the culprit that had paved the way for Hitler's rise to power in 1933; rather, the culprit was the irresponsible dissolution of this bastion of authority, just as it had allowed Napoleon to usurp power in 1799. The worship of an irresponsible demagogue was viewed from the perspective of the political power the rabblerousing radicals had lavished on the ignorant masses.

All of this suggests that the interpretation of liberalism as the paramount value of democracy, as opposed to authoritarian principles, is not the most obvious interpretative framework for understanding what took place at that time. Liberal spokesmen cannot lay claim to having been the main opponent of Nazism.

However, it was not our wartime experience of Hitler, but rather our postwar acquaintance with Stalin that gradually laid the groundwork in the West for anti-authoritarian tales from experiences gained in World War II. In the late 1940s, western politicians clearly saw that their erstwhile ally, the Soviet Union, could no longer be regarded as a reliable ally. With the advent and spread of the Cold War, the need arose for political reorientation in which Germany—or West Germany, at the very least—had to be kept under the thumb of the Allies. Their former ally, the Soviet Union, and the Warsaw Pact countries were now viewed as potential enemies.

For this turnaround, the established habit of casting aspersions on German and Japanese culture was no longer enough. The American film producer, Frank Capra, churned out propaganda films that were repeatedly screened in theaters all over the country during the war, films in which the German dictatorship was vilified as the upshot of long warring and undemocratic traditions in Germany. In other words, Hitler was merely following in the footsteps of Fredrik the Great, Bismarck and Wilhelm II. Furthermore, even Joseph McCarthy's campaign against un-American activities proved ineffectual in the supranational mobilization against communism that took place.[9]

Long after World War II, the western powers suffered from ideological indecision. First, a policy of general disarmament and reconciliation was pursued; mistakes from the aftermath of the Great War were never to be repeated. The United States launched the Marshal Plan for Europe, and played host to a United Nations that was open to all countries subscribing to a democratic charter. Subsequently, the western powers became entangled in the Korean War with the support of the UN, fighting against what was considered at the time an attack on a friendly nation by aggressive world communism.

It was only several years after the Second World War that the notion of communism and Nazism being two sides of the same coin took root. At that time, both ideologies were considered to be authoritarian and anti-liberal dictatorships bent on conquering the free world. The new political us-against-them identity sapped the strength of the long-established image of a familiar enemy. In this light, both the United States and the European democracies could justify their defense alliance against the Soviet Union—not as a change of course, but as an extenuation of their earlier front against Nazi Germany. The western powers came to represent freedom in opposition to totalitarianism and dictatorship. Historical and contemporary opponents were thus defined on the basis of a common denominator.

The Soviet Union had been able to use capitalism as a common denominator for both Nazi Germany and the NATO countries. Soviet-led socialism was the opposite of capitalism.

Earlier, Hitler had used Judaism as a common denominator for his two opponents. Ideologically and economically, Jews were seen as calling the shots with the Bolsheviks as well as the western plutocrats. Hitler's Germany was the opponent of Judaism.

Such a simplification of the political reality is necessary for getting a world view to conform to a mythical duality, with all the motivational force that myths are capable of mobilizing. Strong myths require strong beliefs on the part of those who are spreading the myths. This exceeds the tactical calculations that have characterized a number of ideological interpretations. At the same time, the myth spreaders were bound to what they were spreading, which made correction difficult and eventually led to fatal errors of judgment.

A number of groups put their stamp on the liberal orientation that became predominant during the 1950s. Politicians kept saying that peace depended on moving toward universal freedom instead of remaining trapped within the narrow confines of nationalism. Freedom and rights turned out to be a potent combination indeed. Political programs with this foundation were able to integrate minorities in their own country, generate support among potential allies across national borders, and cast dictatorships in a bad light. An increasingly powerful commercial sector, which had a vested interest in political stability, lent its support to new liberalism. Representatives of the cultural sector, who wanted personal freedom along with market access and government support, did the same. Nevertheless, it was on the research front that new liberalism derived its most important authority.

In social research, which after World War II had largely displaced the previous biological and evolutionary interpretations of human behavior, a number of landmark works appeared. Perhaps it was Hanna Arendt who dug deepest in her quest to understand the prerequisites for the breakthrough of totalitarianism.[10] But it was a different work, *The Authoritarian Personality* from 1950, which first suggested the link between non-liberal ideologies and psychological authoritarianism.[11] This happened despite strong objections from researchers to the scientific integrity of this work.[12] In this book it was claimed that psychological research had shown that Nazis, communists, and even frenzied nationalists actually thought and spoke from a common authoritarian personality structure. Seemingly principled and persistent attitudes manifested a psychological defense of inner insecurity and an inability to come to terms with a multifarious reality. This type of personality, called the F-type—where F stood for "Fascistoid"—was prone to prejudice toward the unknown and to viewing the world in terms of stereotypes. The authoritarian attitude was supposed to be related to an uncritical respect of authority upward, combined with aggression downward, toward those in weaker social positions. In brief, this type of personality was typically undemocratic and politically dangerous.[13]

The Authoritarian Personality rested on a very specific interpretation of relationships between personality and philosophy. On pg. 11 we read the following: ". . . since all ideologies, all philosophies, derive from non-rational sources, there is no basis for saying that one has more merit than another. But the rational system of an objective and thinking man is not removed from the personality. Such a system is still motivated. What is distinguishing in its source is mainly the kind of personality organization from which it springs." The naturalistic interpretation of ideas simplifies the linkage of liberal attitudes with specific notions of soundness and facilitates the adaptation of thought processes to political categories as well.[14] This kind of interpretation could function as a principle of immunization against non-liberal thought: such thinking became not only ideologically unreliable; those who thought that way were deemed questionable, as well.

Several authors followed suit. This gave the discipline enhanced relevance and legitimacy. The social anthropologist Claude Lévi-Strauss claimed that his discipline could explain all the differences between groups of peoples in terms of cultural differences, without having to draw upon dissimilarities in genetic make-up, unlike the Nazis and other authoritarian theoreticians had claimed.[15] The psychologist Milton Rokeach expanded the diagnosis and exposure of radical right-wing dogma with a primary thesis in "The Authoritarian Personality" to include radical left-wing thoughts and attitudes.[16] The authorization of this use of psychology legitimized the rejection of thoughts as non-liberal or dubious, based on the distinguishing characteristics of certain standpoints or attitudes. Undesirable thoughts were interpreted psychologically and rejected, without having to be subjected to a dialogue for examining argumentation. Even philosophers joined the bandwagon and supported this exposé of non-liberal thought. Karl Popper divided western thinkers into those who were in favor of an open society and those in favor of a closed one. His book on the subject was made required reading at many universities.[17] He attacked "nationalism" for being psychologically irrational, virtually unworkable, utopian and, lastly, reactionary. In fact, many intellectuals of that period used their disciplines to support the view that democracies were fighting for the best, and against the worst, in western culture when they took a stand for new liberal interpretations of various controversial questions as opposed to non-liberal ones.

From the 1950s on, the intelligentsia in the West increasingly reflected a duality, with the free, open and democratic on the one hand, and the authoritarian, closed and dogmatic on the other. During the 1960s, this dichotomy showed up in literature, films and the printed press. Lopsided simplifications of all kinds of conflicts, cast as the pitting of freedom-loving and peacemaking ideals against all that was repressive and prone to violence, fit in well with economic market strategy and cultural and political strategy. Liberal notions of individual equality and the right to self-expression eventually became legitimized as hallmarks of modernity, and not just popular culture.

This way of understanding freedom differs radically from system analyses, in which freedom and order constitute two principles that were in equilibrium. These principles, when out of balance, can lead to dissolution and calcification. Paradoxically, what began as an impetus for openness and relativity became an absolute standard of measurement in cultural life. The victory of freedom over suppression became a recurring theme in historical interpretation. Tales about this same duality have been retold countless times in political settings. In educational circles and the entertainment industry, it has long since assumed the form of a myth.

HUMAN RIGHTS AS A BELIEF SYSTEM

Myths of wars—as a struggle of good against evil—are very old. But notions of the good as representing individual freedom and of evil as representing social suppression don't go all that far back. It is these ideas, however, which have given moral and mythical support to the new liberal ideology. But, as we stated earlier, a myth will not have persuasive force unless its vital elements correspond to a belief system. One vital element in the new liberal ideology is a belief in the blessing of individual freedom.

The notion that man is "born free" may have its origins in the philosophy of Rousseau, but we also find it in Article 1 of the United Nations Declaration of Human Rights, where we read: "All people are born free and with the same human dignity and human rights. They are equipped with reason and conscience and should act toward one another in the spirit of brotherhood." This is followed up by Article 2, which states: "Everyone is entitled to the rights and freedoms mentioned in this Declaration, without prejudice of any kind, e.g. on account of race, color, sex, language, religion, politics or other opinions, national or social origins, property, birth or other factors."

This leads us, in turn, to a focus on contemporary concepts of human rights. What is unique about these concepts is the status they impart to the individual in relation not only to the state, but also to society and culture. There were sound political reasons for emphasizing individual rights in 1948, when the UN Declaration was ratified, in view of the world's experiences with

Hitler and Hirohito in the recent past and with Stalin and Mao as contemporary fixtures on the political scene. But this does not fully account for the the status of the Declaration, or the approach it takes. We can say that certain fundamental concepts in this Declaration are based upon a belief system, not only on political experience and an indisputable logic, which otherwise has been considered to be crucial when claiming supranational moral authority in the modern world.

The Preamble of the UN Declaration makes a strong moral appeal for its authority, but offers very few intellectual arguments. In the preamble we read:

> *Whereas recognition of the inherent dignity and of the equal and inalienable rights of all members of the human family is the foundation of freedom, justice and peace in the world,*
> *Whereas disregard and contempt for human rights have resulted in barbarous acts which have outraged the conscience of mankind, and the advent of a world in which human beings shall enjoy freedom of speech and belief and freedom of fear and want has been proclaimed as the highest aspiration of the common people,*
> *Now, therefore,*
> *The General Assembly*
> *Proclaims this Universal Declaration of Human Rights as a common standard of achievement for all peoples and all nations, to the end that every individual and every organ of society, keeping this Declaration constantly in mind, shall strive by teaching and education to promote respect for these rights and freedoms and by progressive measures, national and international, to secure their universal and effective recognition and observance, both among the peoples of Member States themselves and among the peoples of territories under their jurisdiction.*

This text might have an uplifting effect, or it could be construed as pompous or insufferable. Whatever the case, it is far removed from a discursive openness about its own status. A more deep-seated justification preceding the many "whereas" assertions is lacking altogether. Those who wish to discuss the legitimacy of the purported relationship between aims and methods, and those who refuse to accept the claim that freedom from fear and want is, of necessity, the people's highest goal, are all outside the scope of the declaration's terms. They are simply thrown into a class together with those who had promoted "barbarian acts that have outraged the conscience of mankind."

The United Nations Declaration of Human Rights is, as its name states, a declaration of rights. In a legal context, "rights" can have several meanings. In hindsight, philosophers and researchers have been saddled with trying to determine whether the declaration could be defended as valid natural justice and, if so, on what grounds.[18] The declaration has to assume that there is an area for natural justice (*ius naturale*), which stands above and sets limits to both valid international law (*ius gentium*) and civil law (*ius civile*). The validity criteria must remain now, as before: meaningfulness, truth, and justice.

Rights can be formulated as civil rights. Citizens of a particular society are provided with legal protection to circumscribe the power of government over them. Rights can also be formulated as universal rights valid for all people, irrespective of their social identity. This means that all persons are deemed to have qualities that qualify them for specific demands—negative or positive—in relation to the governing authorities. The United Nations' Declaration of Human Rights of 1948 was written—or interpreted, at any rate—on the basis of these assumptions. Some researchers maintain that this declaration presupposes a philosophy of natural rights.[19] This means that those who would defend the declaration's exalted status must be able to show that universal rights are valid and that both the letter and the spirit of the declaration fall within the bounds of natural rights.

The fact that something is called a natural right does not mean that it derives from nature, but rather that it is based on something more fundamental than provisionally accepted political decisions.[20] A demonstration of common norms in all societies would justify a case for natural rights. Otherwise natural law norms are usually based on the consideration of necessary prerequisites for what purports to be assumed truth.

Down through history, attempts have been made to determine natural rights in substantive forms; but spokesmen in later generations have found the results to be non-universal. Classical and Christian Medieval thinking maintained the existence of a natural order of justice, proceeding from God and natural reason. In time, the will of the individual came to be stressed, at the expense of natural reason. Later, the right of the individual to make personal choices came to be regarded as a mark of human nobility. Thus the doctrine of the natural order of justice was changed to what some felt was its direct opposite: a doctrine of the natural freedom of the individual, irrespective of moral or religious regulations.[21] Substantive arguments have also been made in favor of human rights. All such arguments may be based on the premise that a human being can develop into a person, which means that human beings possess reason, a will and a conscience—all traits that distinguish humans from other living beings and give them preeminence in the hierarchy of nature. Objections to this type of justification for universal rights have been made, to the effect that not all individuals of the human species are equipped with the potential for developing these qualities. Furthermore, not everyone who has had such potential has developed it in a way that suggests an exalted moral status. Moreover, the chances of developing such qualities depend largely on the characteristics of the society and the culture in which the individual is raised.

Theoretically, an emphasis on the human potential to become a worthy person could justify a universal law defense for fetuses and children, but hardly for all adults who have realized their potential in a poor way. However, legal thinking is used for the purpose of lending legitimacy to the right of parents to take the life of fetuses—i.e. potential human beings—while the lives of all adult individuals, including those who have used their personal development in the service of manifestly destructive behavior, are defended as sacrosanct simply because they belong to the human species.

From a logical point of view, this is strange indeed. The utilitarian philosopher Peter Singer has argued that there is no intellectually tenable justification for allowing the limit for what is sacrosanct to coincide with delimiting all examples of our species on this earth.[22] In any case, this would be impossible unless we were willing to assign metaphysical references to every human being with a task in life. But the framers of the Declaration of Human Rights kept both metaphysical and theological arguments at bay.

Nevertheless, there are articles in the Declaration that could be defended as aspects of a universally valid natural right, in the sense that no one who takes issue with the Declaration can lay claim to a rationally superior position. For example, if anyone tries to legitimize the treatment of another person as a mere object, that person has violated the conditions for communicative rationality and thus the prospect of a rational justification of their own view as superior.[23] It is not possible to argue logically that other people with communicative skills must be regarded as subjects and not only as objects, for economic, political or sexual use. This could have been part of the premise for Article 5: "No one shall be subject to torture or to cruel, inhuman or degrading treatment or punishment." But certain other articles cannot be assigned a corresponding status adapted to a natural law argumentation. Thus it is a dubious principle to defend all the articles as a "package" and make the defense of the entire package subject to a moral taboo.

Some of the articles in the Declaration are bound to run counter to demographic and ecological boundaries in the not-to-distant future. This applies to the combination of Articles 3 and 25. In Article 3, it is claimed that "everyone has the right to life, liberty and the security of person," while Article 25 claims that "everyone has the right to a standard of living adequate for the health and well-being of himself and of his family, including food, clothing, housing and medical care and necessary social services, and the right to security in the event of unemployment, sickness, disability, widowhood, old age or other lack of livelihood in circumstances beyond his control." In practice, this means that one species on this earth has a moral right to multiply as much as it wants and help itself to everything it finds necessary for its own well-being, without setting any ecological limits to the species' rights in this regard.[24] The authors of these articles have either had a pre-ecological orientation, or they must have assumed that we live on a planet with virtually unlimited resources, or that future members of the human race will be so reasonable and moral that, of their own free will, they will only reproduce and consume within ecologically defensible limits. Such assumptions are so extravagant that they verge on the irresponsible.[25]

The Declaration of Human Rights has an emotional appeal and a moral authority. It could be called a testament for a secular religion. It would be more accurate to regard it as a belief system. This in itself is not a negative term. But it might be wise to recognize the intellectual status of a belief system, if it tries to pretend it is something else. Otherwise it might become a dysfunctional guide for orientation.

"FALSE, IMMORAL AND DANGEROUS"

In his book about civilizations and a changing world order, the historian Samuel Huntington criticizes the view that western culture and civilization has a global validity that would suggest it took precedence over all other civilization-dependent interpretations. He characterizes the western faith in its own universality as false, immoral and dangerous.[26]

To the extent that the UN Declaration of Human Rights is irrevocably linked to western civilization, this characteristic of his applies to the Declaration as well.[27] This is particularly true of the key role the individual occupies in this declaration, as the beneficiary of all kinds of rights. No other civilization than the western variant of recent European and American civilizations has developed fundamental premises for the distinctive brand of individualism that is taken for granted in the Declaration of Human Rights.

The pattern for this declaration is first and foremost the American Declaration of Independence, in which it was claimed that the American people regarded it as "self-evident" that human beings were born with a number of individual rights. We should note at this point that Thomas Jefferson, who wrote the draft of the American declaration during the 1770s, lived during a rather special time in western cultural development, a transitional period flanked in the past by theological interpretations of original sin, and in the future by a coming to grips with the French Revolution and more recent research on human nature. We should also add that those Americans during the 1770s who lent their support to the Declaration of Independence were thinking primarily of their rights as free citizens, and had no notion of extending these rights to apply in full to women or slaves. Jefferson himself was a slave owner.

Moreover, the American declaration of 1776 and the UN declaration of 1948 had practical political agendas that were directed toward traditionalistic and monarchical England, on the one hand, and toward modern totalitarian regimes on the other.[28] None of them were written as recipes for an inner moral order, which was more or less taken for granted. None of them questioned people's right to self-expression within the context of an environment with ecological limitations.

The UN declaration takes human beings as individuals as its point of departure. In doing so, it assumes that social morality and natural morality can be derived from binding conventions framed by moral individuals. A more functional starting point would have been the ecological, material and cultural conditions for sustainable life, which could serve as an initial framework for an acceptable social morality. The conditions for a viable social morality could then constitute the framework for an individual morality.

A system-oriented counter-perspective could make it easier to see the relativity of the present Declaration of Human Rights. Instead of postulating that all human beings are born free and equal, it could have stated that human beings, despite their propensity for being the cleverest of creatures, also possess the potential for fatal forms of maladjustment. This suggests that every individual should allow his or her freedom to be limited by cultural boundaries as well as social regulations. Human beings are one of many species interacting on a planet with limited resources. In an adaptation marked by a struggle for living space and resources, by reproduction and consumption, human beings must adapt to an ecological framework if they are to command moral respect.

The moral respectability of a human society depends on its ability to balance consumption with renewable resources. Societies that permit a high consumption per inhabitant should be obliged to keep their population at a relatively low level. Likewise, societies based on a large number of inhabitants in proportion to available raw materials should be obliged to counter-balance this by a more modest rate of consumption per inhabitant. Societies not in compliance with ecologically acceptable consumption rates would be in violation of the moral framework upon which international support and solidarity are based.

Such ecological perspectives are far removed from those presented in the UN Declaration. The individualism in this Declaration is also subject to criticism on social and cultural grounds. It is hazardous to postulate so many human rights without serious concessions to human duties, with respect to the environment, culture, and society.

There is something disingenuous about the claim that western interpretations of human rights represent universal morality norms for human beings. It can even be claimed that postulating this as immoral does not have to be related to dubious despots who may make their claim when they wish to dispense with a supranational monitor. Even many decent people in other civilizations can be suspicious of being under the moral thumb of former colonial powers when the principle of human rights are regarded as universal moral principles, regardless of local ecological conditions. In fact, these people can argue that a western form of individual morality has an adverse moral effect on circumstances in their own country. Western moral rules are thought to stand in the way of a necessary limiting of population growth, and to hinder effective sanctions on various exploiters. It is also claimed that the idealization of individual freedom, without a concomitant restraint of the outgrowths of this freedom, is in itself immoral.

Within western civilization, it is possible to defend individual liberty in terms of norms of conscience, institutionally grounded in a theological and philosophical context. But contemporary western states have not managed to maintain the connection to their moral roots, much less come up with functional equivalents. References to a good conscience have, instead, made having a good conscience a goal in itself. Feeling good is considered reason enough to assume that something must be right.

The western human rights philosophy current today is part of an anthropocentric conception of morality, developed as a reaction to the political abuse of a theocentric moral philosophy. This context, with its elements of faith and anti-faith, is important for understanding how former humanists thought that the individual would have a strong enough conscience to make a loosening of constraints morally defensible. Especially in certain Protestant circles it was taken for granted that the voice of conscience and the sanctions of the environment would be enough to promote responsible individualism.

But the collective sanctions eventually changed, and so did individual conscience. Where the conscience remained strong, the sense of guilt had a crushing effect on one's zest for living. While an ecclesiastically imparted sense of guilt has been coupled with a doctrine of substitutionary guilt and an offer of forgiveness of sins, the secular humanistic guilt was devoid of any institutionalized redemption. This, in turn, led many secular humanists to avoid guilt feelings and then to explain moralistic reactions as a result of inheritance and environment. Thus a psychological foundation has been laid for interpreting not only morality, but culture in a broader perspective, partly from an objectivist, causal perspective, but also from a subjectivist outlook on experience.

This means that, even in western countries, such an ethic can legitimize dysfunctional forms of adjustment, particularly when it is linked to a new liberal ideology and a mythical understanding of the freedom of the individual as part of a historical struggle between good and evil.

It is probably just a question of time before spokesmen for non-western cultures begin demanding a declaration for international morality other than the one adopted by the UN in 1948. Some countries, instead of regarding themselves as developing countries that need to look to western models for their development, could champion alternative models. In the debate on Samuel Huntington's book *The Clash of Civilizations,* Koshore Mahbubani wrote an article entitled "The Danger of Decadence. What the Rest Can Teach the West," in which he describes the West as a bunch of countries in moral decay.[29] He said that the US has had a population increase of 41% since 1960, but during the same period it has experienced a 56% rise in registered violent criminal acts, a 41% rise in the number of single mothers, a 300% rise in the number of divorces, and a 300% rise in the number of children in one-parent families. Mahbubani regarded this as an unequivocal manifestation of social decay.

This kind of "decay" can be regarded as a suspicious manifestation of the moral development in the West. It is possible to analyze this development in terms other than those that are most congruent with the new liberal ideology and mythical interpretations of the struggle between freedom and bondage. Such analyses must make allowances for the possibility that new liberalism not only limits our attention span, but is also instrumental in promoting dysfunctional adjustment. We should take a closer look at key interpretations of social and moral developments that have been overshadowed in recent years by the new liberal ideology.

ANOMIE

The new form of welfare liberalism might appear less repressive than earlier ideologies. But this impression may spring from a common but misguided way of analyzing suppression. In countries with culturally dominant liberalism, the critique of liberal values will usually be limited to cases where freedom for some neutralizes freedom for others.

Sociological traditions provide a better framework for criticizing contemporary liberalism than vituperative left-wing and right-wing political opponents. Sociology offers better-equipped models than political ideologies for understanding internal relationships between disparate consciousnesses and cultures. These models may imply criticizing the liberal notion of freedom as emancipation from cultural structures.

Emile Durkheim is widely regarded as the first sociologist to provide empirical evidence of individual dispositions within a microcosm of the integrative structures of society. In his study of suicide during the late 19th century, he showed that high suicide rates did not correlate with material hardship, but were linked to religious affiliation and to family fragility. From a sociological point of view, one of his most interesting analyses is the claim that the correlation between marital dissolution and suicide was not just an isolated phenomenon, as would have been the case if people committing suicide had for the most part been those with a history of divorce. The relationships between suicide and divorce rates were supraindividual in nature. Durkheim discovered that the highest suicide rates were to be found in regions, or cantons, that had legalized divorce and where married people often separated. However, those who committed suicide were not usually people who had been through a divorce.[30] These findings inevitably led to structural explanations. The parallel variations in the divorce and suicide rates had to be read as manifestations of circumstances in an underlying social structure that influenced both an intrapersonal variable as a disposition for suicide and an interpersonal relationship as a disposition for divorce.

Durkheim highlighted the social and moral integration of society in his explanation of parallel variations in suicide and divorce rates. To the extent that society was morally integrated, the individual could be integrated as well, and gain strength from that integration.

This link between society's macrostructure and an individual's self-development is of an entirely different nature than explanations adjusted to liberal thought, where the relationships between the individual and society have been lopsidedly regarded as external, partly in a contractual relationship: The implicit assumption has been that the weaker the society—particularly in the sense of the state—the stronger the individuals will be.

A sociological perspective might thus purport to understand freedom in a different way than liberalism perceives it. Freedom must relate to the potential of individuals to realize their predisposition. If an individual from a receptive background is socialized into an integrated culture, and if that same individual goes on to live in a society where the same basic rules apply, we will then have found an important qualification for self-realization.

From a model of the ideal balance between various orientation methods, we can find many types of socio-cultural deviations. One typical deviation may result, on the one hand, from the differences between the predispositions and expectations of an individual that have been accumulated during a given period of his or her life, and on the other hand from the various factors with a potential impact on that individual's surroundings further down the line. Such conditions can lead to painful experiences with feelings of betrayal and a society that lacks integrating norms. In Durkheimian terminology, this was called *anomie*—an absence of regulating norms.[31] The word has been used not only to characterize a lack of motivation in individual moral effort, but also a decline in social solidarity.

Anomie cannot be understood merely as the flip side of freedom, nor yet as a regrettable but unavoidable cost of progress within a differentiated society. On the contrary, we are justified in claiming that human freedom requires laws and regulations that build trust between people. Durkheim regarded anomic conditions as an example of pathological adjustment.[32] Anomie was taken as a sign of crisis. To the extent that anomic conditions are promoted or legitimized by liberalism, liberalism itself becomes a part of the crisis.

Durkheim associated anomie with privatized religion and family relationships. Other sociologists associate anomie with the structure of economic and political institutions, and thus consider several forms of anomic adjustment to be related to liberalism.[33] For instance, in societies based on surplus production, the sale of commodities depends on factors related to potential buyers rather than material necessities and good taste. The advertising industry not only bombards people with information on commodities; it systematically links the advertised product with symbols of brand identity. The less people identify with religion, nationality and family, the stronger their need becomes for personal identities, which may give rise to high regard among reference groups. A major industry sells commodities as symbols of a modern life style. Forms of strength and styles of beauty are sold as identity symbols. At the same time, beckoning success means that most people will never be at ease with themselves, meaning that they are willing to invest, even when they get what they want. This kind of culture can give dispositions for high suicide rates, drug abuse and a narcissist mind-set.[34]

In May, 1995, the news agency Reuters issued the following bulletin: "Levels of crime, depression, suicide, eating disorders, and alcohol abuse have all sky-rocketed among teenagers in industrialized countries over the past 45 years. British and American researchers are now convinced that the growth in the youth culture, which created a generation gap between teenagers and their parents, must bear the brunt of the blame for this development. Researchers feel that an increase in individualism and unrealistically high expectations in life are two of the most important causes of this increased chaos."

These factors highlight personal tragedies. Even worse, the signs could be interpreted as an impending dysfunctional culture with consequences for entire societies. These implications will be discussed in later chapters.

NOTES

1. Michael Freeden, *The New Liberalism: An Ideology of Social Reform* (Oxford: Clarendon Press, 1978)—John Allett, *New Liberalism* (Toronto University Press, 1982).

2. Even in recent times, attempts have been made to revitalize the principles from old liberalism. One example can be found in Richard Nozik, *Anarchy, State and Utopia* (New York: Basic Books, 1974).

3. There are several factors that speak in favor of regarding the principles of the socio-political safety net in the West as being different from similar programs in other parts of the world,—cf. Leiv Ellingsen and Ulf Torgersen, eds., *What Kind of Safety Net?: The Welfare State in Norway and Eastern European Countries.* (Oslo: INAS Report 1992:6).

4. In the last articles in the UN's Declaration of Human Rights, culture is referred to as something everyone has a right to enjoy, not a set of organizational conditions for a community and for the preservation and development of a civilization.

5. Susan Mendus, *Toleration and the Limits of Liberalism* (Hundsmill: MacMillan, 1989).—Alastair MacIntyre, Peter Berger, Charles Taylor, Michael Walzer, Michael Oakshott, *Liberalism and Its Critics* (London: Basil Blackwell, 1984).

6. An example of substantial ideological command based on radical liberal principles, with a condemnation of "communitarian" objections, can be found in Veit Bader's article entitled "Citizenship and Exclusion. Radical Democracy, Community and Justice," (*Political Theory* vol. 23, 2/1995): 211–246.—Contradictions between principles of liberalism and principles of democracy is discussed in Chantal Mouffe, *The Democratic Paradox* (London: Verso, 2000)—The philosopher Hans Skjervheim has written an important article in Norwegian on these issues, entitled "Det liberale dilemma" (*The Liberal Dilemma*), first printed in a book called *Deltakar og tilskodar* (Oslo: Tanum 1967).

7. In a book by Stein Ugelvik Larsen, Bernt Hagtvet and Jan Petter Myklebust, *Who Were the Fascists?* (Oslo: Scandinavian University Press, 1980), reference is made to a number of international studies on who supported Nazism in occupied Europe and who resisted it.

8. Catholic interpretations of Nazism are found in Renzo De Felice, *Interpretations of Fascism* (Harvard University Press, 1977), in Graham Maddox, *Religion and the Rise of Democracy* (London: Routledge, 1996) and in. Jaques Maritain, *Christianity and Democracy*, (New York: Scriber, 1996).

9. The ambiguity of Joseph McCarthy's activities is brought out in two books in which the authors have very different sympathies: James Godbolt, *USA in Our Time—Excerpts from Recent American History* (Oslo: Gyldendal 1994), and in Richard G. Powers, *Not Without Honor. The History of American Anticommunism.* (New York: Free Press, 1995).

10. Hannah Arendt, *The Origins of Totalitarianism* (New York: Harcourt & Brace, 1951).

11. T.W. Adorno, Else Frenel-Brunswik, Daniel J. Levinson, R. Nevitt Sanford, *The Authoritarian Personality. Studies in Prejudice* (New York: American Jewish Committee, 1950).

12. Richard Christie and Marie Jahoda, *Studies in the scope and method of "the Authoritarian Personality"* (Glencoe: Free Press, 1954)—David W. McKinney, David W., *The Authoritarian Personality Studies: An inquiry into the failure of social science research to provoke demonstrable knowledge* (Hague: Mouton, 1973)—W.F. Stones., Gerda Lederer, Richard Christie, eds., *Strength and Weaknesses—the Authoritarian Personality Today* (New York: Springer, 1993).

13. The attempts to expose headstrong people as Fascist F-types must be seen as a countermove against Erich R. Jaench's strongly anti-Semitic book *Der Gegentypus*,

which was published in Leipzig in 1938. Here an unreliable J-type was contrasted with an S-type with strength of character.

14. Sigurd Skirbekk, *Psychoanalysis and Self-Understanding. A Critique of Naturalistic Interpretation of Man* (Pittsburgh: Duquesne University Press, 1976).

15. Claude Lévi-Strauss, *Race and History* (Paris: UNESCO, 1952).

16. Milton Rokeach, *The Open and Closed Mind. Investigations into the Nature of Belief Systems and Personality Systems* (New York: Basic Books, 1960).

17. Karl Popper, *The Open Society and its Enemies,* Vol. I, *The Spell of Plato*; Vol. II, *Hegel & Marx* (Princeton University Press, 1945 and 1956).

18. Ian Brownlie, *Basic Documents on Human Rights* (Oxford University Press, 1981)—Ian Shapiro, *The Evolution of Rights in Liberal Theory* (Yale University Press, 1986)—Jürgen Habermas, *Faktisität und Geltung (Facticity and Validity)* (Frankfurt a.M.: Suhrkamp, 1992)—John Rawls, *Political Liberalism.* (Columbia University Press, 1993).

19. Martin Kriele, *Einfürung in die Staatslehre, die geschichtlichen Legitimitatsgrundlagen des demokratischen Verfassungsstaates. (Legitimation of Democratic Constitutions)* (Hamburg: Rowolt, 1975)—Cf. also Raimondo Panikkar, "Is the Notion of Human Rights a Western Concept?" *Diogenes* (no. 120, 1982):75–102.

20. Leo Strauss, *Natural Right and History* (Chicago University Press, 1953).— Roger Masters, and Margaret Gruter, eds., *The Sense of Justice. Biological Foundations of Law* (London: Sage, 1992).

21. Henrik Syse, *Natural Law, Religion and Rights* (Oslo: PRIO/Dept. of Philosophy, 1997).

22. Peter Singer, "Unsanctifying Human Life," in *Ethical Issues Related to Life and Death,* ed. John Ladd (Oxford University Press, 1979): 41–66.

23. Karl-Otto Apel, "Das Apriori Kommunikationsgemeinschaft und die Grundlagen der Ethik," in *Transformation der Philosophie* II (Frankfurt a.M.: Suhrkamp, 1973): 358–435.

24. Bernado Colombo, Paul Demeny, Max F. Perutz, eds., *Population. Natural, Institutional, and Demographic Dimensions of Development* (Oxford: Clarendon Press, Oxford, 1996).

25. Cf. discussion between Sigurd Skirbekk and Wendell Bell on these issues in *Forum for Development Studies* 1 (Oslo: NUPI, 1999).

26. Samuel P. Huntington, *The Clash of Civilizations and the Remaking of World Order* (New York: Simon & Schuster, 1996): 310.

27. The question of the western dependency on human rights is discussed in Johan Galtung, *Human Rights in Another Key* (Cambridge: Polity Press, 1997).

28. The cultural and historical prerequisites for the American Declaration of Independence are discussed in Paul Johnson, *A History of the American People* (New York: Weidenfeld & Nicolson, 1997).

29. Kishore Mahbubani: "The Danger of Decadence. What the Rest Can Teach the West," reprint in Samuel P. Huntington et al: *The Clash of Civilizations. The Debate* (New York: The Council on Foreign Relations, 1996): 36–45.

30. Later studies have confirmed the social relationships between suicide rates and divorce rates. According to one American study, a 1% rise in the divorce rate will be

followed by a 0.54% rise in the suicide rate. Cf. Steven Stack, "The Effect of Marital Dissolution on Suicide," *Journal of Marriage and the Family,* Feb. 1980.

31. Freda Adler and William S. Laufer, eds., *The Legacy of Anomie Theory* (New Brunswick: Transaction Publishers, 1995)—Christopher Herbst, *Culture and anomie. Ethnographic imagination in the nineteenth century* (University of Chicago Press, 1991).

32. Emile Durkheim expounded his theory of anomie in his book on the division of labor from 1885 and in his book on suicide from 1893. Durkheim's original text, describing four forms of suicide, has been variously interpreted.—Cf. Victor Karady, *Emile Durkheim—Religion, morale, anomie* (Paris: Minuit, 1975).

33. Daniel Bell, *The Cultural Contradictions of Capitalism* (New York: Basic Books, 1976).

34. Marie Coleman Nelson, Marie Coleman, *The Narcissist Condition. A Face of Our Lives and Times* (New York: Human Science Press, 1977)—Charles Tylor, *Sources of the Self. The Making of Modern Identity* (Cambridge University Press, 1985).

Chapter Five

The Dysfunctionality of New Liberal Morality

MORALITY—A FUNCTIONAL-ANALYTICAL APPROACH

In our culture, morality is usually perceived in terms of attitudes toward others and of self-development, but also to a lesser degree in terms of approaches toward social structures. This expresses an individualistic tradition with deep roots in moral philosophy. The self-oriented moral philosophy is steeped in Christian tradition, with an emphasis on the salvation of the soul. In time, however, such perspectives were subsumed by secular moral theoreticians, although it would be wrong to say that all these theoreticians labored in the service of modern liberalism. A self-oriented and secularized perspective on morality nevertheless fits well with a liberal conception of society as the sum total of all individuals.

It has often been said that sociology cannot replace moral philosophy. It is impossible to justify morality in terms of scientific observation alone, whether on a biological, psychological, economic or sociological basis. With the aid of these and other disciplines, however, the visible consequences of disparate moral doctrines in various aspects of life can be touched on. This kind of consequence analysis can tell us about more than the relationship between players' intentions and the realization of goals within a limited sphere.

A consequence analysis of cultural systems can to some extent be kept separate from individuals' personal motives. Still, a consequence analysis has to distinguish between good and bad consequences. That is to say, methods that cannot be ultimately determined solely by empirical measures must be used. Functional adaptation can be said to be a minimum goal for survival. Strictly speaking, the claim that life is better than death and survival better than destruction, is a meta-empirical standpoint. But we can safely ignore those who disagree, since they will not live long enough to further their protest. Empirical research disciplines should try to tell us something about which system-based processes point in the direction of life forms inside or outside the scope of viable adaptation.

In other words, the subject of sociology should, without hesitation, embrace cultural and social moral analyses and warn against system-based processes which, over time, will lead to the disintegration of institutions, society and civilizations. The political preferences of the masses are not necessarily the acme of moral discernment.

When function is perceived as contributing to the survival of a system, a functional analysis will ultimately involve the adaptability of systems that are crucial both to the formation of civilized societies and an individual's odds of survival. If functional analyses are recognized as analyses of the framework conditions for essential systems, then such analyses will take precedence over moral and philosophical discussions on what constitutes the best kind of life. More precisely, this means that if social scientists can show probability that a given form of adjustment is dysfunctional—in the sense of self-destructive consequences—then arguments that take this fact into account will weigh more heavily than potential counter-arguments about how such forms of adjustment have been acclaimed by either philosophers, politicians or popular spokesmen.

A functional-analytical approach to liberal moral philosophy involves investigating whether a liberal culture's typical perceptions and life forms provide us with a satisfactory framework for viable, long-term adaptation. In reality, this approach has longstanding sociological traditions. Emile Durkheim wrote about anomic challenges in a differentiated society. Max Weber wrote about the moral challenges of a bureaucratic, rationalistic social philosophy. Other sociologists have subsequently been concerned with structural conditions for moral cohesion in modern societies.

However, social cohesion is not the only moral challenge facing liberal societies. Morality involves regulation by norms in every area of society, not just those related to politics and economics. Social scientists would do well to ask whether the moral changes occurring are manifestations of functional adjustment to contemporary challenges, or whether we are dealing with an adaptation to a liberal ideology, which over time does not need to be functional.

It could be said that a liberal social philosophy predisposes us to certain types of self-oriented moral perceptions—viewed ideologically as liberation. These, in turn, can predispose us to promote specific types of family formation. An institutionalization of particular family forms might limit the kind of tasks distinct family groups can be expected to cope with.

System analyses, measured in terms of functionality, may lead to different conclusions than those derived from a perspective of historic evolution, with progress and reaction as the main standards of measurement. However, it is possible to take 1,000 years of historical development as representing progress in terms of individual freedom and yet still view the challenges of this trend as a dramatic showdown between functional and dysfunctional forms of adjustment. Instead of elaborating on this from a purely theoretical standpoint, let us consider an example of moral development in a specific western country as an illustration of the types of challenges.

It is only natural for the author to use Norway as an example—partly because he knows the country well, but also because this is a country with a relatively clear history. In short, his reason for introducing this historical perspective is to exemplify the vulnerability of cultural change, and to show how past functional responses provide no guarantee that contemporary and future response will also be successful.

A CHANGE IN MORALS IN NORSE HISTORY

A thousand years ago in the pagan era of the Norse kingdom, when heathen morals predominated, Norwegian moral history had markedly different traditions from the later Christian ones. But there was no absence of norms at that time, as Viking morality prescribed the rights and duties of both sexes and their offspring. For example, a child had to be publicly "adopted" by its father, in keeping with Viking rituals, before the child's rights could be legally protected. Inflicting retribution for transgressions against members of one's family was a matter of honor—by blood vengeance, if necessary. The family lineage was the protective unit for the individual; an individual's morality was closely linked to ancestral subservience and to demonstrating a show of courage and sacrifice in upholding family honor and perpetuating the family line.

With the introduction of Christianity, clan morality gradually disappeared. The local sacrifices, made to ensure the continuation of a family line, were replaced by the Christian Mass and by a God who was supreme. Many not only regarded this transition as a challenge to tradition and family, but also as an omen of impending moral decay. When this failed to materialize, it was because the Church—and later on the State, as well—gradually became a new moral arbiter, replacing clan society. A unique feature of the new Faith was that it commanded superseding authority over both society and the State. This enabled both Church and State to develop their own individual framework without too much destructive tension between them.

In turn, the tension between Church and State provided a framework for a new form of individuality, developed through the morality of conscience introduced and sanctioned by the Church. The individual was, in a new sense, held accountable for his or her own sins. The individuality that grew out of this cultural framework was not anarchistic. In fact, it had many functional advantages over the old clan morality. The Christian code of honor had a broader moral range than heathendom. A moral order geared toward the individual and the State, rather than toward the clan and the local community, had functional advantages for promoting a broader society capable of holding its own against adjoining societies. Internally, conscience-based morality became an important prerequisite for the development of monogamous families. Monogamy became law, which gradually led to improved rights for individuals, including women. Eventually, a marital union was not considered valid without the woman's consent. Giving away unwanted children became illegal. Keeping mistresses was frowned upon, partly through drawing a sharp distinction between children born in and out of wedlock. Even though sin was not eradicated, the Church's norms do appear to have gradually won acceptance.[1]

The Reformation challenged the accepted moral order, even though this transition was far less profound than the previous shift in religion. Nevertheless, Lutheranism represented a break with ingrained notions of a sacrosanct society. *Ecclesia* became the Church and the congregation, whereas the relationship between the Church and the State came to be regulated by the Lutheran principle of two separate "regiments." Monastic life was dissolved and the worship of saints' relics prohibited. Marriage was no longer considered a sacrament. Contemporary critics could interpret this as a weakening of the moral restraints on narcissistic individuals, from kings green with envy at the staggering wealth of the Catholic Church and in dire need of filling their empty royal coffers, to greedy, self-serving merchants alike.

The Reformation did not bring about the moral disintegration of northern European families. The Church's weakened political position was replaced by a stronger national State authority, one that gave a cooperative Church wide-ranging legal authority. Rules on marriage and the dissolution of a marriage were strictly regulated by law. Moreover, the new order led to a greater emphasis on individual accountability and responsibility. This not only confirmed the moral framework of marriage and the family, but also the development of individuals governed from within, i.e. people equipped with what would become known as the Protestant Ethic. We not only gained an equivalent to the previous moralistic restraints on human egotism, but also saw the Protestant individualists, in many ways, become unrivaled in their development of differentiated and rationally-regulated societies.

Family morality was not, however, an unqualified success after the Reformation. In certain districts, priests and peasants didn't see eye to eye, especially as to when a sexual relationship could commence, even though neither party took the matter lightly. This disparity grew out of a desire on the part of some peasants to determine whether a prospective wife was fertile and thus able to carry on the family line before committing to a formal marriage. Many regarded engagement, which eventually came to be Church-regulated, as a starting point for acceptable sexual intercourse. Nevertheless, the period prior to formal engagement remained subject to a host of regulative rituals.

The first systematic data on the status of sexuality in Norway dates back to the sociologist Eilert Sundt's work from the mid 1800s.[2] Sundt found major variations in sexuality in Norway during the 1840s, which he chalked up to the spread of "nocturnal visitors" and the way in which servants were treated. Nevertheless, the main impression gained from Sundt's studies from the mid 1800s is of a society in which marriage-oriented morality generally predominated. Even though he found relatively many births of the first child among couples who were not yet married, 10 out of 11 children were nevertheless found to have been born within monogamous marriages—and this during a time when, to all intents and purposes, birth control was unknown and the average age for marrying was 29–30 for men and 25–26 for women. Moreover, most children born to affianced couples grew up in wedlock.

In the old agrarian society and urban bourgeois families alike, family and financial considerations—not impulsive acts—were long considered to be acceptable grounds for choosing a mate. The parents' views were decisive, even though young people could usually veto their choice. It was felt that love might grow out of dependable marital life, especially if the couple's earthly lives were modeled on holy examples. Passionate love alone was not considered a sound basis for entering into marriage. To the extent that love was thought of in terms of erotic passion, it was usually considered a threat to marital stability.

These views were challenged by new ideas throughout the 19th century, during what later became known as The Romantic Revolution.[3] Romantic authors presented the ideal of a "marriage of love," which was not only an ideal, but was also considered the only acceptable and worthwhile reason for getting married at all. Instead of waiting for love to mature in a relationship in which both parties were trying to live up to certain ideals, love was regarded as a force of nature—beyond the bounds of rationality—a force that would transform both partners, bind them together, and make their married life strong and happy. This emotional love, or infatuation, gradually came to be regarded as a prerequisite for pairing off individuals. Ideally, this would lead to marriage and a sexual union with mutual obligations of fidelity. Conservative critics were quick to question the marital consequences of this romantic cultivation of an erratic, unpredictable eroticism.

The breakthrough of Romanticism cannot be understood solely in terms of an artistic and revolutionary program for giving priority to one's feelings. Even though Romanticism appeared to be new and revolutionary, the pietistic fervency of the 1700s lay sandwiched between the moral orthodoxy of the 1600s and the romantic ideals of the 1800s. Romanticism can also be viewed as an extension of the concepts of liberation inherited from the French Revolution. It fits into a liberal notion of the supremacy of the individual. Romantic authors were often spokesmen for both young people and women, in contrast to what came to be known as a cold and conventional marriage. Romanticism was also able to tap into processes that led to a further liberation of the core family from its binding relationship to kin and tradition, and could thus assist families in becoming mobile units in differentiated industrial societies.

There are several reasons why the Romantic challenge did not undermine family stability. The increased emphasis on the voice of the heart and the enthronement, so to speak, of the individual, were counterbalanced by stricter sexual morality throughout the 1800s. This strengthened both the social authority, production norms in the new industrial society, and—not least—the families themselves. Romanticism helped establish the view that marital life was a kind of reward, bestowed on a couple in the wake of mutual longing and many hard-earned victories before the final "union." For men, this period of waiting involved the development of occupational skills: becoming gainfully employed and establishing an income. For women, it meant acquiring social skills and cultivating their femininity. Marriage was the goal for both partners. In terms of content, the early Romantic period was as much characterized by emotional sublimation—that is, a restraint on sexual drives—as it was by the cultivation of impulsive urges.

Even though the Romantic ideals could never be fully realized—the unobtainable was part and parcel of the essence of Romanticism—in some ways the 19th century's establishment of families with romantic ideals worked even better than the ideals of the previous century. This could partly be due to the improved standards of health and lower mortality rates among parents. At the dawn of the 20th century, morality was held in high regard as a bulwark for marriage. Most people got married; families were stable, with a high rate of childbirth, and many were determined to pass their moral convictions on to future generations.

However, the defense of family morals was closely linked to a general defense of tradition and to the moral derivatives of a theologically-based faith. The new century would witness a breakdown in traditions and the rise of secularization, presenting morality with a raft of new challenges. Some branches of science could have opened new doors for a moral upsurge as regards family formation as well as social and civilizational culture. The question as to whether science in general should have developed in the same direction cannot be answered satisfactorily without taking the dominant ideology of the time into account.

INTERPRETATIONS OF
FUNCTIONAL MORAL EXPLANATIONS

The foregoing is not intended to be an exhaustive history of moral development in a particular country. What we have sought to highlight are some circumstances and factors that are important in a functional analysis. The fact that an institution such as the family has survived into modern times need not be explained in terms of suppositions about human nature or even in terms of general laws of development. Historic development has been on the verge of failure on more than one occasion. The fact that all went well is because certain conditions for the maintenance of a family system were gradually superseded by other practices, which were also able to provide meaningful answers within a functional framework.

Preceding generations arrived at more or less functional equivalents when old guidelines for the support of the family weakened. Moreover, the new circumstances all have one thing in common: they have facilitated a greater degree of individuality, with all the functional advantages this entails for a differentiated adjustment. These same circumstances, however, have also held society hostage to the successful development of individualism in the direction of a strong inward morality, one that can compensate for the weakening of external structural support. In functional terms, individual morality has become more important in modern society than in more tradition-bound societies—not least with regard to the regulation of gender relationships.

In a rational culture we would have expected a deep, broad-based development in the understanding of the various functions of morality, both those that were manifest and known and those that were inherent in the demands and prohibitions of tradition. It would be unreasonable to assume that no functions existed at the heart of the most widespread and inherited moral conventions, or that functions did not account for the fact that all known societies have found the regulation of sexuality necessary.[4] This suggests that researchers in a range of fields would develop rational theories for replacing the functionality of traditional morality. Such a development of morals-based interpretations would have been important for meeting the new challenges with answers that were equal to the task.

It soon became apparent that with the new century came the emergence of serious challenges to traditional moral imperatives. Birth control techniques were steadily being improved and could be expected to alleviate the fear of unwanted pregnancies and STDs, making them less suitable as a justification for moral regulation. Increased mobility and new references to larger societies would make people less dependent upon moral patterns in their local community. Higher educational standards, combined with a more pervasive media presence, could be expected to make young people feel less duty-bound to accept the authority of their parents' attitudes and views. The differentiation of society would make it harder to argue for morality as a direct consequence of one world view.

By and large, this meant that external guidance on the regulation of morality had weakened. From the perspective of the individual, this could be understood as a kind of liberation or as a new right, one designed to serve the individual's needs. From a social perspective, it would be tempting to say that the absence of external necessities had to be compensated by stronger internal norms to maintain development within functional limits.

The simplest functional argument for the necessity of moral regulation is related to "the civilizing process."[5] The development of humans as bearers of civilization not only assumes a process of enlightenment, the acquisition of new skills, and the adoption of "the rules of the game"; it also involves shaping the personality in a more rational and less primitive direction.

Morality doesn't just act as a negative restraint; it also has functions for positive character formation. Disciplining one's urges is related to the development of the will and to long-term planning, and to an ability to give more important principles priority over short-term considerations. Psychologists and sociologists alike have developed a number of explanations for this.[6]

Sociologically speaking, the challenge of modernity should be met by taking the different functions of various institutions into account. As social policies gradually assumed tasks that were once family matters, those that remained took on greater importance for the family's institutional integrity.[7] Seen from such a perspective, the regulation of norms in the direction of particularistic attachment within the family institution would become more—not less—important than before.

From a functional viewpoint we could also argue in favor of a development of norms and institutions to prevent a large number of young men from remaining unattached and aggressive.[8] One could argue that monogamous marital morality has a functional role to play in maintaining a balance between individuality and the social ideals of equality, customarily regarded as "left-wing" values.[9] Major social differences make it easier for men from the upper classes to exploit women from other social strata, because there is less mutual identification. In most predominantly stratified societies, those who saw themselves as belonging to a higher social class tended to demonstrate their superiority by exceeding the moral limits applicable to the lower social classes. "As long as society remains one of class distinctions, the challenge remains of uniting life-long monogamy with human nature," writes Robert Wright.[10]

All societies are dependent on interpersonal ties of various kinds. If these mutual ties are to represent more than constraint or opportunism, special forms of emotional development are required. What is termed "love" in modern-day language actually represents different forms of human bonding. In differentiated societies it is important to distinguish between the various meanings of the word: from impulsive lust to something approaching fervent religious devotion. Certain forms of love are necessary, both for the development of interpersonal experiences and for enduring bonds of loyalty.[11] On the other hand, it is far from certain that all types of relationships covered by the expression "love" are mutually complimentary or that their meanings run in the same vein.

Nor is it an incontrovertible fact that everything definable in words actually reflects a multifarious reality. The focus on sexual love and jealousy as opposites—the former supposedly being admirable and the latter supposedly being wrong—is but one example of concept-based confusion. It is more realistic to regard both phenomena as two sides of the same coin. Some psychological studies suggest that couples who are incapable of feeling jealous are less committed to one other than others.[12]

Societies that aim for more than survival and aspire to spearhead new trends in civilizational development need models that require more than minimum demands. Comparative cultural research leads us to expect a close link between the level of morality and the level of civilization. To be sure, it is not easy to devise supra-cultural solutions with a conceptual apparatus developed in our own culture. Nevertheless, as a rule of thumb we can say that the establishment of a morality that transcends egotism calls for the regulation of human drives. Society, with its many rules and rituals, can make the quest for sexual gratification a highly challenging one. This may exacerbate tensions in several areas of life. Psychological tensions seem to be a prerequisite for creative minds. We might also add that if such tensions are to be constructive, they require a culturally-defined system of meaning. In this connection, the studies conducted by Joseph Daniel Unwin are classics. The data from various cultures that he discussed cannot be summarily dismissed as moralistic, even though Unwin did use certain categorical terms that people today would find discriminating.[13] One of the strengths of his studies is their historical dimension, in addition to their cultural and geographical structure. He felt he could provide convincing evidence to support the conclusion that cultural change, in the direction of higher or lower forms, would be established three generations after a change in morality in the direction of higher or lower thresholds for needs satisfaction. The moral/theoretical conclusions that may be drawn from this type of study are supported, by and large, by psychological explanations.[14]

We live in a differentiated society, one that is dependent on the institutionalized establishment of boundaries between different areas of life. As mentioned previously, families are dependent on other types of norms than those that dominate politics and economics. In order to function, the familiar norms—characterized by reproductive tasks, imputed loyalty and comprehensive reciprocity—must be institutionally protected from both economic and political norms. Historically, the institution of marriage has been perceived in terms of sacrosanct heroes and norms such as those reflected in the maxim, "blood is thicker than water." The obligations of members of close-knit groups are more far-reaching than for the more peripheral members of society.

Marriage as an institution was intended to regulate the family's internal life, as well as its relations to other institutions in society. This suggests that a family-oriented and functionally-based sexual morality must be defined in terms of marriage as an institution. This institution can provide couples with a list of "do's" and "don'ts." Morality, for its part, can help safeguard this institution. The American family historian Robert O. Blood has pointed out that married individuals in all societies are perceived as having a different social status than the unmarried. Clear-cut borders between rights in different institutions, combined with ceremonies to mark the transition between them, could promote a sense of solidarity for the status of marriage.[15]

An analysis of the institutional conditions for sexual morality must involve something more than the characteristics of marriage as an institution. It must also come to grips with other institutions. There are many ways to narrow the field for the legitimacy of market norms; the same applies to rules for when it is functional to apply bureaucratic norms.

In addition to what could be said about the functions of morality in general terms, we could field arguments to support the potential of moral development within distinct cultural frameworks. It is only reasonable to expect that people upholding distinctive traditions that qualify for functional advantage would want to cultivate these qualities and not be intimidated by objections that the moral restrictions thereby embraced might not be universal.

ACTUAL DEVELOPMENTS

Admittedly, the list of all the expectations from the development of sexual morality from a functional point of view could have been much longer and far more detailed, but this would not have altered our main conclusion: Actual developments on this front have differed strikingly from our expectations in terms of functional considerations.

This does not mean, however, that actual developments during the past century took place in spite of a confrontational moral debate. During the past few decades, hardly a day has gone by when this issue has not been the object of media attention in some form or another. Characteristically, the media has presented change in terms that are congruent with liberal ideology. These changes have often been explained as "the march of progress," or as the potential for realizing needs and values, in terms of the choices and goals of the individual. Scant attention has been paid to the institutional prerequisites for moral norms and to their importance in enabling modern society and civilization to adapt.

This focus on the individual has also predominated in various client-oriented and practical-oriented reports that have not played a direct part in the moral debate. This is particularly true in the health sector's approach to these issues. But above all, the focus on individuality has predominated in the popular media's coverage of moral choices and dilemmas. As for sexual morality, the glorification of individual love's victory over strong morality and the intolerant and narrow-minded has been a favorite frame of reference for countless stories. Morality has been viewed as the direct opposite of an individual's happiness. Where morality *is* defined favorably, this has usually involved an appreciation of an individual's courage in asserting his or her convictions, devotion and care for others, of his or her magnanimous attitude and tolerance—and, not least, faithfulness to his or her own feelings and way of life.

Sociologically speaking, we might expect that such a strong focus on problems centered on the individual would result in a tepid defense of marriage as an institution. In fact, this does indeed appear to be the case. Available and reliable data point to a radical weakening of the institution of marriage over the past few decades. This has manifested itself in diverse cultural codes and altered attitudes and patterns of behavior, particularly with regard to marriage as a framework for sexuality.

In the United States, statistics on sexual behavior have been compiled over a long period of time. Lewis M. Terman was probably the first person to submit statistically significant data for changes in sexual conduct within marriage. His investigation was of great value for a comparative study, since during the 1930s he was able to obtain information about people who had been born before 1890.[16] Terman showed that during the first half of the 20th century, there had been a liberalization of marital-oriented morality. The percentage of those who had had premarital relations had increased for both sexes; however, men continued to score higher than women in this regard. Nevertheless, during the 1930s, more American women had premarital sex than men did earlier in the century. Other studies paint a similar picture, one of widespread extramarital sex, fewer marriages and more divorces.

It is not only data on actual behavior that tells us something about the changes that have taken place. Studies of attitudes also show major changes in our part of the world, especially among young people after the 1960s. It remains to be seen whether these changes should be primarily interpreted as precursors to changes in behavior or as individual attempts to adjust to an aggressive development.[17]

In the United States quantitative studies have been carried out that document how graphic depictions of sexual intercourse in the audiovisual media have become widespread.[18] Even though it is not meaningful to compare films from the early 20th century with television programs from later in the century, we can safely assume that the current profile would never have been accepted in earlier periods. Nor is it certain, for that matter, whether the majority of people today would accept the current state of affairs had they had a choice. However, the powerful national media tends to be a one-way communication system; thus, those who control the media also control what information reaches the public.

For media producers, the most important feedback from the public consists of purchasing and consumption statistics. However, these can be unreliable as gauges of popular support, partly because choice is limited, and partly because many people use the media to identify with and respond to a particular reference group, and not because they like what they see, read or hear. So a large pinch of salt and a certain amount of caution is advisable when drawing categorical conclusions about general consumer attitudes from value patterns presented by the media.

The way the media has profiled sexual relations cannot be understood solely in terms of self-oriented accounts of needs, recognition and choice. In a modern information society, a sexual presentation with a broad outreach may constitute a common point of reference for people who do not know each other but who need to relate to something they assume others also feel is important. Sexual "enlighteners" are not the only ones who have a role with unique social potential. The entertainment and porn industries also have latent functions and dysfunctions. Extensive studies suggest that the porn industry has undergone far greater development than expected. This trend is hardly as innocuous as many liberal spokesmen would have us believe.[19] When pornography becomes a widespread cultural pattern, persons of the opposite sex tend to be regarded as mere objects of sexual stimuli, with little in the way of human bonding. So we are talking about a change in family-related morality and not merely "dirty pictures."

Schematically, over time, these changes could be referred to as changes in the order of love, sexuality and marriage. Where the traditional couples' relationship was founded on family-based marriage that entitled the partners to a mutual sex life, one that could gradually develop into a deeper love, the Romantic rebellion sprang up and made love the prerequisite for both marriage and a sex life. It was long taken for granted that dedicated infatuation enlightenment campaigns such as those that came and went throughout the 20th century were all centered around the individual, in the sense that they all played on an individual's needs in determining the criteria for the establishment of strong unions. In time, premarital sex became more common, not just because of the widespread availability of birth control techniques, but also because of weakened traditional and theological moral imperatives.

Radical cultural interpretations, with references to psychoanalytical interpretations, had the effect of bringing infatuation and sexuality closer together. In many circles, premarital sex was perceived as part and parcel of a mutual testing process on the part of the couple, in order to determine compatibility before having children and making a definitive commitment to each other. Such perceptions could seem reasonable enough, when viewed from the standpoint of the individualistic market mentality, but this does not appear equally reasonable from an institutional standpoint. In time, marriage as a goal was relegated to the sidelines, and came to be regarded as a prize for particularly lucky, successful couples. As long as couples could establish lasting relationships without having to be formally married, this was increasingly the accepted practice throughout the 1970s and '80s as a matter of choice. Sweden was a pioneer in this regard.[20] If a relationship did not last, this was interpreted as evidence that it had probably not been viable from the outset, despite having provided a certain amount of satisfaction for the couple as long as it lasted. Sexology could offer categories corresponding to an experience at this level of development. Sexologists have spoken of "life, lust and luck" as a guideline for successful relationships.

The development thus outlined has been referred to as a double-barreled sexual revolution: first the gradual breakdown of the bond between marriage and sexual love, followed by a separation of sexuality and love. Even though this by no means suggests a generally accepted change, or development traits that everyone is trying to live up to, it does tell us something about the direction of change; it tells us that we are on the threshold of a shift in attitudes with regard to marriage, love and sexuality.

Stories and fairy tales from the past can tell us something about these changes. From some older societies, in which love was looked upon as a reward for those who had faithfully lived a life of virtue and had overcome many difficulties, we can note the story about the bear that became a prince and the one about the cow that turned out to be an enchanted princess. In societies founded on the Romantic ideal, we find the fairy tale about Prince Charming who finds and wins his chosen one. In societies which assumed that infatuation and sexuality would lead to marriage, we find stories about people who have bowed to the destiny of their passions. In societies that have primarily regarded sexuality as a need, entitling one to certain rights, we find stories about rebels with a zest for living who locked horns with malevolent and oppressive moralists. In societies where sex is regarded as a stimulus for lust, the media presents people going to bed with one another merely for the sake of an experience. Pornography, as we see it, is a modern cultural phenomenon, not simply a variation of something found in all ages.

In his day, Emile Durkheim maintained that the status and meaning of marriage changed when more and more people got divorced; it was as if married couples would then become "less married." In light of recent developments, marriage is not the only thing that has been devalued; it shares this dubious downsizing with our perceptions of what love is all about. The expression "to make love" has become virtually synonymous with "having sex." In many communities this is looked upon as a form of experience to which people should have broad access, either as an argument for some form of self-realization, as a means of coping with sadness in life—or as sheer fun. For some, it is "making a statement" about a way of life, often used in a power play directed toward citizens considered oppressive and who thus deserve to be provoked by liberated people.

Many have reacted to what has been termed "the sexual revolution." The fact that these reactions have had little impact can be ascribed to the strength of forces for change. An increasing legitimization of the individual's quest for happiness, new power usurped by the media, simplified birth control, and an institutional power shift from the familiar to the social and political spheres are just some of the changes in question. However, for the sake of completion, explanations such as these must be put into a cultural context, where certain interpretations have been suggested as natural and others as suspect. Developments have not taken place in a vacuum, apart from interpretations. We should take a closer look at these.

TYPICAL INTERPRETATIONS OF DEVELOPMENT

Even though the assertion has repeatedly been made that changes in contemporary sexual relationships are merely the manifestation of modern trends, some have nevertheless felt a constant need to justify and legitimize these changes—while at the same time "delegitimizing" the critics. We find the same kinds of arguments in research papers, in popular scientific literature, in articles designed for popular enlightenment and in the popular media.

Given this wealth of literature, it is tempting to restrict our attention to material that is explicitly research-related.[21] In a study of legitimizing cultural forms, such a choice is not a matter of course. It is when new trends are on the verge of a breakthrough, whether in research, popular science, or the entertainment media, that predominant interpretations gain inroads with most people. We can see distinct patterns in the way the media determines which technical material should be given preference. A comparison between statements in the technically-based debate about the more popular media confirms our suspicion that the media tends to focus on research that supports liberal values.

As for popular accounts, there are certain types of recurring explanation. One set of interpretations is based on the premise that changes in morality follow in the wake of technological change. If such interpretations had been compatible with the notion that people's wishes and needs had remained virtually constant over the years, much relativistic criticism could have been avoided. Moral changes could then be interpreted as a consequence of increased leisure time, more cars and efficiency apartments and, above all, greater access to birth control techniques. To be credible, these interpretations must be based on the premise that sexual needs are innate and constant, and that what has changed is the external circumstances for satisfying those needs. Those who make this assumption often try to downplay the differences between popular attitudes, past and present. They claim that, given the opportunity, people would have acted in much the same way in the past. An ancillary explanation is that people used to suppress certain aspects of their nature, at great cost, in order to avoid having unwanted children, or out of regard for their social reputation.

References to nature and to innate needs are a recurring theme in several contexts. This kind of interpretation has its self-immunizing side, as mentioned earlier. It would be futile and somewhat comical to protest against something innate and constant. However, it is not immediately apparent how references to an unchanging nature can explain radical changes adapted to a cultural pattern. Here is where psychoanalytical references come into play, with concepts such as "the suppressed and subconscious nature" representing an important link in the ancillary explanations. If, indeed, moral perceptions were stricter in the past, one could say that people in earlier times played false and pretended to be better than they really were—in which case they were hypocrites! Or it could be claimed that people believed in what they said because they were bound by the attitudes of their time—in which case they were superstitious!

From references to the innate, there are several strands that lead to another kind of legitimizing explanation, one that has to do with liberation. This is a kind of explanation that has a high degree of validity in relation to embodied frameworks of opinion. As for sexual relationships, liberation can mean that people have become liberated from external pressure that used to put a damper on their innate needs, whereas they are now at liberty to own up to human tendencies shared by all. In our culture, accounts of liberation have a pronounced sexual undertone. This is due in part to the Romantic tradition, in which eroticism is assumed to exert a transformative power over an individual's life. At the same time, it is claimed that eroticism must be understood in a positive light. Modern people needn't feel bound to the Romantic notion of fate and suffering. A somewhat offbeat or humoristic view claims to be able to hinder the development of negative feelings such as jealousy.

Liberation can also mean that people now possess greater freedom of choice and that they now choose a way of life based on their individual personalities and preferences, which is on course for a more pluralistic moral situation. Those who would interpret developments as a form of liberation find themselves having to defend how people in the past had in fact been suppressed or "unfree" in a way that is no longer the case.

From freedom of choice, there are links to the next anchor for the legitimizing explanations, those that link change to an increase in democratization. It is claimed that people used to be in bondage to the moral views of the Church and the elite and were now free to govern their lives as they wished, including their sex lives. Democratization, then, is referred to here not merely in political terms, but just as much in a cultural context. The change in the way the mass media deals with sex can be seen as part of this democratization, as it offers something the public wants and is willing to pay for.

The changes in the cultural framework of people's sex lives are often expressed in the context of a supposed transition from prejudice to enlightenment, from non-disclosure to openness. Whereas people once had no choice but to eke out a living in abject poverty in a narrow-minded environment full of prejudice, research and popular opinion have gradually beaten back these forces. Both psychologically and biologically oriented sexologists have crushed the power of prejudice—though not in the case of those who deliberately choose to embrace their prejudices.

The Enlightenment is assumed to have given people a more advanced, more realistic picture of sexuality, which supposedly laid the groundwork for a healthier relationship between the sexes. Far into the 20th century, it was taken for granted among popular opinion-makers that greater enlightenment would counteract fragile relationships and lead to more stable families. The escalation in the divorce rate was often explained as a cultural repercussion of a suffocating, loveless relationship, governed by outmoded sexual roles and based on an inequality that favored paternalism.

Feminists have explained the changes in sexual morality as a function of women's quest for greater sexual equality. They claim that modern women demand equality in order to achieve satisfaction in their marriage. When men fall short of this goal by not sharing household chores, this places a double burden on women, which in turn puts a strain on many relationships.

Now and again, one can hear the drums beating for a historical development from traditional morality to a puritanical production-oriented ethic, and on to a norm system adapted to a hedonistic lifestyle and an anti-puritanical consumption mentality.[22] At other times, we hear people say how changes in morality ought to be regarded as representing not only liberation from society's value system, but also an individual's general disentanglement from social constraint. Change is regarded as a manifestation of a slackening of the reins of both political authority and capitalistic discipline. We hear it said that the development of a more anti-authoritarian morality is due to the weakening of public social norms, and to the fact that people are now largely left to their own devices. The hotbed of love works best when the family, Church and Government avoid involvement in people's private affairs—or so it is claimed.

Most arguments on behalf of liberation have focused on the individual. Overarching moral arguments have been regarded as ideologies suitable for domineering people. But some theories have tried to explain the changes in morality as functional adjustments to major changes in society. Among sociologists it has been customary to claim that modern families have fewer functions than traditional families had in the past. Whereas the family was once a production unit with a variety of social responsibilities, modern families have supposedly become specialized units centered on emotional functions. For an individual, the family unit might well retain its importance, but the nature of the bond between family members has changed character. Under the new regime, a couple could develop their complimentary distinctiveness and at the same time lay the groundwork for stronger emotional ties to each other.

If the establishment of married families is not the matter of course it once was, this is because marriage as an institution lost some of its importance after social trends had altered its functional status. Greater instability has also been termed the price of freedom, or the manifestation of a more honest, mature relationship with respect to the chaotic forces of love.[23]

CRITICISM OF INTERPRETATIONS

First impressions from all these arguments can be overwhelming. It is as though some have anticipated every conceivable objection to trends and have offered explanations to counter any weak points that could possibly leave any doubt. Viewed in context, these interpretations merely give the impression of a dogged attempt at hedging one's bets.

Nevertheless, creating the opposite impression is not really that difficult. Other ethical perspectives could be conceived for the entire development process and thus portrayed in a highly dubious light.[24] Where some speak of liberation, others speak of dissolution. Where some speak of naturalness, others speak of primitivization. Where some speak of being unshackled, others speak of an amoral egotism. Where some speak of tentative ethics, others speak of exploitation.

As a rule, moral aims are countered by opposing moral standards. Discussions along these lines, however, seldom lead to anything more than aggravated conflict, or possibly an appeal to accept public opinion or advice on more tolerance toward other views—a kind of "we agree to disagree."[25]

Still, these interpretations are not intended as an exclusive domain for select groups. These claim to be modernism's self-awareness, or to consist of interpretations derived from science and reason, modernism's grounds for authority. Criticism of these interpretations in terms impossible to regard as historically outdated requires consideration of the scientific status of the interpretations that have been set forth. If their status proves valid, we should then accept them. If not, they should be accorded a different status than the one to which they falsely lay claim.

Scientific argument, as previously discussed, is not just a way of referring to certain experts making judgments. To claim that something is scientific, or that it stems from scientific research, must mean that it has passed the falsification test without being proved incorrect. Even though no scientific interpretation can be expected to encompass every kind of empirical experience, no unequivocal empirical material should exist to contradict the interpretation. Nor should interpretations contain logically self-contradictory elements, even if these might seem necessary for a successful presentation. If a scientific claim is contradicted by these criteria, then perhaps we are dealing with an ideology in which pretensions of scientific authority are an aspect of its self-immunization.

At first glance, the interpretations in question might appear to be overly general and imprecise. But such an impression is not necessarily an objection to repetition. For the most part, interpretations are shared on exactly this level. However, presentations require more precise research. This kind of research is pervasive, but we needn't travel far back in searching the literature to discover that the grounds for research are far more varied than those we find in popular accounts. To the extent that unequivocal conclusions can be drawn, these are often at variance with popular interpretations. We can point to scientifically relevant objections to all interpretations presented, both logical and empirical.

Attempts to explain trends as an inevitable result of technological change defy general experience, which has its own tale to tell about the causes of extensive cultural change. The development of birth control techniques can hardly be regarded as an overwhelming interpretation, partly because the record from a number of countries indicates that the introduction of birth control does not coincide with the time frame for accelerated changes to couple's habits. The technological explanations also mesh poorly with experiences from official and semi-official government agencies that have waged active contraception campaigns.

The spread of HIV was seen by many during the mid 1980s as proof that "the sexual revolution" had gone wrong. In the years that followed, however, public health authorities stated that the AIDS threat should be met with information rather than moralizing. With public funds, some Nordic countries initiated campaigns with a humoristic touch, under the motto "safe sex is fun." During the mid 1990s, doubts were raised as to the medical benefits of these campaigns in fighting the spread of HIV. The behavior-motivational effect, on the other hand, was not questioned. There are clear indications that moral repugnance toward casual sex and prostitution weakened as the 1990s wore on.

There are several explanations for this trend. The notion that we were dealing with an unchanging human nature runs counter to our experience with short-term change. Attempts to interpret human motivation as being governed by innate needs have led to a number of flawed predictions. During the 1950s, many predicted that a more tolerant attitude toward sexuality would cut the ground out from under prostitution and pornography alike, an interpretation that might have made sense if human nature had consisted of a predetermined set of needs. During the 1990s, sexual tolerance had legitimized both pornography and prostitution on a scope scarcely anyone during the 1950s had dreamed of.[26] This says something about the significance of an altered framework of opinion. During the 1990s, the issue of whether prostitution should be accepted was usually viewed in light of what best serves categories of individuals, women and consumers rather than the institution of marriage and society's functional capacity.

Psychological interpretations of nature as a set of "needs" are not derived from something indisputably innate, but rest on a linguistic organization of biological impulses for linguistically-determined interpretive categories in our culture. The substantival category "needs" is just a nominative form of "to need." Freudian-inspired theories about a subconscious nature, which is assumed to be suppressed if it gives rise to manifestations that confound our expectations, rest on a number of non-falsifiable statements and cannot automatically be granted scientific status.[27] Furthermore, no branch of science can argue that individual realization of needs is civilization's highest ethical goal, or that a specific ranking of needs should enjoy an uncontested status exalted above the standards of a specific culture.

In terms of research, the term "liberation" can enjoy a similar status as the term "need." Terms like these can have a strong emotional and ideological appeal and still not represent anything scientifically observable or falsifiable. In a number of contexts, liberation comes across as the basis of an appeal to people with mutually incompatible interests. Attempts to develop a universal, neutral conception of liberation, understood as the absence of cultural bonds, has led to untenable conclusions. It is far from certain that people from other cultural circles, or people educated in past cultures, for that matter, would regard lifestyles in our type of society as particularly liberating.

Nor can moral trends within our society be said to represent the choice of the people. Few referenda have specifically dealt with morality. To the extent that people have expressed their opinions through demonstrations, petitions or opinion polls, their vote has usually pointed in directions that have run counter to actual moral trends.

Nor have interpretations in various research collectives provided any clearcut or unbiased form of enlightenment. This is shown all the more clearly by references to the logical assumptions of research, the dependence of various disciplinary traditions on concepts and models, and experience with the relationship between personality types and perception.[28]

Nor does the suggestion that the so-called sexual revolution has given people a richer and more fulfilling emotional life seem very convincing—in any case, not if the basis of comparison is anything other than barren and emotionally poverty-stricken. In his book about the intellectual fall of the West, Allan Bloom writes that a lack of passion is the most conspicuous effect of sexual liberation, and perhaps the one distinguishing characteristic that renders the younger generation so incomprehensible to its elders.[29]

The value of interpretations which claim that sexual relationships are healthier now than before is also in the eye of the beholder. It is always possible to find comparisons that seem to bear this out. By the same token, it is equally feasible to argue that the way in which people experience health is distinctly culture-related and that this is an ill-suited goal for independent judgments over time. More openness about sex doesn't automatically lead to a greater sense of reality. On the contrary, the kind of reality provided by the popular media can often lead to a fixation on symbols of happiness and to an escape from unpleasant realities. At the same time, attitudes toward sex tend to lead to less protection for vulnerable individuals than before, which in turn leads to new forms of exploitation. The increase in registered sexual offenses reflects a genuine trend, which can be explained most naturally as the unintended effects of a new form of development, legitimized as sexual liberation, not as a by-product of conditions in the past.

It is no foregone conclusion that the battle for greater gender equality should be reckoned as a modern phenomenon with the development of more recent sexual perceptions. In many ways, feminism comes across as a protest movement against development traits that were previously perceived as humiliating.[30] A phenomenon such as greater participation by women in the professions is primarily related to educational levels and new occupational trends, and cannot automatically be coupled with gender attitudes typical of the times.

Some might disagree with this criticism, claiming that interpretations can be valid even if they are not strictly scientific. It could be said that each type of interpretation referred to merely represents parts of a whole and that these explanations must be viewed in context before they can provide a more comprehensive explanation. The authority of the interpretations should then depend upon the inner logic between them. Interpretations grounded in different subject areas do not have to supplement each other in a way reminiscent of modules in order to comprise a whole. However, at the very least, they must not be logically contradictory.

However, when we consider the presented interpretations, they may indeed seem to represent precisely these logical contradictions—and not just one contradiction, but many. It is logically contradictory to base a conclusion on developmental processes on claims that the development of morality is a consequence of some culturally-unrelated technical change, and that this is a consequence of specific values of individual freedom in western culture. It is self-contradictory to regard developments as the realization of a collective human nature, as well as individual freedom of choice and pluralism. The desire to idolize Eros as a transformative power over our will and to trivialize eroticism as a kind of leisure time activity is self-contradictory. The same can be said of regarding developments as originating from the victory of the enlightened elite over popular prejudices and as the democratic realization of popular rights in opposition to an elitist morality. Explaining developments in terms of greater gender equality and as a realization of complementary distinctiveness is self-contradictory. The same is true of arguments claiming that a particular brand of liberation will strengthen emotional ties and couples' relationships and asserting that this same sexual liberation has inherent value and that marital instability is the price that must be paid for freedom, or that

instability is the normal state of affairs. Ascribing the change in sexual relationships as an adjustment to modern conditions for the establishment of families and at the same time asserting that the family unit is no longer all that
important is self-contradictory. To claim that liberated sexuality will promote
love between the sexes is also self-contradictory, as is perpetuating the claim
that liberation means people can have sexual relations without having to em-
bark on complex loving relationships.

Even though it may be possible to reason one's way out of some of these
self-contradictions, the mere fact that we have not fully come to terms with
others, which are blatantly self-contradictory, leads us to conclude that there
is more than reason and science at the root of these interpretations.

Varying portrayals of sexual morality in the service of popular enlightenment down through the ages tell us a great deal about the relativity of past
claims on scientific authority. In older encyclopedias, the subjects of sexuality and sexual morality often used to be found under the heading of "theology." Subsequently, medical personnel, followed by psychoanalytically-
oriented psychologists, felt qualified to provide the most factual enlightenment on the subject of sexual morality. In recent years, a number of natural
scientists and evolutionary psychologists have invoked similar authority and
positioned themselves accordingly. Not all that many years ago, Desmond
Morris, in *The Naked Ape*, felt competent to expound on human nature as being essentially monogamous, which he took as evidence that it was perfectly
acceptable to use nature as a moral standard. Later, when Robert Wright
claimed that even though nature had made us prone to polygamous relationships, society would endure by putting a premium on monogamy, and the major newspapers presented this as evidence of natural morality bursting the
bands of monogamy. This, in turn, was used as a scientific argument to support the notion that de-emphasizing monogamy was the way to go.

As mentioned previously, those claiming scientific authority in support of
their interpretations must be prepared to substantiate which tests their interpretations have passed without contradiction. Advocates of interpretations
claiming to be scientific must be prepared to explain which logical objections
and contradictory data might cause them to modify or relinquish their current
interpretations. A precautionary defensiveness does not boost scientific credibility; on the contrary, it is a sign of interpretations not grounded in science.

SEXUALITY AND MARRIAGE

Predominant interpretations in the debate on morality would be in for a rough
time if they were to be confronted with scientific viability criteria. The fact

that research and reason are constantly used to legitimize these attempts springs from the need for some kind of authority to rebuff potential opposition, as long as we are not dealing with more the mundane applications of ideologies and myths.

In the debate on sexual morality, the adjustment to an overarching framework of opinion on individual self-realization is clear-cut in many contexts. Much the same can be said about the adaptation to a new liberal ideology based on individual freedom and public accountability. We should also touch on the mythical aspect, particularly in the many media dramatizations of sexual conflicts. Conflicts with many possible dimensions are compressed to a duality, with enlightenment, liberation and modernity on the one side and obscurity, repression and reaction on the other. Thus, conflicts become a struggle between Good and Evil, in which the liberal codes are on the side of Good. The use of the key words "liberation" versus "puritanism" is striking, even though many moralistic bones of contention have completely different cores than these terms imply. "Puritanism" is a term borrowed from reformist theology; it fits neither the Lutheran pietistic tradition, nor stoic heroism, nor functional theories, nor any of the more popular forms of moral arguments, for that matter.

In much of the moral debate, however, Puritanism has remained a coded expression, coupled with specific interpretations with a psychoanalytical origin, for interpreting people's attitudes toward how they realize purportedly subconscious natural drives. Those expressing strong support for moralistic ideals are likely to have suppressed the demands of their drives in relation to the superego, and to have projected their own psychological defenses onto others. This interpretation, originally intended to serve as a precedent for self-awareness and liberation, has long since become part of the liberal technique of domination. When moral views clash with liberal ideology, they are branded as "puritanical." This is nothing short of an attempt to neutralize potential threats and becomes part of a defense mechanism for the new liberal ideology.

Spokesmen for the key ideologies of the 20th century have made selective use of history, economics, biology and psychology to neutralize spokesmen for system-threatening argumentation. The new liberals' defense is certainly less brutal than that of National Socialists or Marxist Socialists with respect to public sanctions against critics of the system. On the other hand, the recourse to a psychology of subconscious needs opened the floodgates for certain forms of self-punitive sanctions. In view of the many standards for sexual gratification and self-realization adopted as reference points for the entertainment industry, most people are doomed to feel they have foundered. Even if they could accept living with this stigma, most people will understand that if they express themselves in a "puritan" manner, this will influence others' opinion of them.

Nevertheless, we cannot reject all liberal arguments with the cavalier claim that they correspond to a recognizable ideology and with certain myths. Scientifically untenable arguments might very well possess other qualities. As for the predominant interpretations of sexual morality, one accommodating approach might be to regard these as tentative arguments for the adaptation of modern family relationships. These arguments could have a positive function, even if the argumentation itself were to prove dubious.

From a functional perspective, these changes could theoretically have been presented as follows: Earlier forms of the family were based on family members' many essential chores and on several forms of mutual dependency. Since people today have fewer duties directly tied to the family, emotional relationships assume greater importance. A realization of partners' emotional potential can presuppose the liberation of erotic energy as well. This involves a huge transition from the morality of necessity to something new which, for the time being, must be characterized as a process of trial and error. In a turbulent situation, some people may well have succumbed to the temptation to use research and reasoning in their efforts to legitimize their work. This can be defended for a while as a fundamental strategy for neutralizing criticism and for establishing a counter-position. Nevertheless, the main concern today is acceptance of the fact that attitudes toward sexuality and love must change if modern people are to find any meaning in establishing a family. Through viewing this prospect in a positive light and by demonstrating that marriage holds out the promise of a certain kind of security, marriage may stand a chance in the future. But if the majority still chooses to live together outside the bounds of formalized families, it is probably because they find it unnecessary to institutionalize their relationship. The relationship between institutional frameworks and individual liberty will always be prone to conflict.

This is how one could argue the case for legitimizing the liberalization process. Since the above is a clear-cut functional argument, we should take a closer look at both the premises and conclusions for laying down a functional chain of arguments. We should also ask whether the contemporary family has in fact become more dependent on erotic emotions in bringing people together and whether it is reasonable to assume that the form of sexuality that typifies our culture points toward something that would promote the popularity of marriage and family stability.

Furthermore, we should ask whether it is reasonable to explain the changes in sexual morality as an exploratory adaptation to new conditions governing the formation of families. If this is indeed a correct interpretation, then we can expect a number of family crises in a transitional period. Nevertheless, at the present level of development, the most highly-developed societies should be able to identify family forms that had become more stable than those we would expect to find in an anomic transitional phase. The credibility of this argumentation depends on our being able to find a detectable manifestation as proof. To make the tradition of trial and error plausibly functional, we should be able to point to a number of leading groups with a degree of stability and functionality well above average after a hundred years.

A lot of official statistics could be presented for checking the viability of these suppositions. But when we look at the annual statistics on the family, we find little to indicate a moving on from what Emile Durkheim would have termed an anomic transitional phase into more stable forms. Nor do internal comparisons among groups with different attitudes suggest that we will find more stability among people who purport to represent the most advanced modernity.

In this connection, we should consider Sweden—in part, because the Swedes have kept good statistics on family relationships, but also because Sweden has long been regarded as an avant garde society, particularly with respect to sexual mores.[31]

Ever since the mid 18th century, the Swedes have kept statistics on the percentage of births registered as illegitimate children. Experience showed that children born out of wedlock became a greater burden on society at large. The statistics also tell us something about the status of marriage as an institution.[32] A few decades into the 20th century, there was an alarming increase in the number of illegitimate births in Sweden. By the 1920s the rate had risen to 15% of all births. It was during that time that progressive doctors, psychologists, politicians, and particularly spokesmen for The National League for Sexual Enlightenment decided to take matters into their own hands. This came about through a sex education campaign and through non-moralizing information about birth control techniques. Contraceptives became more readily available, for young and old alike, and the results soon became apparent. The rate of children born out of wedlock began to drop. This appeared promising, and sex education programs were intensified and expanded. But then the unexpected happened. The percentage of children born out of wedlock began to rise again—slowly, at first, then explosively. By 1976, the rate had escalated to a third of all births, and during the 1980s it was the highest in western Europe.

If Swedish politics can be credited with having had an impact on this development—and it should, since developments in Sweden have taken more of a marked turn than anywhere else—it has clearly unleashed processes that mitigated against the original goal of reducing the number of births outside stable, marriage-regulated families. However, this policy proved unsuccessful, in part because the introduction of a supposedly neutral form of sex education changed the balance between influential institutions and led to alternative attitudes toward sexuality. Sexual habits changed markedly during the 1960s and '70s. This, in turn, altered the status of marriage from that of being a safe haven and the only commonly accepted framework for having a sex life, to being just one of a number of tolerated frameworks for relationships between couples. In addition, marriage involved many commitments and legal formalities in the event of the breakup of the relationship. With its new status, in the eyes of many, marriage was simply unable to compete in popularity with the other more informal form of cohabitation, which was called "love marriage" during the 1970s, as opposed to "institutionalized marriage."

The fall-off in marriages in Sweden throughout the 1960s was so drastic that the authorities appointed a commission to look into how marriage was adapting to the times. A report entitled "Family and Marriage" was published in 1972.[33] Interestingly enough, psychological and sociological arguments, rather than theological or legal ones, were used as a justification for the formation of families as a public matter. One such argument was that institutions concerned with children's welfare favored families with a father. The report said: "Theoretically, the birth of children in modern societies, with their medical opportunities, specialization and differentiation of work could be separated from the family and reduced to a mere biological event. As far as we know, sociology has not been able to report of any society where this has been the case. [...] In psychological, pedagogical and sociological literature we are often confronted with the view that a harmonious development of the personality of the child—the combined dispositions based on nature and nurture—depends on security and solidarity during the first years of their life. [...] The more norms a child encounters, and the less unanimous these norms are, the family's responsibility for uniting the norms becomes all the more important. [...] The father's role as breadwinner outside the home limits his opportunities for participation in the development of his children's personality, while the mother, on the other hand, is considered to have an overly dominant influence through her constantly being together with the child."

The argument that marriage had to do better at competing with cohabitation was promoted in order to encourage fathers to have more contact with their children and to help more people establish committed relationships. The Committee wrote the following: "The difference between living together outside marriage and within marriage can conclusively be narrowed by a combination of limiting the legal implications of marriage and introducing rules for actual living together, with the same implications as those for marriage."

The Committee's proposal, with a few modifications, was incorporated in new marital legislation that took effect on January 1, 1974. Later statistics indicate that family politics did have an impact. By the end of 1974, the decline in the marriage rate had reversed and an upswing had begun, which soon flattened out, albeit at a lower level than was the case in the mid 1960s. But if the new legislation was to be credited with halting the decline in the marriage rate, it also had to share the blame for the sharp rise in the divorce rate during the same period. In 1973, the number of divorces stood at about 16,000, after having stood at around 10,000 per year during the 1950s and 1960s. In 1974, the numbers skyrocketed to 28,802. After that, the divorce rate dropped a bit and appeared to stabilize at about double the rate of the 1950s. In Sweden, marriage was an institution that was easier to enter into, but also easier to leave than previously, and the Swedes availed themselves of both options. In recent years, Sweden has had the lowest marriage rate and the highest divorce rate in the West, in relation to the number of marriages.[34] This indicates that increasing numbers of children had begun to live without regular contact with both parents, especially their fathers, which had been one of the main rationales for the new marriage reform legislation.

There was nothing inherently wrong with this logic, nor with the good intentions of the Swedish reports. The subsequent inventiveness in redefining new goals in order to make them accommodate unforeseen developments has been fairly impressive. Nevertheless, something went wrong, and this led to an acknowledgment of the need for further reform.

The committee members and all the educators involved in this matter had all regarded sexuality as a matter of the needs and rights of the individual; they had judged the preservation of marriage to be dependent on its popularity in a competitive market. They had been focusing too much on the individual, even though they thought they were being neutral. They had lost sight of the fact that marriage is an institution with social functions and assumptions that cannot be derived from individual-based premises. Instead of putting sexuality into a functional context, as a reward for contributing to the preservation of the family and the continuation of society, they had defined sex as everyone's individual right.

Self-oriented diagnoses have not only been characteristic of certain public reports. We find the same choice of perspective in a number of fields. Typical here is the way in which sex is exploited in advertising and the entertainment industry. Contemporary sexology, which purports to represent specialized expertise, is also characterized by the idea that individuals' feelings determine family structure, rather than vice versa. One reason for this striking effect is its evasion of the sociological perspective, as well as the many empirical studies which give the lie to a hypothesis suggesting that successful family life ought to be governed by the right of individuals to seek happiness in their own way. Several studies indicate correlations between early and non-institutional sexual debuts, between many partners before and after a marriage, and a high rate of marital failure.[35] In a Norwegian study conducted during the 1970s on the reasons given for divorce among 87 divorced men and 84 divorced women, it was found that about 50% of those interviewed cited an extra-marital relationship with a third party.[36] In an American study, we find the claim that 40% of both partners, in some way or other, were actively involved with a new partner during divorce proceedings.[37] Systematic studies have also cast doubt on the notion that the stability of marriage can be determined by the degree of satisfaction among selective couples. One American study reports that "the investment in the future that a couple represents in a relationship is a better measure of stability than various expressions of satisfaction."[38]

This suggests that we are not only faced with a number of unintended negative effects on how some individuals adapt. The de-institutionalization of marriage confronts us with changes that could have far greater dysfunctional repercussions. In fact, it could be argued that we are facing a form of adjustment that is bound to have civilizational consequences, since it will adversely affect the reproductive ability of the very people one would expect to carry on western civilization.

THE CONCEPT OF HUMAN NATURE IN NEW LIBERALISM AND IN EVOLUTIONARY PSYCHOLOGY

A common feature in all liberal moral perspectives necessitates specific assumptions on human nature. If one could take for granted the fact that human nature is conditioned for harmonious social adjustment—as long as the personality is neither suppressed nor perverted in any way—one could reasonably draw the conclusion that this personality liberation also represents the liberation of human beings as social creatures.

Certain assumptions are taken for granted, at least where commercial culture is concerned. New liberal thinking must gain trust in the usual course of events in order to appear positive and progressive.

Natural perceptions lie outside the sphere of social scientists' routine tasks. If key research in the field is consistent with notions of a harmonious innate human nature, new liberal spokesmen could lay fair claim to exemplifying a realistic view, even though they represent specific interests as well. If important research in the natural sciences contradicts these notions, this is all the more reason to suspect new liberal notions of having ideological inclinations.

A number of perspectives exist on naturalness in subjects within natural science. Explanations provided in evolutionary psychology and neo-Darwinian literature are without doubt of greatest interest in this instance, not least because this literature discusses the issue of morality from a functional perspective.[39] One starting point within evolutionary psychology is the notion of how people bear the hallmarks of selective genetic material over long periods of time, not only by their outward, evident behavior, but also through their mental attitudes. Few communities have lived for more than a century under contemporary living conditions, for more than a thousand years in cities or for more than three thousand years in agricultural communities. On the other hand, we all have ancestors who perhaps lived as hunters and gatherers three million years ago. These are functional for a specific lifestyle, and distinguish our personalities through inherited predispositions. The example of how small children in New York betray an instinctive fear of snakes, but not of cars, is sometimes used to lend credibility to this assumption.

From the Darwinian camp, claims have been forwarded to suggest that one mechanism for human adaptation, over and beyond individual survival, is a chance to put one's stamp on future generations by leaving descendants—i.e. by passing on one's genes. Richard Dawkin has gone so far as to claim that the battle of the genes actually characterizes individuals' adaptation, and not vice versa.[40] No matter how we might choose to regard this, our nature is undeniably predisposed to a struggle to pass on our genetic material. Furthermore, we are prone to disseminate ideas in order to legitimize our own lifestyle.

In the animal kingdom, we find both polygamous and monogamous forms of reproductive adjustment, both of which are illustrated in this context. Polygamy might seem advantageous for dominant males who want to distribute their genes to as many offspring as possible. In the animal kingdom, the gender war between males and females is central. Dominant males killing other males' offspring is commonplace.[41] For example, some scientists consider the monogamy of male gibbons as representative of a functionally-developed lifestyle that is geared toward defending its own young and toward preventing other males from killing them.[42] Monogamy has a number of functional advantages, the most conspicuous being that it offers individual progeny a better chance of survival.

Among human beings, there are societies that permit polygamy and others that prohibit it, just as we find variations in the scope of sexuality that are not linked to marriage. Interpreting these variations purely as an expression of degrees of liberation or of inadvertent convention would be unreasonable, as they are an intrinsic part of social patterns with disparate adjustment strategies. Some societies are adapted to large families, with relatively little protection for the individual and a high rate of mortality. Other societies are adapted to smaller families, with strong protection of the individual through strict regulation of families and kinship ties.[43]

In ancient times, polygamy characterized the first civilizations, which were governed by despotic leaders. These despots allowed themselves many privileges, such as keeping large harems and a bountiful supply of offspring. This was common among despots in all the early civilizations in Babylon, Egypt, India, China, Central America and Peru.[44]

If the despot's genetic characteristics were superior to all the other men's, this could be regarded as functional for the population. However, this adjustment seems to have advanced the selection of individuals with inherited aggressive character traits. Moreover, these kinds of community demanded strict social hierarchies, in which few rights existed for concubines or for single men. This state of affairs came at a price. The Incas practiced extreme inequality and a rigid distribution of rights for men. The Sun King Atahualpa was said to have kept several "houses of virgins," each one holding 1,500 women, so as to guarantee an ample supply of royal concubines. State officials just below royal rank were permitted to keep harems of more than 700 women. Other important citizens were allowed 50 concubines, leaders for liege nations 30, heads of large provinces 20, heads of small provinces 15, overseers 12, managers 8 and minor leaders only 7, 5 or 3 concubines—all according to their status. Less privileged men were not allowed any wives at all.[45] The Aztec king Montezuma amassed a staggering total of 4,000 concubines, and imposed a strictly hierarchical society with hideous punishments meted out to wrongdoers. History verifies how these societies were not adept at fostering public support or creating an alternative elite when heads of state were under threat. The American civilizations were easy prey for the invading *conquistadores*.

There are a number of explanations why South American Indian civilizations were so easily conquered by the Europeans during the 16th century. Military superiority among so few invaders can hardly be the only answer here. The Aztec king's belief in the Inca god, Quetzalcoatl, sailing across the sea in the reed year, explains some of the Indians' ineffectual resistance. Feudal tribes' desire to topple a bloodthirsty despot from power could explain this turn of events even more. The Inca culture and social structure started to crumble once their god-king had been deposed and put to death. Speculation abounded as to whether genetic inbreeding was a causal factor for the Incas' susceptibility to the medley of infectious diseases brought over by the European conquerors, diseases to which they would most likely have been exposed sooner or later anyway.

One distinguishing feature of despotic governments has always been how violence was rewarded. All ancient civilizations used access to sex as a reward system for subjects that enjoyed the most favor and acquired the most power.[46] This could imply that it was only by means of a counterforce, and by supervision of the established system of power, that another moral view could be accommodated.[47] Nevertheless, despots' sexual lusts and lascivious nature was not the sole reason for potential conflicts and escalating violence within these societies. In prehistoric times, societies seem by and large to have been violent. One study has estimated that as many as one in four men from primitive societies were killed by another man, a rival within the community, and that murder may often have been sexually motivated.[48]

A well-known 18th century example can be mentioned at this point. In 1709, nine mutineers from the HMS *Bounty* came ashore on the Pacific island of Pitcairn to settle and establish a peaceful community. They were accompanied by six men and thirteen women from Polynesia, a Pacific archipelago regarded even then as notorious by European standards for the inhabitants' sexual permissiveness. The colony was discovered eighteen years later. By that time, only one of the men and ten of the women had survived. Of the original fifteen men, only one had died a natural death, one had committed suicide, and twelve had been murdered. The lone survivor was, quite simply, the only person remaining in the wake of an orgy of violence, apparently motivated by sexual competition. After his discovery, he immediately converted to Christianity and drew up legislation prescribing monogamy for Pitcairn Island. Up until the 1930s, this little island community was prosperous and law-abiding. And so far, apart from sporadic infidelity, the Pitcairners have remained monogamous.[49]

Monogamy has a lot of advantages in comparison with polygamy. It has facilitated greater social equality, enhanced women's rights, provided greater protection for children and created closer bonding with parents. Above all, communities regulated by monogamy produced less sexually-motivated violence. Nevertheless, the functional superiority of monogamy does not prove that human beings are monogamous by nature, even though evolutionary psychologists would claim that most hunters could not possibly have supported several wives and that this mentality has been passed down to us as part of our genetic inheritance.

From an evolutionary standpoint, it could be objected that absolute monogamy does not generate a particularly diversified selection. Monogamy gives most people a fairly equal chance of passing on their genes. Exceptionally capable or valuable individuals yield relatively minor benefits to populations. People with high-ranking executive positions could carry desirable genetic material, but acquiring adequate resources to maintain larger families would be functional.

Different forms of research show that men and women generally differ in terms of attitude and preference with respect to sexuality and cohabitation. Sociologists have tended to explain this on the basis of divergent roles and dissimilar socialization. These differences can also be explained in terms of evolutionary psychology. For over thousands of years, the two sexes have been adjusting to their different roles in the cycle of life. Evolutionary psychologists argue that men can have more pronounced promiscuous tendencies on account of being able to spread their genes in this way. Promiscuous women don't have the same advantage, nor do they usually show much interest in this direction, although women's sexual digressions are not an unknown phenomenon and, more often than not, are liasons with men in high-ranking positions of influence.[50]

This does not mean that evolutionary psychology may be used as an argument in favor of promiscuity. This kind of activity may have either a positive or negative impact on genetic selection. For the preservation of monogamous marriages and equality between the sexes, the effects are primarily negative. The evolutionary psychologist Matt Ridley concludes that infidelity and the condemnation of infidelity are both "natural" in the sense that evolution has left us predisposed in both directions.[51] On the other hand, it would be a misunderstanding if this conclusion were presented as an argument in support of liberal tolerance as the most natural choice. Ridley also claims that repressing men's natural tendency toward violence cannot be effectively brought about through gentle admonition alone. The Fifth Commandment is worded in an unconditional and judgmental manner; the same can be said of the Sixth Commandment.

Women have traditionally been condemned in stricter terms than men when marital norms have been violated. Even Trobriander women, once central in cultural liberals' mythical imagery,[52] were condemned to death for infidelity. This is commonly regarded as manifest male chauvinism or inhibited gender equality nowadays. But this interpretation does not ring entirely true, as no known society has punished women more severely than men for other acts of lawbreaking, such as theft or murder. A functional perspective here makes other explanations plausible. From a historical and an evolutionary point of view, different reaction patterns could be attributed to a family unit not necessarily feeling threatened by a man having children by another woman. On the other hand, having to feed other children could diminish the family's procreative ability to produce more children with the parents' own genes. We must not ignore contemporary data on infanticide. Contemporary American studies suggest that stepchildren are at greater risk of death than children living with their biological parents.[53]

From a natural science perspective, the grimmer aspects of the relationships between men and women and between parents and children can all be placed in a historical functional framework. Before we condemn everything that runs counter to humanist values, we should at least try to understand the kind of functions that various arrangements and reaction patterns may have had. It isn't certain that we can eliminate everything before we have discovered more humane, but equally functional, alternatives than those we inherited. The desire for more children than can be fed, a limited willingness to care for other people's children, and the urge to take a competitor's life all constitute elements within a natural selection process that might have been both quantitatively and qualitatively crucial to human development. For the same reason, it can be a mistake to believe that the old order, with lots of children and a high mortality rate, resulted in a satisfactory functional alternative represented by families with few children, all of whom are expected to survive into adulthood. The fact that many people only want to deal with the positive emotional aspects of human reproduction seems to suggest some form of wishful thinking rather than future-oriented rationality, as does the wish to cultivate emotional states related to love as an intrinsic value, regardless of the functionality of those states.

Where a humanist sees a flower garden, a natural scientist might see a battlefield. For a variety of reasons, Darwinian and psycho-evolutionary moral interpreters may represent an important corrective to ideas based solely on humanist concepts. But even so, naturalistic interpretations of human nature can hardly be regarded as representing a superior ethical standard in the art of civilization-building.[54] A natural conclusion to this chapter might be Katherine Hepburn's reply to Humphrey Bogart in the film *The African Queen*: "Nature, Mr. Allnut, is what we have been put in this world to rise above."

NOTES

1. Einar Hovdhaugen, *Ekteskap og kjønnsmoral i norsk historie* (*Marriage and morality of the sexes in Norwegian history*), (Oslo: Samlaget, 1976): 31–32.

2. Eilert Sundt, *Om Giftermal i Norge* (*On marriage in Norway*), (Oslo: Gyldendal 1976; orig. 1856)—Eilert Sundt, *Om Sedelighedstilstanden i Norge* (*On morality in Norway*) (Oslo: Gyldendal 1976; orig. 1857).

3. Stuart Hughes, *Consciousness and Society* (Brighton: Harvester Press, 1979).

4. Kingsley Davis, "Sexual Behavior," chpt. 5 in: *Contemporary Social Problems*, eds. Robert Merton and Robert Nisbet (New York: Harcourt, 1976).

5. Norbert Elias, *The Civilizing Process—the history of manners and State formation* (New York: Urizen Books, 1978).

6. Sverre Lysgaard and Louis Schneider, "The deferred gratification pattern"; *American Sociological Review*, 18, 2, (1953).

7. Talcott Parsons and Robert Bales, *Family, Socialization and Interaction Process.* (London: Routledge and Kegan Paul, 1956).

8. American data suggests that a man between twenty-four and thirty-five years of age is three times as likely to commit murder if he is unmarried than if he is

married.—Cf. Robert Wright, *The Moral Animal.* Pantheon, (New York: Partenon 1994): 100.

9. Wright, *The Moral Animal: "Darwinism and Moral Ideals."*

10. Robert Wright, *The Human Animal. Evolutionary Psychology and Everyday Life.* (New York: Pantheon): 106.

11. William J.Goode, "The Theoretical Importance of Love," *American Sociological Review,* 14 (Feb. 1959): 39–47.

12. M. Wilson and M. Daley (1992): "The man who mistook his wife for a chattel," in *The Adapted Mind,* eds. H. Barkow and L. Cosmides (New York: Oxford University Press, 1992): 232–289—Cf. also Matt Ridley, *The Red Queen, Sex and the Evolution of Human Nature* (New York: MacMillan 1993): 237.

13. Joseph Daniel Unwin, *Sex and Culture* (Oxford University Press, 1934)—An abridged version: J.D. Unwin, *Sexual Regulations and Cultural Behaviour, An address delivered before the Medical Section of the British Psychological Society* March 27 1935, ed. by Frank M. Darrow, (California: Trona, 1969).

14. The classic example here is surely Sigmund Freud, *Das Unbehagen in der Kultur,* (Vienna, 1930). But even non-Freudian behavioral scientists can give evidence for this kind of interpretation; cf. Hans. J. Eysenck, *Genius* (Cambridge University Press, 1995) and Dean K. Simonton, *Genius and creativity: selected papers* (Greenwich, CN: Ablex, 1997).

15. Robert O.Blood, *Marriage.* (Glencoe: The Free Press 1978): 157.

16. Lewis M. Terman submitted interview data from a selection of 174 American men and 104 women born before 1890. Of these, 50.6% of the men and 86.7% of the women denied having had premarital sex. After this period, the rates decline for men: from 41.9% (N = 291) for those born between 1890–1899, to 33.6% (N = 273) for those born between 1900–1909, to 13.6% for those few people in his selection who had been born after 1910 (N = 22). For women in the same birth cohorts, the rates sank from 77.0% (N = 227) to 51.2% (N = 336), to 33.7% (N = 060). Cf. Lewis M. Terman, *Psychological Factors in Marital Happiness* (New York: MacGraw Hill, 1938).

17. The profound changes of the 1960s are in large measure reflected by a study of attitudes carried out by the English researchers Wright and Cox, who claimed that the number of English teenagers who felt that premarital sexual relations were always wrong had sunk from 55.8% in 1963 to 14.6% in 1970; cf. Christie Davies, *Permissive Britain. Social Changes in the Sixties and Seventies,* (London: Pitman 1975). 65.

18. American media analysts have found that popular "daytime soap operas" contain on average between 3 and 4 sex acts per hour, compared with between 2 and 3 in so-called "action series" and situation comedies. In these cases, only 1 in 6 people, on average, was married with their sex partner. Cf. Bradley S. Greenberg: "Content Trends in Media Sex," in Dolf Zillmann et al., *Media, Children and the Family.* (Hillsdale, NJ: Erlbaum, 1994): 170–172.—Cf. also B.S. Greenberg et al., *Media, Sex and the Adolescent,* (Hampton Press, NJ: 1993): 45f.—The same media analysts reckon that the average American household watches television about 4 hours per day.

19. Cf. David Copp and Susan Wendell, ed., *Pornography and Censorship.* (New York, Prometheus, 1983)—Neil M. Malamuth, Edward Donnerstein, ed., *Pornography and sexual aggression.* (Orlando: Academic Press, 1984)—Robert J. Stoller,

Porn: Myth for the Twentieth Century (Yale University Press, 1991).—Maurice Yaffé and Edward C. Nelson, *The Influence of Pornography on Behavior.* (London: Academic Press, 1982).—Diana E.H. Russell., *Against pornography: the evidence of harm* (Berkeley: Russel Publ., 1993).—Dennis Howitt and Guy Cumberbath, *Pornography: impact and influence: a review of the available research evidence on the effect of pornography* (London: Home Office Research and Planning Unit, 1990).

20. According to an opinion poll quoted in an official Swedish publication, *Ej till salu (Not for sale)* from 1981, the proportion of Swedish women who regarded love as a prerequisite for sex sank from 73% to 54% between 1967 to 1979; for men the drop was from 47 to 43% (p 321).—Cf. the discussion in David Popenoe, *Disturbing the Nest. Family Change in Modern Societies,* part II "The Case of Sweden," (New York: Aldine de Gruyter, 1988) and in chpt. 3.2 in Christopher Prinz, *Cohabiting, Married and Single?* (Avebury: Aldershot, 1995).

21. An argumentation survey and literary references may be found in Anthony Giddens, *The Transformation of Intimacy: sexuality, love and eroticism in modern society.* (Stanford University Press, 1992) and in Michel Foucault, *The History of Sexuality (Histoire de la sexualité)* (Copenhagen: Rhodos, 1978).—Cf. also Robert E. Michod. and Bruce R. Levin, *The Evolution of sex: An examination of current ideas* (Sutherland, MA: Sinauer, 1988)—Mike Brake, *Human Sexual Relations. A Reader* (London: Penguin 1982).—Shery B. Orner. and Harriet Whitehead, *Sexual Meaning. The cultural construction of gender and sexuality* (Cambridge University Press 1981).

22. Colin Campbell, *The Romantic Ethic and the Spirit of Modern Consumerism* (Oxford: Blackwell, 1987)—Cf. also Daniel Bell, *The Cultural Contradictions of Capitalism* (New York: Basic Books, 1976).

23. Ulich Beck and Elisabeth Beck-Gernsheim, *The Normal Chaos of Love* (Cambridge: Polity Press, 1994).

24. Gertrude Himmelfarb, *The De-moralization of Society. From Victorian Virtues to Modern Values* (London: IEA Health and Welfare Unit, 1994).

25. Jeffrey Weeks, *Sexuality and its discontents* (London: Routledge, 1985).

26. In *US News and World Report* No. 5 1997 there is an estimate of the extent of the porn industry in the USA.

27. Hans J. Eysenck., *Decline and Fall of the Freudian Empire* (London: Viking 1985).

28. The relationship between personality types and forms of perception has been studied in many contexts. A number of principles for interpreting these relationships may be found in Graham Powell, *Human Nature, Selected writings by Hans J. Eysenck* (Aldershot: Dartmouth Publishing, 1994).

29. Allan Bloom, *The Closing of the American Mind* (New York: Simon & Schuster, 1988).

30. Dorchen Leidholdt and Janice G. Raymond, ed., *The sexual liberals and the attack on feminism* (New York: Pergamon Press, 1990).

31. Richard F. Tomasson, *Sweden: Prototype of modern society* (New York: Random House, 1970)—Another author, Roland Huntford, has interpreted the Swedish program for sexual liberation as a covert social art of decoration; cf. chpt. 5 in *The New Totalitarians,* (London: Allen Lane, 1975).

116 Chapter Five

32. During the 1750s, the percentage of registered illegitimate births in Sweden was as low as 2.5%—cf. Jonas Frykman, "Sexual Intercourse and Social Norms. A Study of Illegitimate Births in Sweden"; *Ethnologia Scandinavia* (1975): 111.

33. *Familj och äktenskap.* 1 (*Family and marriage. 1*) (Stockholm: SOU, 1972:41).

34. Cf. analysis of Dorchen Anderson and Michael Leidho, "Quantitative indicators of family change" in: *Sociology of the Family, ed.* Michael Anderson (London: Penguin 1980).

35. An interview study of young people in the age bracket 16–24, conducted by Scantel for MTV Europe and published in 1997, shows that English young people debut earlier and have more partners than boys and girls of their age in the rest of Europe. England has recently had the highest divorce rate in Western Europe; all the while, Englishmens' perception of themselves as puritanical is a recurring theme in the major media. For more than a decade, the comedy *"No sex please, we're British"* has been the most popular theatrical play in London.

36. Jan Erik Kristiansen, *Skilsmisse i Norge (Divorce in Norway).* (Oslo: Dept. of Sociology, UiO, 1976): 82.—Svein Blom, *Familieverdier i Norge (Family Values in Norway)* (Trondheim: INSS, Report 22, 1986).

37. Janet R. Johnston and Linda E. G. Campell, *Impasses of Divorce. The Dynamics and Resolution of Family Conflict* (Glencoe: Free Press, 1989), 25.

38. Sally A. Lloyd., Rodney M. Cate, June M. Henton, "Predicting Premarital Relationship Stability. A Methodological Refinement," *Journal of Marriage and the Family,* (Feb. 1984)—Cf. also Bernhard I. Murstein, *Love, Sex and Marriage through the Ages.* (New York: Springer, 1974): 230. The conclusions of these researchers also agree with Naroll's findings concerning the affect of the marriage structure apart from the actual satisfaction of the partners: cf. Raoul Naroll, *The Moral Order* (Beverly Hills: Sage, 1983).

39. Among social scientists, Neo-Darwinism is often associated with the sociobiology that Edward O. Wilson championed during the 1970s; cf. E. O. W.: *Sociobiology, the New Synthesis* (Harvard University Press, 1974) and Carl N. Degeler, *In Search of Human Nature: the Decline and Revival of Darwinism in American Social Thought.* (New York: Oxford University Press, 1991).

40. Richard Dawkins, *The Selfish Gene,* (Oxford University Press 1976).

41. Sahra Blaffer Hrdy, "Infanticide among animals," *Ethnology and Sociobiology* (I;1979): 13–40.—Cf. also Glenn Hausfater and Sahra Blaffer Hardy, *Infanticide* (New York: Hawthorne, 1984).

42. Robin Dunbar, *Primate Social System* (London: Croom Helm, 1988).

43. Philippe Rushton, *Race, Evolution, and Behavior: A Life History Perspective.* (New Brunswick: Transaction Publishers, 1995).

44. Matt Ridley, *The Red Queen. Sex and the Evolution of Human Nature* (New York: MacMillan, 1993): 198f.

45. Ridley, Red Queen, 173.—Cf. also Laura Betzig, *Despotism and Differential Reproduction. A Darwinian View of History* (New York: Aldyne, Hawthorne, 1986).

46. After studying 104 polygamous communities, Laura Betzig discovered that in nearly all of them there was a correlation of power and the size of a man's harem; cf.

L. B., *Despotism and Differential Reproduction. A Darwinian View of History.* (New York: Aldyne, Hawthorne, 1986).

47. Pitirim A. Sorokin. and Walter Lumsden, *Power and Morality. Who Guards the Guardians?* (Boston: Porter Sargent Publishers, 1959).

48. Ridley, *Red Queen,* 205.

49. D. E. Brown and D. Hotra, "Are prescriptive monogamous societies effectively monogamous?" in: *Human Reproductive Behavior, ed.* (Cambridge University Press. 1988): 153–160.

50. Cf. the bibliography after the chapter "Monogamy and the Nature of Women," in Matt Ridley, *The Red Queen*, 1993.

51. Ridley, *Red Queen,* 219.

52. Bronislaw Malinowski, *Sex and Repression in Savage Society.* (Cleveland: World Press, 1927).

53. M. Daly and M. Wilson, *Homicide.* (New York: Aldine, Hawthorne, 1988),— Cf. also Robert Wright, *The Moral Animal. Evolutionary Psychology and Everyday Life* (New York: Pantheon Books, 1994):390.

54. Cp. Richard Wrangham and Dale Peterson, eds. *Demonic Males.* (New York: Houghton, 1996), with Norbert Elias, *The Civilizing Process* (Oxford: Basil Blackwell, 1978).

Chapter Six

Family Structure and Functionality

THE WEAKENING OF MARRIAGE

It is easy to point to data that supports the major changes occurring within family structure in western civilization over a few short decades. Statistics clearly show the changes reflected in recent marriage figures. Fewer couples are getting married, and more couples are getting divorced. It is hard to deny that this downgrading of marriage is related to sexual morality, although changes in social institutions are also partly to blame.

Contrary to times past, marital obligations are not being counterbalanced by marital rights as the sole, universally accepted and legitimate framework for sexual conduct. It is only natural, as an extension of our earlier analysis, to ask whether this change represents a functional adjustment to a modern world, with scope for individual freedom, or a dysfunctional adjustment, temporarily legitimized through ideological manipulation.

To answer this question, we must confront the issue of whether the family in today's society safeguards vital functions that cannot be fulfilled by any other institution, and whether these necessitate a precise marriage-regulated family structure; or whether other institutions, or even other family structures, have satisfactorily taken on these tasks in a functional sense.

Let us start by determining what constitutes a family. The US Bureau of Census has offered the following definition: "A family consists of two or more persons who are living together and who are bound to each other by kinship, marriage or adoption." Others have given more comprehensive descriptions of what may rightly be called a family. Family researcher Dolf Zillmann of the University of Alabama has listed nine characteristics as the most important, durable and valuable hallmarks of a family.[1]

(1) A couple consisting of a man and a woman constitutes the core of a family. (2) This couple commits itself to live together for an indeterminate period of time, potentially for life. (3) The couple reckons with having children, and they ultimately do so. (4) The couple is prepared to care for their children. (5) The couple will support their children with a view to their mental, emotional, moral and financial independence. (6) The couple contributes to a common future financial goal. (7) The couple accepts sexual exclusivity. (8) The couple accepts the fact that family happiness depends on a constant investment of time and initiative. (9) The couple accepts the fact that it must resist temptations that would disrupt the family and cause potential conflicts and violence.

The first of these definitions could be called a "minimum definition" without moral aims; the other could be called a "maximum definition" with moral aims. But the minimum definition does not always warrant referring to a family in every instance where several people live together—let alone instances in which individuals constitute a housekeeping unit.

It is easy to see that both the family structure and ideal vary between societies, and that these have changed over time. This does not imply, however, that all family structures are equally functional in all societies and population groups. Nor does this imply infinite scope in variation. Family structures that we can study—in practice, a selection of structures functional enough to have survived to this day—all share certain similarities. First, every society regards the family unit as an important component of an individual's identity and sense of belonging. Observation tells us that establishing and unifying a family has been universally ritualized in all societies. Marriage rites follow communal rules; they are not created by couples alone. These rituals normally require representatives from both sides of the couple's families to be present. In addition, a priest, shaman or community leader will officiate at rites marking a couple's change of status. This suggests that the establishment of families is universally perceived as a concern for society, and not just a private matter.

In some culturally relativistic socio-anthropological circles it has been common practice to speak of polygamous families as the family type found in most societies, even though the vast majority of people live in societies that have only permitted monogamy. In fact, even the majority of people living in societies that do permit polygamy live monogamously. In a functional context, it is interesting to note that every prominent modern society conforms to the monogamous norm. Furthermore, the social anthropologist George Peter Murdock discovered the nuclear family in all the 250 societies on which data had been collated.[2] The family structures varied, as did the obligations of relatives outside the nuclear family; but the father-mother-child relationship was universally held to be a distinct social unit with vital functions. This means that the nuclear family cannot be considered a new family structure or just some bourgeois construction.

This suggests that something quite dramatic may be evolving in our time—particularly in our part of the world—if the most fundamental social cell throughout history has now become merely a matter of private choice, while global authorities and cultural elites have tried to remain neutral in their efforts to ensure maximum equality between all types of gender relationships.

Historically, there have always been several kinds of relationships between the sexes, although some of these have never gained acceptance—much less the same status. Kingsley Davis has compiled a list of different types of sexual relationships, which he placed on a sliding scale, from casual to steady: cohabitation, consensual unions, common law marriage, and marriage.[3] It is marriage that has been regulated by law and for which specific obligations and functions have been prescribed. And it is this very type of relationship that has been steadily declining.

The eternal dilemma here lies in deciding how far back one should go to gain a comparative perspective on our social development. Carle C. Zimmermann, family historian, thinks that contemporary processes in western civilization can be compared with those in ancient times.[4] He felt there were good reasons for claiming that the decline of the Greek and Roman civilizations was due to similar changes involving the institution of the family. Zimmermann listed eleven hallmarks of the decline:[5] (1) the spread of quick divorces; (2) falling family birth rates, coupled with an overall decline in population; (3) the loss of the true meaning of marriage; (4) support for negative interpretations of heroes and virtues of the past; (5) the spread of theories claiming that companionships or looser family structures would solve our problems; (6) people who had been married in accordance with older family traditions were not allowed to carry on these traditions, while younger people shirked the obligations of their elders; (7) the spread of anti-familism by urbane and pseudo-intellectual circles; (8) the breakdown of most barriers to divorce; (9) the revolt of young people against their parents, making parenthood more difficult; (10) the spread of juvenile delinquency; and (11) a widespread acceptance of various forms of sexual perversion.

We should be careful before hastily jumping to conclusions. However, the current divorce rate suggests that marriage does not enjoy the same status as was once the case. The annual decline in marriage in populations is yet another measure of its declining status. Marriages have become more unstable. More people are living in relationships without the same degree of stability as marriage.

In the mid 1990s, British demographers noted that 56% of all English women over the age of 16 were married, 23% were single, 14% were widowed, and 7% were divorced. These demographers estimated that by 2020, only 48% would be married, 25% would be single, 13% would be widowed, and 14% would be divorced.[6] As early in 1981, the Norwegian demographer Bjørg Moen wrote about Swedish birth cohorts of the time, and estimated that only half of the youngest Swedish cohorts would ever marry, provided they followed a behavior pattern similar to that of older cohorts.[7]

This trend, which is substantiated by various data, can be explained in several ways. Some are inclined to see it as an expression of positive values, such as liberation, equality and tolerance. Others view this trend as a general decline in morality. The responsibility for this development must be shared by culturally liberal spokesmen as well as commercial agents.[8] Part of the trend can be regarded as the unintended consequences of measures taken for noble purposes, such as the desire to ease discrimination against illegitimate children.

Changes in the family's status can be seen as just one aspect of a general disintegration of society. Economic differentiation, political democratization, and cultural rationalism resulted in traditionalism commanding less authority. However, several forms of adaptation could have compensated for this. Different countries have different cultures, and hence different approaches in tackling these issues.

There is little point in using economic development as a global explanation for all the variations in how people get married and get divorced. In 1965, Canada recorded 46 divorces per 100,000 inhabitants, as opposed to 250 divorces in the United States for that year. This deviation cannot be explained in terms of minor discrepancies in economic structure between the two countries.

Nor should contemporay changes be explained as an adjustment to a future form of human liberation. From a functional point of view, there is little reason to assume that the most widespread forms of cohabitation in recent years represent a future pattern of modern adjustment, or that they constitute the most rational and functional response to the challenge of modern times. Interpretations that take this for granted ignore comparative analyses.

Changes on the family front have generated heated discussions. In every country where open dissent is permitted, the predominant change has been subject to criticism. Research groups have certainly not spoken with one voice in these discussions,[9] — nor have the people, for that matter. Only rarely has the majority rallied in support of change in the earliest stages of development, even though most people have tried to adjust to established conditions. This suggests that the liberal interpretations in the media and in some organizations primarily express the strength of specific cultural codes.

It is tempting to interpret this as a sign of strength for the new liberal culture — the operative word at this juncture being "new." The older liberals

viewed the marriage-regulated family as a foregone conclusion. Liberal theoreticians, such as Herbert Spencer, argued in favor of the functional supremacy of strict family morals in predominant societies.[10] Contemporary social liberals and social democrats have not accepted certain original programs
for privatizing or de-institutionalizing the family, even though a number of
Leninist declarations suggest such an interpretation. A study of the Swedish
Social Democrats' policies on the family can tell us more about how de-
institutionalization of the family won political legitimacy. As already mentioned, Sweden pioneered a trend where people associated with the Social
Democratic Party have been a driving force.

THE SWEDISH CASE

In Sweden, Alva and Gunnar Myrdal were the first to put family policy into
a social and political framework. In the mid 1930s, they published a book entitled *The Crisis in Population Development*.[11] The authors pointed out the national dangers posed by the decline in the birth rate at that time and argued
for the introduction of a pro-active social policy geared toward society's
poorest, to aid them in establishing normal families. In the 1940s, Gunnar
Myrdal wrote that there was a consensus among experts to leave no stone un-
turned in deterring illegitimacy.[12] This goal was a crucial reason for radical
Swedish politicians backing the work of a sex education organization, RFSU,
with all its unexpected consequences during the 1960s and '70s. New interpretations of the family policy goals and tasks emerged at a time when radical Sweden was compelled to acknowledge that its policies had had other effects than those originally intended, and that they would either have to change
policies or modify their political objectives.

As early as the mid 1960s, a number of semi-official papers were published
in Sweden in favor of the "new family," in which gender equality was highlighted as a supreme value. The development of individual potential became
an official goal of family policy.[13] Adults were to be given equal treatment by
society, whether they chose to live alone or cohabit with others. The Swedish
Institute, an organization dedicated to disseminating Swedish social standpoints abroad, published a work called "*The Family is Not Sacred*," in which
the author maintained that marriage and divorce should be regarded strictly
as a private matter between individuals, with no moral interference from society.[14] The references to gender equality and women's freedom of choice became important elements in the debates during the 1970s on the impending
shift in the social democratic viewpoint on the goals for a progressive family
policy. This viewpoint was largely institutionalized in Swedish family legis-

lation passed in 1974, and this has also played a significant role in the other Nordic countries in the debate on the family's position.

Developments in Sweden are of particular interest. It is here that the de-institutionalization of family structuring has made the greatest strides, at least in our part of the world; and it is here that the most clear-cut political programs for promoting this policy have had a positive impact.[15] According to some studies, Sweden also stands out as the western country in which marriage enjoys the weakest public support, despite the fact—or perhaps because of it—that the Swedes have come farthest in their removal of some of the bothersome legal obligations that encumber formalized marriage.[16]

In the Swedish study on marriage and the family from 1972, we read the following: "Theoretically, the birth of children in contemporary societies, with their medical opportunities, specialization and differentiation of work, could be separated from the family and reduced to a mere biological event. As far as we know, sociology has not been able to point to any society where this has been the case."[17] Normally, this would suffice to put the burden of proof on the advocates of cohabitation in deciding whether cohabitation can serve as the functional equivalent of marriage. It says a great deal about the strength of a framework of meaning dominated by values associated with individual-oriented liberties, when our society demands justification for the stand that people should get married.

Implicit and explicit arguments for cohabitation have proliferated in recent years; in the popular media this has gone hand in hand with—if not pre-empted by—actual developments. However, these arguments have never risen above the counter-arguments that could be leveled against them. Admittedly, the viability of the various arguments can be legitimately assessed in different ways. In part, they could be evaluated on the basis of the relationship between claims and actual circumstances, and in part on the basis of existing data on differences between marriage and cohabitation. An example of testing for the former would be studies of attitudes on claims that cohabiting couples decided on their type of union more often than not based on their convictions of ideals, e.g. because of their faith in the power of love—cf. the expression "love marriage" that was often used for cohabitation in the 1970s and 1980s.

Contrary to interpretations, a Swedish research report concluded that young people usually moved in together without deciding beforehand not to get married. In fact, there was often no prior decision even to move in with each other; "it just sort of happened. . . ."[18] Another Swedish study, penned by 279 family lawyers during the 1970s, confirms this picture. As to which grounds their clients gave for avoiding marriage, about six in ten lawyers stated that "they didn't want to commit themselves." Only one in ten mentioned that for many, love was such a strong force that they reckoned they could get by without the benefits of a formal marriage.[19]

Even so, the weakening of marriage is not a uniquely Swedish phenomenon. As already mentioned, certain changes have had the effect of "watering down" family tasks, while advances in contraception, a financial safety net, and media ideals in addition to young people's expectations have all increased the appeal of less binding forms of union.

In the United States, it is estimated that the number of cohabiting couples rose from 0.5 million in 1970 to 1.5 million in 1980, and to 2.5 million in 1990. Though these figures may not be completely reliable, it is clear that the position of marriage in the US has suffered in recent years. Relatively speaking, fewer people are entering into marriage and more people are abandoning it.

In sociology, it was long taken for granted that changes in the field of marriage and the family could be interpreted as forms of adjustment to new social circumstances, circumstances that admittedly might pose problems during a transitional phase. This was a recurring pattern for interpretations by family theoreticians during the second half of the 20th century, from Talcott Parsons to Anthony Giddens.[20] There is, however, another tradition, often relegated to the sociological sidelines, represented by men like Carle C. Zimmerman and David Popenoe.[21] These men have borne witness to a decline in support for an important institution. The question as to which of these two interpretations is the more convincing could be resolved if professionals would only agree on whether developments pointed to conditions within or outside the confines of what could be termed minimum functional measures for a necessary reproduction.

THE FAMILY AND INEVITABLE FUNCTIONS

Finding examples of winners and losers in the de-institutionalization of family structures is straightforward enough. On the positive side, the career potential of emancipated women is mentioned most frequently. On the other hand, finding examples of individuals who stand to lose from the proliferation of less tightly-knit family structures is easy to find as well. Children are usually regarded as the losers when they live in dread of their parents leaving each other one day.

It is not easy to weigh the winners against the losers, if the standard is reduced to a run-down on the increase or decrease in individual suffering. However, this goal only indirectly reflects our line of reasoning—determining the way in which culture enhances or impairs society's functionality. By and large, functional analyses have to be based on other types of data than guessti-mates of individual happiness. Before we attempt to determine whether a given form of contemporary living leads to conditions within or outside func-tional limits, we must decide whether the family has any functions that are so important that no society can survive without them. Then we must decide whether these functions depend on a specific institution—in other words, whether a de-institutionalization of families and a transfer of tasks from fam-ilies to other institutions is functionally realistic.

We can start by asking ourselves what the family's social functions are. From a historical perspective, or a comparative social anthropological per-spective, we could compile a list of functions that have long been associated with the family. The family has been a decisive factor in underpinning peo-ple's senses of belonging and security; it has helped ensure the food supply and other necessities of life; it has cared for the young and the old, the sick and the infirm; it has figured in the exchange of goods and services, and served as a link between the individual and society at large. Contemporary life has led to a differentiation and specialization of these functions. Nowa-days we expect more of the family as an emotional arena and as a base for leisure activities. The question is this: can we still find functions that require an institutional framework for the family? We must ask which family-related tasks are so important that a society would suffer a major loss of functional-ity if these tasks were not institutionally legislated.

Talcott Parsons answered this question by pointing to three or four family-re-lated fundamentals without which no society—above all non-contemporary ones—could survive. These involved reproduction, the primary socialization of children, and the role of an identity-preserving primary group, on which most people depend. In addition, the regulation of sexuality has been mentioned as a separate "must." No society can survive without erotic ties between people, or without regulation of these ties. This, in turn, calls for legislation that holds peo-ple accountable for their offspring.

Reproduction is the most indisputable task, and the one that can most eas-ily be dealt with in terms of functional analysis. Without an infusion of new recruits, any society will die out. The extent to which immigration from other societies and cultures can provide such an infusion is limited, if new genera-tions are to pledge primary allegiance to a society with a given historical tra-dition and are willing to defend and carry on that tradition. In olden times, people gave birth to large numbers of children, who often died in infancy. We could conceive of more humane, and yet functional, alternatives to those con-ditions. But we could also conceive of a development that points in a dys-functional direction, even if the first generation were to benefit personally from this kind of development. Overpopulation is one form of dysfunctional adjustment that can threaten a society, particularly where emigration is not an option. Another dysfunctional adjustment would be underpopulation, caused by a birthrate well below reproductive levels for long periods of time.

Functionally speaking, we can safely assume that a society must have a legal framework for dealing with children during the first years of their life. This is necessary not just to ensure their immediate needs, but also to introduce children to a social tradition and help develop their personalities so that they can function in society, preferably in a personal way.

Finally, the family must be held up as the closest and most durable primary group of a society's citizens, even though most people belong to both a family of orientation and a family of reproduction. The family must not only satisfy the material and social needs of its members and support their contact network and private life, but must also act as a coordinating unit for the individual's experiences. In the words of Talcott Parsons,[22] the family assumes importance as an emotional base for popular participation in society.

These are important functions without which no contemporary society can expect to exist, at least not in the long run. But how does this affect our understanding of the way in which marriage functions as an institution? After all, these functions could be taken over by government agencies, kindergartens and training centers, with the marriage-regulated family being merely one of several options for popular social attachment, customized for people who prefer security to liberty.

The answer depends on the extent to which a population needs institutional guidance so that enough people will make life choices that are functional for society. The answer also depends on whether it can be argued that marriage, as opposed to other forms of union, possesses structural qualities that recommend it as the most functional choice even for contemporary societies. Let us stress two characteristics of constituent families: the internal norms, which relate to a couple's roles and obligations toward one another, and the external delimitation, which is meant to protect the family sphere against a normative invasion from other social institutions. This may mean protection from economically-derived norms of market choices and various norms originating in political and bureaucratic organizations. Both sets of norms may contribute to a destabilization of the family unit.

Structural circumstances can have an impact on the way family functions are cultivated. In every society, reproduction depends on far more than biological urges. In contemporary society, where the birth rate is even more dependent on what couples want and on their active decisions more than in earlier societies, reproduction can assume the nature of a long-term investment. Institutional frameworks, which can bolster faith in the durability of couples' relationships and prescribe duties and forms of cooperation for both parties, are key factors in the number of births. Such expectations appear to be borne out in our part of the world. Family statistics show that married couples generally give birth to more children than couples belonging to more informal units. The difference between marital and non-marital reproduction is crucial to a population's reproduction over time, and becomes a measure of the functionality of marriage. Generally speaking, it is also important for the preservation of the family that there are norms and legal guidelines for how various conflicts should be handled. Even this could require institutional guidance.

Successful primary socialization is important for a subsequent secondary socialization into specific social sectors. Even though primary socialization may be perceived as being based on a private relationship between parents and their children, this relationship is nevertheless dependent on institutional frameworks. The way in which mothers and fathers relate to their children usually has to do with models. No functional society can remain indifferent to the *kind* of models given to the new generation. This has implications for the learning of gender roles. A father is a man who has a specific relationship with a specific woman. A mother is a woman who has a specific relationship with a specific man. This implies role models that differ from those derived from identification with a man only or a woman only, which explains why homosexuals and unmarried people do not enjoy the same functional status in adoption cases as do opposite-sex couples.

The family's task as lasting primary group depends on its subjugation to those institutional frameworks that can preserve this kind of durability. The institutional structure can also provide frameworks for the family's rights and obligations in relation to other social institutions.

The arguments in favor of the functional advantages of marriage could be carried even further. Nevertheless, the question many would pose nowadays is this: could other forms of cohabitation become commonplace and adopt more or less the equivalent functions enjoyed by marriage, yet at the same time be more in harmony with modern notions of freedom? This leads us to take a closer look at what we know about the differences between marriage and cohabitation.

THE DIFFERENCE BETWEEN
MARRIAGE AND COHABITATION

The most practical method for testing the status of cohabitation involves comparing its stability with that of marriage. However, there are problems with such a comparison. In the first place, what is termed cohabitation is not just intended as an alternative to marriage, but rather as an alternative to engagement, which has traditionally been easier to dissolve than marriage. In the second place, cohabitation is such a new phenomenon that we lack experience in analyzing its long-term effects. In the third place, both marriage and cohabitation are set in cultural contexts. This means that cohabitation will tend to cater to the expectations of a marriage-oriented culture in societies where marriage clearly predominates. In societies where cohabitation is customary and accepted, this will also affect people's attitudes toward each other in their marriages. This means, for instance, that cohabitation at the end of the 20th century is not entirely the same as cohabitation in the mid 1900s.

On the other hand, the change in these relationships may, over time, provide vital information for a subsequent evaluation of their impact on people. Statistics from the Nordic countries emphasize these changes, where by the 1980s, a marked decline in marriage rates for childless women living out of wedlock could be clearly seen in each new birth cohort during the periods 1936–40 to 1956–60. In Norway, the likelihood of a relationship developing into marriage plunged by about two-thirds, from approx. 90% to 31%. Figures showing the trend in registered cohabitation in Sweden and Denmark were even more dramatic.[23]

By working with data from the fertility study carried out in the late 1970s by Statistics Norway, demographer Randi Selmer was able to show that the probability of a cohabitation ending in marriage had declined even in cases involving children. She discovered that of those born between 1941–45, who had started living together as 15–19 year-olds and who had neither had children nor gotten married, only 12% had discontinued their relationship two years after its onset. The corresponding frequency of dissolution had risen to 26% for the birth cohort 1956–59. For those who had started to live together as 20–24-year-olds, the corresponding dissolution frequency stood at 10% for the birth cohort 1941–45 and 24% for the birth cohort 1951–55.[24]

The increasing instability over time among cohabiters has been succeeded by a rising divorce rate among married couples.[25] Nevertheless, marriages have consistently represented the most stable type of union.[26] This is not just because cohabitation has often been regarded as a kind of trial marriage. Even in instances where a couple has had children together—which ought to indicate their view of the relationship to be a lasting one—cohabiters have a dissolution rate of as much as three times higher than that of married couples with children.[27]

These calculations are not only relevant in a Nordic context. Studies from other countries also confirm the more tenuous nature of non-institutionalized cohabitations as opposed to marital unions.[28]

One of the most frequently used arguments for legitimizing cohabitation is that it functions like a trial marriage, enabling the parties to become better acquainted with each other before they make a firm commitment. This was supposed to facilitate the selection of compatible partners, which would in turn result in more stable marriages. To a large extent, cohabitation unions are also regarded as less binding. Those willing to commit themselves tend to get married.[29] In Germany, it has been claimed that the inherent instability of non-marital cohabitation can be traced back to personal selection. People with the fewest predispositions for a stable family structure tend to shun marriage. Still, this line of reasoning falls short when broadly used to legitimize trial marriage. The proportion of "risk candidates" is periodically erratic and varies from country to country. Sweden, which has gone to great lengths to legitimize non-marital cohabitation, also holds the highest percentage of such risk candidates. American data does not suggest that people who have spent some time in a cohabiting relationship are prone to form more stable marriages than people who have chosen the more traditional route to marriage. As for having lived in a cohabiting relationship with a partner other than the parent of one's children, the available data suggests that the risk of family dissolution rises further down the line.[30]

A range of studies suggest that changes in cohabitation patterns are governed by factors other than functional considerations for family structuring. On the whole, these changes can be explained by changes in the framework of meaning and cultural reference. On an individual level, it can be shown that people living in a "common-law" relationship generally have more liberal attitudes than married people, particularly with regard to divorce.[31] Nevertheless, it would be wrong to regard cohabitation as something that two people choose individually on the basis of a specific prioritizing of values. In the Norwegian family and vocational survey from 1988, we see that while 18% of a selection of 4,019 women stated that they were living with a cohabiter, only 2% supported the claim that "cohabitation is always preferable to marriage."[32] What people do is one thing; what they would have done under different circumstances is another matter.

One Swedish study shows that 53% of a selection of cohabiters stated that both parties wanted to get married eventually, while 33% stated that they, but not their partner, wanted to get married.[33] This dithering with respect to marriage was explained in terms of weak norm pressure in Swedish society for choices of this nature. Data of this type encourages us to consider whether this trend can be explained in simple terms as the liberation of the individual from institutions. It is fair to ask whether, on the whole, women are better off because of these changes.

ARE WOMEN BETTER OFF BECAUSE OF THESE CHANGES?

Today when men take a critical stance toward changes on the cohabitation front, they are often met in predominant intellectual circles with the reaction that men's criticisms reflect their loss of long-standing privileges. It is claimed that the current trend must be regarded as part of women's emancipation. When current trends lead to more family break-ups, it is often the women who have taken the initiative. Men are presumed to be stuck in old, ingrained role patterns, unwilling to come to terms with the laws of gender equality. Recent feminist literature is often used to point up and criticize the patriarchal and subjugating nature of marriage.[34] The mythical arch-image that binds these reactions together can be found in the tale of Nora, in *The Doll's House,* one of Henrik Ibsen's psychologically weakest, but most frequently staged plays.

It is easy to find examples that correspond to this interpretation, and these receive persistent coverage in the media. All the same, the choice of examples is seldom unrelated to the lifestyles of the players producing them. All this suggests that we ought to take a closer look at the issue of whether, when all is said and done, the de-emphasis of marriage as an institution has been in women's best interests.

Many kinds of data can help shed light on such questions. Current conditions, marked by unstable marriages and even more unstable cohabitations, could be compared with historical examples. Our basis for comparison could be the 19th century's approach to marriage, typified by the parents' active role and the couple's veto—and vice versa—or 20th century ideals, in which the couple passes through different stages of infatuation, engagement, and marriage, where the more rights one obtained, the harder it became to break off a relationship. Our comparison could also be a theoretical one. In this case, future family structures could be compared with functions adapted to long-term social adjustment.

A number of commonplace interpretations can be refuted fairly directly. A couple of Norwegian studies are relevant in this connection. On the basis of data on health and well-being, Svein Blom and Ola Listhaug concluded that married partners of both sexes fare best in different types of comparison, even when the data is adjusted for variables of personality selection and age variables. In their conclusion, they state the following: "It should not be regarded as a manifestation of collective irrationality when the majority of adult people get married. Reports of violence and family abuse reveal the shadowy aspects of the institution; and even though the phenomenon appears to have been on the rise, there is nothing in our data to suggest that this is anything but a deviation from the normal situation."[35]

Objections can always be raised against studies of general trends. In this area, violence can be said to take place behind closed doors in families at all social levels, a fact easily confirmed by active duty policemen. The question remains, however, whether this violence is due to marriage as an institution, or whether it is because people spend so much time with their families. To determine whether marriage promotes or hinders domestic violence, comparisons can be made with violence in areas where unmarried people indulge their emotions. We ought to review the validity of the many likely causes of violent outbreaks, as these might well be ideologically tinged. We must also take into consideration the fact that domestic violence can be reciprocal.[36]

Based on American data of recorded incidents of domestic violence, it is estimated that approximately 57,000 married women were physically abused by their husbands annually between 1979 and 1987. But during this same period, 200,000 women were reported to have been abused by their "boyfriends" and 216,000 by their ex-husbands. Of all registered crimes involving domestic violence against women during this period, 65% were committed by these "friends" or by ex-husbands, compared with 9% by husbands.[37] The differences here are too great to be attributed to women being more likely to report violent behavior from ex-husbands than current husbands. Measured in rates for criminal abuse of women aged 12 and above for the period 1973–1992, 43% were unmarried women, 45% were separated women, and only 11% were married women.[38] Another study concluded that for every pregnant woman reporting domestic abuse from her husband, approximately four other pregnant women suffer abuse from their unmarried partners.[39] Even though a variety of selections can be cited for different forms of cohabitation unions, data suggests that marriage, in general, diminishes the spread of domestic violence toward women.

To explain this phenomenon, let us return to Emile Durkheim. He claimed that psychologically, husbands had the most to gain from marriage, because marriage set limits for unlimited needs, which is a prerequisite for inner harmony. The assertion that men have more unlimited tendencies than women can be justified in evolutionary and psychological terms. Elaborating on this point, one could argue that civilizing male urges requires institutional frameworks which, on the whole, tend to benefit women. This, in turn, suggests that a de-emphasis on institutional boundaries regulating the realization of needs could lower the threshold of domestic violence in several areas.

Let us consider the issue of rape in light of a report from the United Nations Human Rights Commission submitted by Radhika Coomaraswamy on April 2, 1997. This report was about the spread of rape, forced prostitution and sexual harassment in recent years. The Commission concluded that women worldwide are victims of a steady rise in violence. Studies at American, Canadian and British universities suggest that one in six women has been the victim of violence with sexual overtones.

Spokesmen for individualized ideologies have often viewed the institution of marriage as a framework for husbands' marital rights. They have been criticized for effectively encouraging men to believe they could avoid showing their wives any consideration. Relationships based solely on emotions were supposed to lead to greater reciprocity. This is the background for attempts to legitimize all mutual consent and to define all sexual relationships lacking mutual consent as rape. In practice, however, determining the existence or degree of consent in the many rape cases tried in court has proved impossible. In cases where one party's word was pitted against another's, courts have normally given the accused the benefit of the doubt. As a result, most female rape victims feel they have too much to loose and too little to gain by taking legal action. Nevertheless, so far there has been no show of renewed interest on the part of the new liberal societies in the institutional criteria for distinguishing between legitimacy and illegitimacy. These criteria have the potential of reversing the burden of proof for men accused of raping women with whom they were not married.

Naturally, gauging the prevalence of domestic violence against women is not the sole method of determining whether women are winners or losers in the de-institutionalization of family structuring. As a rule, women are concerned with their children's situation as well, so some mention of studies on how changes in the family have affected children's lives is in order.

Not all research supports the new liberal interpretations in this respect. It is true that some men do tyrannize their wife and children; but statistically, this is not typical. Recent information on men's maltreatment and abuse of children indicates that quite the reverse is true, as atrocious behavior is overrepresented among men who are not husbands.[40] The independent British research institute Family Education Trust studied family court cases in England over a 6–year period during the 1990s and found a clear connection between child abuse and family structure. British children living with unmarried parents were generally victims of more violence and abuse than children in married families. Among children living with a man who was not the child's father, the chances of being killed were 30 times greater than those living with their fathers.[41] Several studies show that girls living with stepfathers are at greater risk of sexual abuse than girls living with their biological fathers.[42]

Other studies conclude that changes in family structure represent the greatest long-term threat to American children.[43] This threat must be taken seriously in a country which, in the course of just one generation, has witnessed a decline in the number of children living with their biological fathers from about eight in ten to six in ten. What has been termed "the feminization of childhood" is a historical experiment.[44] True, there are cases where children experience parental separation as liberation, but long-term studies in California suggest that this reaction is atypical, accounting for no more than 10% of cases.[45] The argument that children used to experience the death of their father just as often as contemporary children experienced their father's abandonment of the family does not ring true. Family researcher David Popenoe writes that when a father dies, the child grieves. When a father leaves the family, the child experiences worry and guilt. Death robs fathers of their lives, but keeps their fatherhood intact. Abandonment of the family preserves the fathers, but kills fatherhood.[46] Popenoe has subsequently published a book in which he argues that fatherhood and marriage are indispensable for the good of children and society.[47]

We can once again ask ourselves whether the de-institutionalization of family relationships means that women generally have become freer to make their own choices, and whether this has set the stage for new forms of personal development. There are studies of rapes by acquaintances with a weak family-institutional setting.[48] One of the sociologists who first discussed the consequences of de-institutionalized relationships was Willard Waller.[49] He found that those with the least interest in seeing a relationship continue were the very ones who had the most say in relationships that were not constrained by institutionalized forms. Husbands often had a disproportionate advantage in families in which children were involved and mothers had a vested interest in keeping the family intact. Waller's observations fit well with other sociological explanations of the way that institutions tend to regulate conflicting interests, and do so in order to preserve society. Some interpersonal norms were primarily intended to limit infringement; while others were intended to cause people to bond more closely.

Men and women are not only different in a complimentary way, or in a way that sets the stage for mutual attraction. Evolutionary and psychological arguments and explanations related to women's close relationship to their offspring suggest that it is not only masculine role models and emotional seclusion that causes men and women to have different attitudes toward commitment to marriage.[50] Young males are noticeably more favorably disposed to cohabitation than their female counterparts.[51] There is little support for the assumption that an increasing acceptance of cohabitation is an expression of women's rising influence on social norms.

Women's greater social sensitivity can be gainful if an impartial framework exists around social interaction. On the other hand, it is not certain that relationship-oriented ethics, which has typified women more than men,[52] can cope with situations where even the rules of the game are determined by the parties. Women trained to believe that a man's emotional life is basically the same as women's—merely more hampered in terms of emotional expression after the age of four—tend to believe that men will be blinded by love, as long as she shows him love. This can lead to major disappointment upon her discovery that sexual satisfaction often has a liberating effect on a needs-oriented man, whereas this binds a relationship-oriented woman. Women, it would seem, stand to lose a great deal from de-institutionalization.[53]

MARKET AND BUREAUCRATIC NORMS

When most people talk about the emancipation of women, they are usually thinking about the spread of specific lifestyles and behavior, which are considered enlightened, or preferably modern and liberated. People may or may not be in favor of these lifestyles and liberation. Quite often, ordinary people show more willingness to look at the negative aspects of liberation than professionals, who have a closer relationship to ideology-producing environments.

Nevertheless, we rarely encounter people in normal environments questioning the description of lifestyle changes as expressions of liberation. It is easier for those schooled in theory to see that the perception of development as liberation is an interpretation, and that other interpretations might prove more accurate. Where some see changes as a liberation from traditional gender roles and marital norms, others see those same changes as an adjustment to market norms of buying and selling or to bureaucratic norms of legal equality—that is, norms derived from an economic or a political institution rather than from the institution of marriage and the family.

This might all seem extremely theoretical. The relationship between individual forms of adjustment and institutional power might be clearer if we think about day-to-day observations of changes in lifestyle. For instance, many women dress more provocatively nowadays than women tended to do in the past. But we must review the new elements here and invoke contemporary explanations. The fact that women use clothes to heighten their sexuality is certainly not a new phenomenon that requires a special cultural-historical explanation. What is new is not that clothes are used in part to cover up and partly to show off the figure by means of sexual symbolism. In the past, there were strict rules as to what constituted the appropriate way of dressing for a variety of social occasions. It would be hard to find an earlier period in which ordinary women went about daily in tight miniskirts and men in tight-fitting trousers in order to attract attention in public places, or a time when symbols of female sexuality were used to help sell all kinds of products and services. Historically, this is a new phenomenon, one that calls for a special cultural-historical explanation.

If we were content to study ordinary people's verbal response to these phenomena, an investigator might be satisfied with merely recording statements about a woman's right to choose her own lifestyle and general references to tolerance. However, to explain why a given lifestyle has become prevalent, we must resort to theories of institutional macrostructures, which are by no means characteristic of popular explanations.

If we see individual adjustment in relation to norms derived from a variety of institutional subsystems within a society, we can come up with a few explanations. An emphasis on typical norms for different institutions takes us beyond the framework conditions for individual choices. The reason certain norms are more typical of an institution than others is because of the way institutions organize their tasks. Explanations based on institutional systems need not account for special motives on the part of all those who subscribe to the institution's norms. A comparative institutional perspective can provide explanations on a structural macro level.

Going back to the dawn of the modern age, we find social regulations illustrating the functionality of institutional differentiation. Institutionally-related norms used to be clearly characterized by their own respective areas of life. Viewed in a social context, religious norms functioned as taboos for sacrosanct beliefs, and as an example for various rules on living, especially at the level of the individual. Political norms were characterized by legislative rules laid down by the authorities, with citizens' rights and duties originating from official government regulations. Economic norms dominated the retail and commodities markets and the cost/benefit rationality in manufacturing, partly limited by socio-political legislation. Even norms related to family relationships were institutionally demarcated and legally protected. The institution-specific family norms were conspicuously governed by tradition and faith, and were characterized by diffuse and mutual obligations with respect to assigned roles and to a status achieved by marriage. Relationships were collectively oriented, with family and relatives as the orienting units, and these were characterized by loyalty norms for particularistic relations. Marital exclusivity was maintained through sanctioned norms in the local community, through legislation, and through religious ideals and popular examples.

Today's situation appears to be a confused version of a differentiated society, partly because market and bureaucratic norms have gradually come to put their stamp on an increasing number of relations in which these norms are unlikely to be functional.

The institutional perspective shows us that we are not necessarily facing liberation from social pressure when we meet women who dress to attract as much attention as possible from strangers of the opposite sex. Rather, this should be seen as an adjustment to a market-oriented organization of sex. Norms typically associated with an economic institution point to the perception of sex symbolism as a means of bartering in the marketplace. Strong sex symbols take on meaning when they are perceived as an advertisement for evoking the interest of potential customers—with the lucky winner being selected as a potential partner in a lasting relationship. The reason this does not function particularly well is in part because men tend to think it fair to consider women as sex objects in the marketplace for their own personal gratification or as a means of finding a partner who will confirm their own preconceptions.

Institutional norms not only put interpersonal activity into a specific framework; they do the same with people. Women have to admit that, more than ever, they are being viewed as sex objects and therefore risk sexual advances in many situations. To avoid being caught off-guard, they must remain constantly on guard, a situation that often calls for a steady infusion of imagery and musical stimulus. This kind of relational explanation might prove more convincing than an individual-psychological explanation, which explains the same use of media stimuli as a form of needs realization.

The evidence suggests that such a continuous state of alertness can affect a person's concentration on other things, such as work, politics and culture. Nevertheless, other dilemmas can be equally restrictive. Young women must become reconciled to being appraised in the sex market for their value as an experience-enhancing partner. In this competitive situation, women who come across as the most devoted will be most likely to attract a man. At the same time, devotion without a safety net might lead to many painful disappointments. One way of trying to cope with this dilemma involves learning to play the role of a warm woman, while acting out an emotional reserve. A large part of the feminine role repertoire in so-called TV soap operas illustrates this; it is an object lesson in just this kind of adjustment. However, this is hardly the most functional starting point for a modern family union, which should be built on emotional foundations. In other words, market norms have very little functionality where family unions are concerned.

Paradoxically, the commercialization of sex nowadays is related to a certain kind of radical anti-capitalism which, a generation ago, attempted to liberate sexuality *per se* from inhibiting production norms. The result was an emotionally-deprived sexuality that could be exploited by capitalist advertising, commercial entertainment and the global porn industry.

It is not only norms from financial institutions that have invaded the family sphere as the family has become increasingly de-institutionalized. Political and bureaucratic norms have also made inroads, although this has not brought about a more functional family structure.

The socio-political assistance apparatus is concerned with more than employment service, training, illness and care for the elderly—tasks too burdensome for family and relatives in view of contemporary demands on living standards. Spokesmen for health services and social politics have gradually encroached on areas once considered a private domain.[54] Justification for this is based partly on accounts of domestic violence and neglect by the family. In a liberal culture, few object to the notion that all individuals have rights that the State is obligated to accommodate as far as possible. Thus the health services, in the guise of humanitarianism, have become a spokesman for a fairly comprehensive psycho-physiological needs gratification, even after taking into account the task of dealing with individuals' sexual rights against a backdrop of family constraints and limitations. Within this framework of meaning, traditional gender norms can be explained in medical terms as the way people would earlier have sought to prevent the spread of sexually transmitted diseases as well as unwanted pregnancies. This is a situational understanding, which suggests that modern contraceptives can serve as the functional equivalent of moral norms. If the family is to have any chance under the new institutional regime, it will have to compete in offering the individual more tangible benefits inside than outside the framework of the family.

The socio-political bureaucracy has emerged as the administration of an assistance apparatus designed to provide all citizens with additional rights, and not just to deal with those who fall outside familiar and voluntary networks. New liberal arguments for helping those in need with universal rights have given social politics a universalistic goal. This, in turn, has provided the framework for new socio-political rules of the game. Those who successfully portray their clients as people with neglected needs have generally received uncritical political assurances of considerable assistance.

The issue here is whether socio-political institutions should only be construed as agencies serving people with the greatest social needs. In a sharply critical review of Swedish family politics, David Popenoe questioned the logic and child-friendliness of legislation which, in the name of humanity, forbids all forms of corporal punishment, while at the same time placing cohabitation on a par with marriage, even though cohabitation, statistically speaking, is three times as prone to dissolution as marriage, even where children are involved.[55] Today, it is the threat of parents leaving each other that creates the greatest anxiety for children. When sociologists and politicians do not see the inconsistencies in their own activities, this suggests that they are thinking in terms of ideology, rather than in terms of what is best for children, for families, and for society.[56]

From politically conservative quarters, there has been a reaction to a usurping bureaucratization, especially on the family front. The slogan of the day was a return to the old values: "Back to basics." However, neither Thatcher's nor Reagan's politics led to greater stability of the family in their respective countries. On the contrary, the de-emphasis of bureaucratic political influence led to greater market influence. The institution of the family was too weak to reclaim its former position, irrespective of support from surrounding institutions.

FUNCTIONALITY AND FERTILITY

In most countries, ordinary people would regard the increase in family breakups as evidence that something had gone wrong, whether this was deemed immoral, detrimental, or just something unwanted. The fate of children is often used to support and justify this view, along with spouses left in the lurch, and the general feeling that things have spiraled out of control.

One would have expected people in leading positions to have done something to reverse this trend—assuming that they had it figured out, since they profess to be more adept than others in interpreting and influencing social development but otherwise share the values of the general public. On the other hand, if we assume that people sitting in the corridors of power have gotten where they are today because they were smarter than others at exploiting social structures and predominant interpretations, we should think again. It should come as no surprise, for example, to find that several spokesmen for predominant positions prefer to interpret the breakup of families as an expression of individual liberation, or as the result of an implacable trend. The scarlet thread running through all these interpretations is their tendency to disarm criticism of the predominant ideology. However, when these norms are compared with institutional norm systems in a differentiated society, we can identify them as market-oriented and view them in relation to cultural patterns emerging from the institution of economic norms.[57]

Some family functions are hard to clarify. This is particularly true of the relationship between the family structure and birth rate, and of long-term prospects in the face of a decline in population. This has been particularly borne out in Germany, a country with traditionally high welfare costs, a low retirement age, and long-term birth rates below the reproductive level. At the same time, the country's political past has made waging an offensive "population policy" ideologically problematical. According to the August 14, 1995 issue of the magazine *Focus*, 8.8 million married German couples did not have any children at that time; 6.8 million had one child, 4.9 million had two children, 1.2 million had three children, and 0.35 million had four or more children. Of single parents, 1.9 million had one child, 0.6 million had two, and 0.16 million had three or more children.

Over the long term, a birth rate below the reproductive level could be a sign of dysfunctional adjustment—at any rate, when no compelling factors exist to explain a drop in the population figures. But we should stress that chronically low birth figures, rather than year-to-year discrepancies, are critical to the survival of a society and its culture.[58] A temporary decline in the annual birth rate could be ascribed to an economic downturn that prompts some married couples to postpone having children. The situation would be different if an entire birth cohort were to decide to have fewer children. During the 1930s, statistics on periodic figures were interpreted as cohort figures. This subsequently led to the view that people crying "wolf" were just being hysterical. The figures for the period after 1970 are unambiguous with respect to long-term development. In nearly all European countries, birth rates have peaked at a level well below the reproductive level of 2.1 children for women who survive their fertility period.[59]

During the mid 1990s, some European Mediterranean countries, renowned for their sensual cultures, had birth rates, on average, of 1.4 to 1.2 children per woman. We appear to be on the threshold of a new population law: the more sex in culture, the fewer children in families! In some parts of central Italy, population figures are lower than one child per woman.

Calculations based on birth trends up until 1992 led European demographers to predict an average childbirth rate of 1.48 for the younger generation of women in the 12 EU member states of that time.[60] Even more disheartening was the fact that no realistic political action plan had been drawn up to spur any significant rise in the birth rate. It is against this backdrop that we must understand what Gaston Thorn, the former Prime Minister of Luxembourg, said when he claimed that Europe was committing collective suicide.[61]

There is no doubt that this represents a dysfunctional trend in line with every discussed functionality criterion. The question remains, however, whether this dysfunctionality can be broadly linked to cultural forms developed in relation to the new liberal ideology.

Many objections will be voiced by communities dominated by this ideology. Some will elaborate on the decline in birth rate by resorting to economic theories: theories on women's occupational activities and on historical necessity and demographic transition. Above all, this decline will be judged as the result of women's recently-won right to have the last word on their own fertility. The latter provides an explanation with a potential for profound moral mobilization.

These explanations can all be made to fit a variety of contexts to which they seemingly apply, but none of them has gained universal recognition. The reason is clear: they are not comprehensive, nor they cannot replace cultural explanations. Explanations based on inadequate financial resources are contradicted by experiences from other times and societies in which families had far more children than in Europe today, even though these communities had less leisure time and fewer financial resources. Moreover, it is not always the poorest that have the fewest children. If the concept of relative poverty is introduced in order to rescue this theory, we enter straightaway into the realm of value explanations based on the value of children versus commodities. Nor can theories on the increasing numbers of women in salaried occupations account for all the variations in the declining birth rate.

Comparisons of the variations in European women's contribution to the workforce and their childbirth rate cannot in all fairness lay the main blame for the recent low European birth rate at the door of working women. For example, the 1997 national target for children per woman in Italy was estimated at 1.22, while it was 1.86 in Norway. At the same time, OECD figures from 1997 showed that only 44% of Italian women were actively employed, as opposed to 75% of Norwegian women. And comparative studies within Norway do not suggest that occupationally active women have noticeably fewer children than those who have no occupational employment.

As it happens, historically deterministic explanations relating to a so-called law of "demographic transition" have accounted for little more than a general trend, with many national variations.[62] These explanations have rested on the assumption that a decline in child mortality is bound to lead to a corresponding decline in birth rates, following a transitional phase with high birth rates and low mortality rates.[63] Experience thus far tells us that Europe has fallen far below the reproductive level, while the decline in birth rates in most other countries has a long way to go before reaching that level. Within Europe, immigrants from other cultures tend to have more children than the native-born population. In Germany, the disparity in fertility rates has been estimated at 20%. This suggests that certain special characteristics of an individualistic culture in our part of the world cannot be dismissed as a determining factor.

In public debate, if not in demographic circles, the most common explanation for the drop in birth rates has been the availability of contraceptive devices and the fact that women now have the last word on their own fertility. The era of involuntary births is over—or so it is claimed. Therefore, those who bemoan the declining trend in fertility are seen as attacking women's liberation!

The author's familiarity with the fate of certain women leads him to question the latter explanation's validity. A market research institute was contacted in 1975 and commissioned to conduct a survey among Norwegian women to determine whether the declining birth rate could be explained as an expression of women's general desire.[64] Of those with children at that time, 23% responded that they had only one child; 36% responded that they had two; 22%

had three, while approx. 20% reported having four or more children. To the question how many children they thought was appropriate for a Norwegian family, less than 1% of all those polled answered "no children," 2% responded one child, 44% two children, 41% three children, 10% four or more children, and only 4% responded "don't know." This distribution of responses showed even then that the basic desire for children exceeded the number of realized births and the number of expected children. To the degree that there was a mismatch between ideals and reality, this usually ran counter to propaganda, although in some cases there was a match.

Another survey on the same issue was commissioned in the 1980s in several western countries.[65] It showed the same trend, only even more clearly. The ideal number of children for European women at that time was about one child more than they could expect to have. At the same time, comparisons showed that while the number of realized births in all respondent countries except Ireland was under the reproductive level, the ideals in every country were higher than the reproductive limit. The reason Europeans had not reached the reproductive level could not be explained on the basis of women's primary choice.[66]

Studies like these make it all the more relevant to go beyond the players and seek explanations on a structural level. The de-institutionalization and disestablishment of the family appear to be good candidates for explaining the decline in births. In fact, this has been confirmed in more systematic demographic studies. A committee officially appointed to study population trends in Norway wrote in their report in 1984: "Changes in fertility outside of marriage and changes in the durability distribution of marriages mean relatively little. The key factors are fertility in marriage and the proportion of married women. What kept the birth rate high in the 1950s when the population of parents was small was the fact that the percentage of married couples increased sharply. From 1965 there was a sharp drop in marital fertility. This did not have an immediate impact on the birth rate, due to the favorable change in the age structure that was taking place. The full ramifications only appeared after 1970. But the negative effect of marital fertility disappeared after a few years. In the late 1970s, a dwindling percentage of married women contributed most to the fall in the birth rate." We read further: "We conclude that the intermediate variable related to marital behavior has had a marked influence on birth rate trends during the 1950s and the period after 1975. It is clear that cohabitation unions do not compensate for the decline in traditional marriages as far as fertility is concerned."[67]

The fact that more women than ever are giving birth, since it has become more common for unmarried couples to have children, does not compensate for the effects of a weakened marital culture. Comparisons of fertility among cohabiters and married couples must be tempered by the somewhat uneven age distribution; more cohabiters than married couples can expect to have fertile years ahead of them. Nonetheless, the difference in birth rates between groups is so large that it is unrealistic to assume that age variation will ultimately compensate for differences in reproductive behavior.

This suggests that the deinstitutionalization of family unions will be a key link in what is apparently a dysfunctional adjustment. The cultural aspect of the declining birth rate enters into the picture in part through attitudinal changes in the direction of increased emphasis on self-realization instead of family realization. To some extent, this change can be seen as an unintended effect of the privatization of the institution of marriage, in accordance with interpretations congruent to the new liberal cultural complex.

Studies of the difference between what is called the first and the second demographic transition indicate that the changes are cultural in nature.[68] Whereas the first decline in birth rates could be explained in terms of parents' wishes to secure a higher economic and social status for their children, the decline in recent years must be explained in terms of a stronger desire on the part of parents to gain time in which to invest more in their own self-realization and their own well-being. A Dutch demographer describes the new ideals as "secular individualism," with an emphasis on "the individual's right and freedom to define goals and the means of achieving them." [69]

The close connection between changes on the family front and the rather extensive cultural changes in the course of the past few decades makes it highly unlikely that we will see a radical revision of the family as an institution as long as society is dominated by the new liberal ideology and frameworks of meaning that prioritize self-realization. On the other hand, the relationship between a dysfunctional adjustment and a certain ideology makes it unlikely that this ideology will last for a very long time in its present form.

In taking a closer look at this aspect of contemporary culture, we would do well to consider the debate that emerged following the news that western societies were no longer maintaining expected reproductive levels. While the debate on immigration concerns immigrants, it is also about protecting certain frames of interpretation. This has kept important issues from receiving the attention they deserve.

NOTES

1. Dolf Zillmann et al., *Media, Children and the Family* (Hilldale, NJ: Erlbaum Associate, 1994), 200.

2. George Peter Murdock, *Social Structure* (New York: MacMillan, 1949).

3. Kingsley Davis, "The Meaning and Significance of Marriage in Contemporary Society", in *Contemporary Marriage,* ed. K. Davis (New York: Russel Sage Foundation, 1985): 1–21.

4. Carle C.Zimmerman, *Family and Civilization* (New York: Harper, 1947).

5. In addition to the account on p 760 f in Zimmermann's book, this is also cited in Michael Anderson: *Sociology of the Family* (London: Penguin 1980): 175.

6. Cf. *British Stationary Office*, Jan. 1996.

7. Bjorg Moen, in an article numbered *SES 47*, (Oslo: Statistical Central Bureau, 1981).

8. Christopher Lasch, *Haven in a heartless world.* (New York: Basic Books, 1977).

9. Brigitte and Peter L. Berger, *The War over the Family.* (New York: Doubleday, 1983).—Micael Anderson, ed., *Sociology of the Family.* (London: Penguin, 1980),— David Popenoe, *Disturbing the Nest. Family Change and Decline in Modern Society* (New York: Aldine de Gruyter, 1988)—Ferdinand Mount, *The Subversive Family* (Glencoe: Free Press, 1992).

10. Herbert Spencer, *The Principles of Ethics,* Vol. I, (London: Williams & Norgate, 1892): 463f.

11. Alva and Gunnar Myrdal, *Kris i befolkningsfrågan.* (*Crisis in demographic development*), (Stockholm: Bonnier, 1934).

12. Gunnar Myrdal, *Population: a problem for democracy* (Harvard University Press, 1962): 185.

13. Cf. *Jämlikhet (Equality):* The Alva Myrdal report on the Swedish Social Democratic Party, Stockholm 1971: 82.

14. Anna-Greta Leijon, *Swedish Women—Swedish Men* (Stockholm: Swedish Institute, 1968): 125.

15. Cf. "The Case of Sweden" in *Disturbing the Nest. Family Change and Decline in Modern Society Part II,* ed. David Popenoe (New York: Aldine de Gruyter, 1988).

16. According to an opinion poll made public by the Prime Minister's office in Japan in 1984, only 28% of Swedish young people at that time were purportedly in agreement with the statement that people ought to get married, and that it was better to be married than not to be married. In comparison, 78% of Japanese young people concurred in that statement. Cf. Christopher Prinz, *Cohabiting, Married, or Single* (Luxemburg: Avebury, IIASA 1995): 74.

17. *Familj ock äkenskap (Family and marriage)*, (Stockholm: SOU 1972): 412.

18. Bo Levin and Jan Trost, *Att sambo och gifta sig. Fakta och föreställningar. (Cohabitation and marriage. Facts and fiction)*, (Stockholm: SOU 1978:55): chpt. 4 & 5.

19. A. Claesson, R. Lundgren and G. Lundh, "Samvetsäktenskapet och juridiken", (*Marriage of conscience and the Law*) in *Tre sociologiska rapporter.* (Stockholm: The Justice Department 1975:24).

20. Talcott Parsons and Robert Bales, *Family, Interaction and Socialization Process.* (Glencoe: Free Press, 1955)—Anthony Giddens, *The Transformation of Intimacy: Sexuality, Love and Eroticism in Modern Societies* (Oxford: Polity Press, 1993)

21. Carle C. Zimmerman, *Family and Civilization.* (New York: Harper, 1947).-Cp also David Popenoe, *Disturbing the Nest. Family Change and Decline in Modern Societies.* (New York: Aldine de Gruyter, 1988) and Christopher Lasch, *Haven in a heartless world,* (New York: Basic Books, 1977): chpt. 3.

22. Talcott Parsons, *The System of Modern Society.* (Prentice Hall, NJ: Englewood Cliffs, 1971): 100–101.

23. Lars Ostby, *Første skritt i familiedannelse i Norge, sammenliknet med Danmark og Sverige (First step of family structureation. Norway compared to Denmark and Sweden)* (., Stockholm University, Demographic Dept. 1986): Tab. 2

24. Randi Selmer ,*Samliv uten vigsel (Living without marriage)* (Oslo: Norwegian Bureau of Statistics, Article 146, 1983): Tab. 11 and 13.

25. Turid Noack, and Oystein Kravdal, *Divorces in Norway 1965–1985* (Oslo: Norwegian Bureau of Statistics, Report 1988/6).

26. Turid Noack and Nico Keilman, "Familie og husholdning," (*Family and household)* in *Sosialt Utsyn* (Kongsvinger: Norwegian Bureau of Statistics, 1993): cht 8.1.

27. The comparison is based on calculations made by Oystein Kravdal on the basis of data from the Norwegian family and the vocational study from 1988 of dissolution frequencies.—Cf. Oystein Kravdal, *Wanting a Child but not a Firm Commitment to the Partner: Interpretations and Implications of a Common Behaviour Among Norwegian Cohabiters.* (Memo from Department of Economics, University of Oslo. No. 19, May 1997).—Also Swedish data suggests a significantly higher frequency of dissolution among cohabiters with children compared with married parents with children.—Cf. Brita and Jan Hoëm, "The disruption of marital and non-marital unions in contemporary Sweden," in J. R. Trussel, R. Harkinson, J. Tilton, eds. *Demographic Applications of Event History Analysis* (Oxford: Clarendon Press, 1992): 61–93.

28. L. Bumpass and J. Sweet, "National estimates of cohabitation. Cohort levels and union stability." (*Demography*, 1989, no. 26): 615–25.—J.D. Teachman and K.A. Polonko, "Cohabitation and marital stability in the United States." (*Social Forces*, 1990, 69): 207–220.

29. Figures from the beginning of the 1990s show that of all cohabiters who started their relationships at 23 years of age and who continued to be together after five years, 79% had gotten married, while only 21% continued to live as cohabiters.—(Oslo: *Sosialt Utsyn,* SSB, 1993): 293.

30. Alfred de Maris and William MacDonald, "Premarital cohabitation and marital instability: A test of the unconventional hypothesis;" *Journal of Marriage and the Family*; (1993):399–407.—Cf. also Janic M. Saunders and John N. Edwards: "Extramarital Sexuality: A Predictive Model of Permissive Attitudes," *Journal of Marriage and the Family*;(Nov 1984).—D. M. Fergusson, L.J. Horwood, D.E. Dimond, "A Survival Analysis of Childhood Family History," *Journal of Marriage and the Family* (May 1985)—Neil G. Bennett., Ann Klimas Blanc and David E. Bloom, "Commitment and the modern union: Assessing the link between premarital cohabitation and subsequent marital stability", *American Sociological Review* 53 (1): 127–139.

31. Svein Blom, *Famileverdier i Norge. (Family values in Norway),* Trondheim: Report 22, INSS, 1986).

32. *NOS B 959,* Norwegian Bureau of Statistics: Tab 5.5.4.

33. Bo Levin, "Unmarried Cohabitation: A Marriage Form in a Changing Society", *Journal of Marriage and the Family,* (1982):763–773.

34. Jessie Bernard, *The Future of Marriage.* (New York: Bantam, 1972).—Marilyn French, *The War Against Women,* (New York: Summit Books, 1992).

35. Svein Blom and Ola Listhaug, "Family and quality of life", *Tidsskrift for samfunnsforskning, Oslo,*(2. 29, 1988): 5–28.

36. Richard J. Gelles., Donileen R. Loseke, eds., *Current Controversies on Family Violence* (London: Sage, 1993).

37. Carol Wolf Harlow, *Female Victims of Violent Crime.* (Washington DC: U.S. Department of Justice, 1991):1–2.

38. U.S. Bureau of Justice Statistics, *Highlights from 20 years of surveying crime.* (Department of Justice, 18, 1993)

39. Center for Disease Control and Prevention, *Morbidity and Mortality.* (Washington DC: U.S. Government Printing Office, Report 43, (no. 8, March 4, 1994): 135.— David Blankenhorn, *Fatherless America.*(New York: Basic Books, 1992): chpt. 2.

40. David Finkelhor,"Risk factors in the sexual victimization of children." in *Child Abuse and Neglect* (4, 1980):265–73.—D Russel, "The prevalence and seriousness of incestuous abuse: Stepfathers versus biological fathers," *Child Abuse and Neglect* (7, 1980):133–46.

41. Martin Daly and Margo Wilson: "Discriminative Parental Solicitude," *Journal of Marriage and the Family,* 42:277–88,—The independent British research institute *Family Education Trust* has studied family court cases in England for a six-year period during the 1990s and found evidence that supports the American studies. British children who live with unmarried parents are the victims of more violence and mistreatment than children who live in families with marriages. Among children who lived with a man who was not the child's father, the chance of being killed was 30 times greater than for children who lived with their father.

42. Michael Gordon and Susan J. Craighton, "Natal and Non-Natal Fathers as Sexual Abusers in the United Kingdom: A Comparative Analysis", *Journal of Marriage and the Family* (50, no. 1, 1988)—Leslie Margolin, "Child Abuse by Mother's Boyfriends: Why the Overrepresentation?" *Child Abuse and Neglect* (16, 1992): 545–46.—Catherine M. Malkin and Michael E. Lamb, "Child Maltreatment: A Test of Sociobiological Theory"; *Journal of Comparative Family Studies* (no 1, 25,1994): 121–33.

43. Leif Jensen, David J. Eggenbeen, Daniel T. Lichter, "Child Poverty and the Ameliorative Effect of Public Assistance," *Social Science Quarterly* (3, 74, Sept. 1993): 544.

44. Ann Magritt Jensen, "The Feminization of Childhood", in Jens Qvortrup et al. (ed.) *Childhood Matters*, ed. Jens Qvortrup (Aldershot: Avebury, 1994): 59–75.

45. David Popenoe, *Disturbing the Nest.* (New York: Aldyne de Gryter, 1988): 315.

46. Popenoe, *Distrurbing*, 24.

47. David Popenoe, *Life Without Fathers* (Harvard University Press 1999).

48. Nart O. Jissm and Sarag K, Ciij, "Facing the Facts: Date and Acquaintance Rape are Significant Problems for Women", in *Current Controversies on Family Violence*, eds. R.I. Gelles, D.R. Loseke (London: Sage, 1993): chpt. 6.

49. Willard Waller, *The Family. A Dynamic Interpretation*, (New York: Dryden Press, 1951)

50. Sonya Rhodes and Marlin S. Potash, *Cold Feet. Why Men Don't Commit.* (New York: Signet Books, 1989)

51. Keith London, "Cohabitation, marriage, marriage dissolution, and remarriage. United States 1988", *Vital and Health Statistics of the National Center of Health Statistics*, No. 194. 1990.

52. Carol Gilligan, *In a Different Voice: Psychological Theory and Women's Development* (Harvard University Press, 1982).

53. A discussion of this subject is foiund in Geoff Dench. ed., *Rewriting the Sexual Contract* (London: Institute of Community Studies, 1997).

54. Peter Flora and Martin Heidenheimer, *The Development of the Welfare State in Europe and America* (New Brunswick: Transaction Books, 1981)

55. David Popenoe, *Disturbing the Nest.* (New York: Aldyne de Gryter, 1988): 237–335—Cf. also Roland Huntford, *The New Totalitarians* (London: Penguin, 1971): chpt. 15

56. Cf. the argumentation in Robert O. Blood, *Marriage,* (Glencoe: Free Press; 1978), in ROB, *Husbands and Wives, the Dynamics of Married Life.* (Glencoe: Free Press, 1965) and in Robert Haveman and Barbara Wolfe, *Succeeding Generations. On the Effect of Investment in Children.* (New York: Russel Sage, 1994).

57. Larry Bumpass, "What's happening to the family? Interaction between demographic and institutional change.". *Demography* 27 (4) 1990:483–498).

58. John R. Gillis., Louise A. Tilly, David Levine, ed., *The European Experience of Declining Fertility: A Quiet Revolution,1850–1970.* (Cambridge: Blackwell, 1992)

59. Ansley J. Coale. and Susan Watkins, *The Decline of Fertility in Europe* (Princeton Univ. Press,.1986)—Oystein Kravdal, "Fruktbarhet under reproduksjonsnivået i Norge", (Fertility below reproduction in Norway), *Samfunnsspeilet* , Oslo, no 1 1994.

60. Cited in *The European*, London, December, 1993.

61. Cited in *Newsweek* December 15, 1986.

62. Charles Hirschman, "Why Fertility Changes," *Annual Review of Sociology* (No. 20, 1994): 203–233.

63. Warren Thompson, "Population," *American Journal of Sociology* (34, 1929)— Parvitz Khalatbari, *Demographic Transition* (Berlin: Akademie-Verlag, 1983).

64. Norsk Gallup, Nov./Dec. 1975: "Barneantall," (*Number of children*) ordered by S. Skirbekk, Dept. of Sociology, Univ. of Oslo. The study was based on interviews with 436, 419 and 421 women during weeks 40, 42 and 45 1975; the selection proved to be reasonably representative according to standard control measurements.

65. Svein Blom, *Familieverdier (Family values).* Report No. 22, (Dept. of Sociology, Univ. of Trondheim 1986): Tab 9.8. Women's attitudes were studied in the following countries: Belgium, Denmark, England, France, Ireland and Northern Ireland, Italia, The Netherlands, Norway, Spain, Sweden, West Germany and the USA.

66. Tone Schou Wetlesen, *Fertility Choices and Constraints: A qualitative Study of Norwegian Families* (Oslo: Solum, 1991).

67. Norwegian Bureau of Statistics, *Befolkningsutviklingen (Population development in Norway),* (NOU 1984):267f.

68. D van de Kaa, "Europe's second demographic transition" in *Population Bulletin*, Washington (No 1, vol. 42, March, 1987).

69. R. Lesthaeghe, "A Century of Demographic and Cultural Change in Western Europe: An Exploration of Underlying Dimensions" in *Population and Development Review,* (3, 9, 1983): 429.

Chapter Seven

Migration—Research, Ideology, Myth and Belief

DEMOGRAPHIC TRENDS AND MIGRATION

There are a number of reasons for supplementing a study emphasizing birth rates as a measure of functionality with a chapter on population growth and migration. In numerical terms, a country's population growth is determined by the sum of its births and immigrants minus deaths and emigrants. A quick calculation will tell us a few facts about ecological adjustment in territories with limited resources, provided we take a population's consumption patterns into account. Public opinion on immigration tells us something about the culture of argumentation and about how the new liberal ideology depicts common forms of understanding.

At first glance, migration to western countries would appear to be a clever combination of self-help and help for others. Imported labor can be seen as a domestic ploy to compensate for a low reproduction rate in the West, while at the same time helping the Third World reduce its population surplus. A change in perspective is vital in order to understand that migration cannot provide a steady influx of help from countries with high birth rates and that reproduction based on immigration levels can stymie efforts to maintain key values in western civilization.[1]

The chosen perspective for presenting these issues is not the only element of interest here. The forms of argumentation, as well as the methods used in neutralizing antagonists' credibility, are in themselves interesting fields of study. The choice of emphasis and de-emphasis plainly demonstrates the selection principles in the dominant culture of interpretation. Some psychologists claim that studies of taboos are some of the most rewarding avenues to cultural understanding. The stronger the taboo, the greater the potentially harbored insight. How heated the debate on immigration becomes will indicate whether we are dealing with positions rife with taboos, all of which might have a major impact on the way we relate to our culture.

Before we say more about the debate itself and turn our attention to the media's argumentation style, we will briefly describe the trends in population growth, as clearly as demographers have been able to verify them.

Global population growth figures in modern times are quite dramatic from a historical standpoint. The number of people living on this planet is thought to have reached its first billion during the time of Napoleon Bonaparte, two hundred years ago. The two billion milestone was reached shortly before Hitler came to power in around 1930. The three billion mark was reached during the post-war 1950s. The four billion mark was reached during the period of colonial liberation during the 1970s. The five billion mark was passed when Soviet communism collapsed at the end of the 1980s.[2] The six billion mark was reached by the end of the 20th century. Population growth in the 20th century was primarily due to improved survival rates in the poorest parts of the world. The so-called developing countries experienced an overall explosion in population of around 1.3 to 4.1 billion people during a dramatically short time span, from 1930 to 1990.[3] However, considering developing countries as a separate category may be misleading. Birth rates vary tremendously among Thirld World countries.

Future estimates of population growth must be based on statistical computations of birth rates and conditions affecting them. Even though expert demographers differ in their predictions, these variations are not pronounced enough to cast doubt on their overall calculations. Based on figures released from the UN's demographic division in 1999, a mean estimate of global population growth suggests that a figure close to 9 billion people could be reached by 2050.[4] If birth rates were to continue to escalate at current levels —although few believe this likely—the projection would reach 14.9 billion people already by 2050, and 296 billion by 2150.

Based on the UN sources, mean estimates suggest that the population of North America will rise from 172 million to 392 million during the period 1950–2050. The figures for Latin America, based on the same estimates, are expected to rise from 167 million to 809 million. The greatest increases are expected to occur in Africa and Asia. Relatively speaking, the population of Africa is expected to escalate most, from 221 million in 1950 to some 1760 million by the middle of the 21st century. The African rise is particularly worrying, as it is not expected to stabilize during the 21st century; on the contrary, it could even rise to three billion, according to some projections. All in all, African fertility during the 1990s was estimated at an average of 5.7 children per woman.[5] Nevertheless, in absolute terms, the Asian population is expected to rise most rapidly during the 21st century; from about 1.4 billion in 1950 to 5.2 billion by 2050.

Asia's urban population is expected to double during the next thirty years, and Asia as a whole could account for over half the world's population. This will lead to dramatic domestic social changes, such as new, vast population concentrations in major cities. The Asian Development Bank estimates that the number of "mega cities" harboring more than 10 million inhabitants will soar from nine to twenty by the year 2025. Half of these will contain more than 20 million inhabitants. It is estimated that, by 2025, more than 4 billion people will be living in urban clusters scattered around the Third World, as opposed to barely 1.5 billion today. Mexico City is expected to swell to more than 24 million inhabitants, with Sao Paulo mushrooming to more than 23 million inhabitants.

All this will lead to a rise in overpopulation, with attendant social stress and, in all likelihood, weaker regional cultural ties than is customary in traditional rural towns. This trend is bound to exert enormous pressure on emigration to areas with a relative shortage of people. As for the Mediterraneann region, the population of northern Africa is expected to rise by more than 100 million between 1990 and 2025,[6] while the birth rate in southern European countries currently stands at between 60% and 70% of the reproduction level. While Europe as a whole contained twice as many people as Africa in 1950 (547 million to 224 million), the figures at the turn of the century were almost identical. However, the population of Africa is expected to reach 2,046 million people by 2050, as opposed to Europe's 638 million, according to the modest scenario described by UN demographers.[7]

Another factor putting pressure on emigration to Europe is the advances in communications. Both technical modes of transport and audio-visual communication, which project an idealized image of living conditions in the North, are significant in this context. In addition, most potential target countries will have established immigrant environments capable of absorbing new immigrants.[8]

Demographers are predicting major discrepancies in Asian population growth. While China, on account of its birth control policies, can only expect a "modest" rise from today's 1.2 billion people to approximately 1.5 billion in 2050—a rate that largely reflects age distribution and the fact that people are living longer—the situation in other Asian countries will vary. According to some estimates Pakistan, one of China's neighbors, could expect a population growth on an altogether different order. Pakistan is a country 778,720 km in size, with 74 million inhabitants in 1975 when the country's present borders were fixed. This figure has almost doubled within a single generation, and might double again by the middle of this century.[9]

The net rate of emigration from Pakistan during the mid-1990s is estimated at 17 per 1,000 inhabitants. With such a huge increase in population, one might expect emigration levels to have risen proportionately. Conversely, emigration appears to be determined for the most part by domestic social tensions, which in turn are linked to overpopulation levels. When overpopulation levels rise, the emigration rate tends to climb. A demographic and economic imbalance between different parts of the world will change the terms for migration. As several quantitative studies show, the risk of conflict between population groups rises in proportion to the number and concentration of immigrants.[10]

In view of the anticipated rise in growth rates in countries with limited resources, a broad political consensus exists in the West that we bear a fair amount of responsibility for these countries. This accountability is reflected in our moral obligation to provide emergency aid, medical and technical assistance, as well as economic development aid to enable these countries to develop on their own terms. The philosophy behind this approach has always been that, when living standards begin rising, the desire to have many children will taper off—and, with any luck, stabilize—voluntarily and at an acceptable level.

These expectations are questionable and unrealistic for a number of reasons. As already mentioned, the so-called "law of demographic transition" does not operate in a cultural vacuum. Furthermore, counting on living standards to bring population growth to a halt does not seem ecologically rational, especially if we assume that everyone has the right to a consumer-oriented lifestyle consistent with the western pattern.

Access to arable land worldwide is limited. According to some estimates, the Earth's land-based ecosystems have enjoyed an annual production potential of 150 billion tons of organic material. Human beings have already destroyed approximately 12% of this resource potential, in addition to confiscating 27% for their own purposes. This means that a single species on this planet has granted itself sole user rights to almost 40% of the Earth's organic production, leaving only 60% to be shared among the millions of other land-based fauna and flora. Moreover, the 40% that we have claimed for our own use is the easiest to exploit. It is unlikely that we would be able to utilize an additional 40%, even if we felt entitled to do so, and even if a doubling of the global population might suggest that we ought to.[11] But access to resources is not the only discouraging factor here. To be environmentally sound and not prove destuctive to vital ecosystems, waste management will require vast tracts of land According to one estimate, humans would need 1.2 planets the size of Earth just to maintain long-term conditions for ecosystems and simultaneously provide today's entire population with living standards on a par with those of the West.[12]

Whether these projections are completely reliable or not, it is indisputable that natural ecosystems limit our culturally legitimized right to self-realization. This means that ecological stumbling blocks will also pose a challenge to a liberal ideology that has created open-ended values out of economic growth and individual self-realization.

Ecological challenges cannot be defined solely in terms of consumer patterns in well-developed countries or merely in terms of population surges in less developed countries. In the early 1990s, population experts from the London School of Economics estimated the ecological responsibility for the "consumer societies" and the "birth societies" at a 60/40 distribution rate. They also reported that it was difficult to pin down guesstimates with exact figures, so their conclusions were based on the premise of sudden change. In 1997, the London-based World Watch Institute singled out the following countries as the greatest threat to ecological development: The United States, Russia, Japan, China, India, Brazil, Indonesia, and Germany. Vast numbers of consumers, as well as a high consumption rate per person, can have serious consequences.[13]

THE IMMIGRATION DEBATE: PURELY A QUESTION OF MORALITY AND COMBATING RACISM?

One might have expected that demographic and ecological factors had formed a united front in terms of the commentary on migration. The debate on migration encompasses a range of topics. Migration influences demography and ecology, cultural patterns and family structures, economic disparity and employment prospects, and legislative resolutions in the West—apart from its influence on human resources in poverty-stricken, overpopulated areas of a world in which conflict is rife. In view of this multifarious reality, the basic premises of the ongoing immigration debate appear to be severely restricted.

Instead of presenting statistics and information from many sources, the major media have been selective in their approach, making immigration policies look like a simple choice between good and bad, instead of acknowledging that they are an attempt to resolve the dilemma of how to weigh concern for individuals against concern for cultural, demographic and ecological systems.

A typical aspect of public discussion has been the general references to racism and anti-racism, two symbols with a range of undertones, but invariably used as a reference to good and evil. People claiming to represent anti-racism, while labeling their opponents as racists, have assumed an attitude of moral superiority, exploiting their position to set the terms for debate and preempt conclusions.

The fact that the popular media seldom refers to demographic and ecological arguments could theoretically be explained in terms of pandering to the majority. But this does not rationalize the profile of the presentations. Public opinion and media opinion do not coincide.

In 1994, the German periodical *Focus* pointed to opinion polls conducted in Germany, France and Great Britain in which 55%, 52% and 50%, respectively, felt that their countries accepted too many immigrants.[14] The figures for the Scandinavian countries are similar. A representative Norwegian survey from 1987 showed that 51% of respondents felt that Norway should accept fewer immigrants, 25% felt that politicians should adhere to current practice, while only 8% wanted to accept more immigrants.[15] A similar survey conducted in Sweden a couple of years later showed that 54% felt that Sweden accepted too many immigrants.[16] A subsequent survey in Denmark showed that 59% of Danes wanted to limit the number of immigrants to Denmark.[17] Figures have varied somewhat in recent surveys; but those favoring a restrictive policy have always outnumbered those favoring liberalization.

The extent of recent immigration cannot be explained in terms of popular opinion. So the question naturally arises: Can this be explained on the basis of a superior moral insight among groups that have dominated the debate in the public arena? If so, it should not be easy to contradict their arguments.

A commitment to individual humanitarianism is seen as an investment in future peace and mutual understanding among nations. Liberal immigration regulations are thought to be consistent with a generous foreign aid policy, even though migration often involves a brain drain from underdeveloped countries. Nevertheless, involvement on behalf of the most diverse values — such as human rights, economic growth, ecological responsibility, population control, women's liberation and political peace — is thought to reinforce these values in one direction or another.

It is hard to find fault with the good intentions in these references. Still, they often betray limited knowledge on the part of their many protagonists. There is no indication that all positive values will be able to coexist in harmony within some form or other of a future utopian society. Ecology and unlimited human rights are simply irreconcilable. A policy that prioritizes human rights and humanitarian aid will not necessarily promote the development of civilized societies and peaceful relations between societies, even though generous aid may clearly benefit most people. However, if we endorse random measures to reduce mortality rates without lowering birth rates at the same time, we could end up promoting overpopulation, which will only compound the problem for future generations. In time, debt relief and a realistic alternative to self-sufficiency may have a more humane effect than an unrelenting emphasis on human rights that was adopted in the 1940s to protect citizens against authoritarian regimes.

Paradoxically, the only developing country of any size that has been able to stabilize its birth rate to around two children per woman is China. And as Virginia Abernethy pointed out, the Chinese authorities were forced to solve this problem on their own terms, without waiting for foreign economic support or relief from the pressure of overpopulation. At the same time, they avoided an overly critical foreign scrutiny of the way the UN's norms for human rights were being practiced on this issue.[18]

As already mentioned, the governing reference in understanding the issue of migration in moral terms has been the contrast between racism and anti-racism. Trade unions, political parties and the media's editorial executives have all assumed that any opposition to liberal immigration policies is tantamount to racism.

This linkage has always been so strong that we could speak of an anti-racist front on the part of certain prominent, problem-defining parties. Even though spokesmen for this front may disagree among themselves on certain issues, their opposition to racism has been their unifying hallmark. This suggests we ought to investigate anti-racism arguments more closely.

ANTI-RACISM BASED ON RESEARCH

What could be termed an "anti-racist front" has been partly legitimized by purely moral arguments. Nevertheless, its presumptive authority is tied to the widespread conviction that it represents scientific research. This means that these arguments should be subjected to critical tests.

Before asking whether the typical tenets of anti-racism conform to scientific reasoning, we must define racism. The *Encyclopedia Britannica* defines it as follows: "Racism is the theory or idea that there is a causal link between inherited physical traits and personality traits, intellect or culture and, combined with it, the notion that some races are inherently superior to others."[19] According to this definition, to be called a racist, an idea must be consistent with a theory of causal relationships between people's physical characteristics and their collective character traits, consistent with the notion that whole population groups can be categorized as superior or inferior to each other; and finally, that these relationships must remain constant over time, since they involve innate characteristics.

Such notions can be linked to the racial philosophy of the Third Reich. Brutal encounters with this philosophy caused many to react against racism after the Second World War. A great deal of research on racial ideas was subsequently carried out in a number of countries, revealing similar attitudes in a variety of fields, even in countries not directly associated with the policies of Nazi Germany.[20]

Today a vast body of research has undermined key assumptions of the original concept of racism. Numerous differences, once explained in biological terms as congenital character traits of certain populations, have since proven to be variable and culture-dependent. Both sociological and biological research proves the implausability of earlier racial categorization, alongside political and civilizational distinctions. Widespread consensus exists today on rejecting previous categorizations of separate races in which everyone assigned to a racial group had common physical and mental features that distinguished them collectively from other groups. In fact, intra-racial differences reflect greater variation than average racial differences. There is also a concensus that traditional methods of measuring intellectual differences— e.g. IQ testing—fail to reflect the potential inconstancy of these differences over time. Nowadays, variations indicated by IQ tests are generally believed to manifest the properties of the tests themselves, the differences in environmental backgrounds, and the genetic variations between tested individuals.[21] On the other hand, no one has been able to create environments that enable all ethnic groups to achieve the same average test scores.[22] This suggests that we are dealing with populations of people spread out in overlapping normal distributions.

It doesn't take an expert to see that research in this area is far from complete, with much left unclear, and there is widespread disagreement over the soundest interpretation of deviations in findings. All the same, it is easy to identify patently absurd or clearly untenable interpretations. Nor is it difficult to find examples of irrational explanations among racists and anti-racists alike. Some of these absurdities can be linked to ideologies and to the social attitudes of their guardians.

From an evolutionary viewpoint, it seems presumptuous to assume that hereditary explanations for physical differences between ethnic groups apply to external traits only, such as hair and skin color, whereas all mental differences can be put down in their entirety to environmental influences. This interpretation is bound to overlook the extensive research findings on the interplay between inheritance and environment, as well as internal and external predispositions for dissimilar adjustment. Furthermore, it overlooks the possibility of dissimilar, environmentally-governed selection over a period of many generations.[23] Some evolutionists consider it likely that African and European populations have lived relatively separate from each other for about 100,000 years. This means that these populations have undergone approximately 4,000 generations of selection, each having had a certain impact on progeny selection and subsequent inheritance of population mutations and genetics.[24] It would be strange indeed for this selection to have transpired in exactly the same way under different living conditions, just as it would be unreasonable to assume that a different environment than our own would only select traits that are deemed negative. So the assumption that all ethnic groups, statistically speaking, must have the same mental aptitude, or that some groups must be intellectually superior to others by every standard of measurement, is a highly dubious proposition. Even though the evaluation of the relative significance of inheritance and environment is fraught with uncertainty, it would be foolhardy to presume that future research will confirm full equality of mental aptitude in all populations, in linking all assumptions about human value to a notion of equality. Not even reports from the recent Genome project, showing that human beings are 99.9% alike in their genetic makeup as opposed to a 98% match with chimpanzees, have resolved disagreements on whether heredity, and even "race," is a constructive category for understanding human differences.[25]

Nevertheless, the immigration debate is rife with anti-racist statements which take as fact that research has confirmed the concept of full equality between populations with respect to hereditary mental aptitude. This is usually argued in negative terms. Given that the Nazis' interpretation of racist dissimilarities was untenable, it follows that equality must be right. In the attempt to determine the right interpretation, the distinction between research findings and democratic aspirations has not always been respected. There are no doubt many reasons for the confusion surrounding this issue; it can't all be blamed on a poor dialogue with researchers. After the Second World War, some research scientists were invited to UNESCO to speak on the subject. They must share some of the blame for the ensuing confusion.

For many involved in the public debate, pronouncements made by UNESCO have been invoked as an authoritative source for research-based anti-racism. There are a number of well-founded explanations as to how this perception took hold.[26] In 1950, a scientific conference was called at UNESCO in Paris, where the Secretary General expressed his wish to combat discrimination based on racial prejudice. On that occasion, he said that if only researchers could produce reliable scientific data, racism as it was known before the Second World War would no longer be defensible. A number of noted geneticists and physical anthropologists either could not, or would not, attend the meeting. On the other hand, a far less renowned researcher and publicist, Ashley Montagu, did attend. He also offered to spread the conference's final report, which was not supposed to be published until all geneticists and physical anthropologists had been given the opportunity have their comments worked into the report. However, Montagu, who had a reputation as an anti-racist,[27] publicized an incomplete summary in the Saturday Review the following week. Among other things, he stated: "For all practical purposes, race is not so much a biological phenomenon as a social myth." A number of geneticists disagreed with the published article, but UNESCO found it awkward to correct an article that had already been published in its name.[28]

At a subsequent UNESCO conference on the same subject, the final communiqué was formulated in negative terms, like the article following the first conference. It stated that there was a lack of scientific evidence to prove there are racial dissimilarities in mental capacity, and that the same was true of the effects of racial intermarriage. This is the kind of negative deduction that researchers will normally support, provided there are stringent falsification criteria and the matter at hand involves complicated issues such as distinguishing between hereditary and environmental factors. Nevertheless, only 22 of the 108 researchers who subsequently submitted papers to this UNESCO conference gave their unqualified support to the communiqué.

ANTI-RACISM AS SCIENCE

The rest made negative comments of greater or lesser import. Unofficially, as many as 80% of the geneticists had claimed that science must leave open the possibility that demonstrable differences between population groups were, in part, genetically determined.[29]

The statements from these conferences can be interpreted in various ways, as indeed they were. Media moguls and geneticists have apparently gone their separate ways. For quite some time, it appeared that modern research had become the chief guarantor for the new interpretations, since many researchers shunned old interpretations and adopted social and cultural explanations of differences once considered innate instead. However, major media journalists have gradually begun to suspect researchers of having lapsed into a traditional racist mentality. For their part, these researchers felt that the media hype had been unbalanced and to some extent distorted.[30]

Compared with the extensive ongoing discussions among research scientists on these subjects, the debate in the public media comes across as singularly one-dimensional. A striking characteristic is how references to race, with respect to immigration, are linked to factions that are opposed to immigration —almost without exception. Few have discussed the possibility that race could also speak for different types of immigration, as a "genetic upgrading" of a population. The protagonists' assumption that "race" is an explanatory category that stands to benefit the opponents of immigration strengthens the impression that the various viewpoints in the debate are based on political ideals of equality, rather than on research-based analysis.

Another striking characteristic, which also makes it hard to see how predominant views are out of synch with research, is the fact that spokesmen for these positions do not mean the same thing when they talk about "racism." Now and then reference is made to the original biological philosophy of racism, such as the one quote from the Encyclopedia Britannica. But reference is made just as often to a new and expanded philosophy of racism, in which anything that might lead to social discrimination of people from other cultures is perceived as racism.[31] A number of researchers have pointed out that this leads to a form of confusion which, though it may well serve some ideological purpose, is inconsistent with the assumptions of researchers.[32]

The possibility that there might be a link between cultural forms and varying genetic predisposition has generally been absent from the debate. The major part of this discussion has focused on intelligence studies and on averages in the different populations. To the extent that these studies reveal innate limits to human potential, and in particular if they show that these limits are unevenly distributed among different population groups, this can be taken as a challenge to typical views on social equality.

A survey carried out during the mid 1990s among United States immigrants can perhaps shed some light on this confusion.[33] It found that 87–88% of all immigrants to the US over the past 10 years replied that they had felt welcome, both on arrival and at the time of the survey. At the same time, 48% of the same respondents stated that they agreed with the claim that the United States was a "racist country." At that time, the vast majority of immigrants were classified either as "Hispanic" or "colored." The fact that nearly 9 in 10 immigrants felt welcome in the US, and almost 5 in 10 felt that the country in which they felt welcome was in fact racist, suggests that the popular use of the term "racism" no longer reflects its original meaning, but refers instead to a milder form of discrimination based on ethnic traits.

Not all contemporary debate on racism is related to the new social definition. In the dispute over Herrnstein and Murray's book *The Bell Curve*, the focus was on the original biologically-oriented philosophy of racism.[34] These two researchers submitted many bivariate tables on aptitude tests and social placement, arguing that social differences based on class and race also involved a genetic component. Objections can be raised to some of their conclusions, particularly to their failure to utilize multivariate analyses.[35] But this fact, which could be termed standard scientific criticism, is not sufficient grounds for rejecting all their conclusions—such as the claim that there are innate limits to human development, and that these limits have somewhat differing mean values with respect to different populations and social groupings.

There seems to be a huge gap between research-based criticism and the kind of positions many seem eager to defend.

Even extreme radicals concede the point. To neutralize the argument over *The Bell Curve*, the book was accused of building on scientifically invalid premises. To provide a "definitive disclaimer" of Herrnstein and Murray's reasoning, some scientists claimed that it was impossible, strictly speaking, to draw conclusions on the innate dissimilarities between population groups on the basis of empirical data, for the simple reason that environment and heredity are too closely intertwined to be gauged separately.[36]

Perhaps such critics underestimate researchers' skill in finding a way out of these problems.[37] However, in this case, the key principle in deciding the status of anti-racism is the claim that researchers have no method for separating heredity from environment, and that they are therefore unable to even potentially falsify the assumption that all mental differences between populations can be traced to environmental factors. In view of the claim that science has no way of falsifying fundamental anti-racist beliefs, this premise of anti-racism must imply something other than science, since nothing that cannot be falsified can claim scientific status.

ANTI-RACISM AS IDEOLOGY

If research alone cannot legitimate the contemporary status of predominant anti-racism in the migration debate, then we must ask what alternative explanatory principles are available to us. We shall start by asking whether aspects of anti-racism that cannot be explained as research-governed ought to be construed as a separate ideology, or as part of one.

Ideologies have been defined in terms of five hallmarks: system context, particularistic interest-dependency, distortion of reality, unintended victims, and self-immunization. The first criterion, system context, refers to arguments that are mutually supportive, so that the system of thought gains credibility—when viewed from within, at any rate.

Casting the participants in the migration debate as racists or anti-racists reflects an anti-racist mind-set and constitutes a certain structuring of social reality. Both moral and political viewpoints can then support each other. While racists can be linked to violence and anti-democratic thought, anti-racists can be linked to humane, democratic ideals.

It is not difficult to find participants in the debate with particularistic interests. These interests may apply to preferences for exclusive immigration; but this also applies to those who want to see individuals from different cultures as players in a collective human arena, and who would then gladly disregard the significance of cultural differences. These interests may belong among people involved in political bureaucracy and liberal marketing, and among people with specific humanitarian interests. Liberal attitudes are far more prevalent among individuals in elitist positions than among ordinary people.[38] Particular interests may in this case even be linked to lifestyles favoring the multicultural as cultural stimulation.

If all conflicts surrounding immigration are linked to racism or anti-racism, this will obviously lead to oversimplification, and eventually to a distortion of the facts. Anxiety over global population growth and the ecological consequences of our lifestyle simply cannot be laid at the door of racism, in whatever guise. Neither can concern for cultural conflicts. If the categories of interpretation are too narrowly defined, key aspects of the immigration issue will exceed the scope of public concern.

Optimistic views that mass immigration will reduce racial tension as people with different backgrounds become more used to each other, are not completely supported by systematic research. Conflicts tend to escalate in proportion to the volume of immigration within populations, especially in times of high unemployment.[39]

Nor is it altogether realistic to assume that problems of integration are due solely to the attitudes of the majority population. Asian immigrants living in the West are reluctant to embrace contemporary western culture in all its complexity. For example, a number of immigrants have branded contemporary European gender relationships as immoral. With Sweden in mind, they claim that only half the women in our part of the world will ever get married. In the case of the United Kingdom, they claim that 50% of married couples are destined for divorce. In the case of Italy, they claim that the native population has no more than half the number of children necessary to ensure survival. Faced with conditions such as these, immigrants often deliberately select marriage partners for their children from their native country, in order to maintain their own traditions as long as possible. It has been estimated that over 80% of all Pakistanis that were married in Oslo between 1986 and 1996 got their spouse from Pakistan.

In all probability, ecological and demographic challenges may ultimately call for restrictive solutions that will conflict with contemporary liberal values, including human rights. The introduction of a political/economic initiative has been tried as a type of restrictive agent. In China, parents have been penalized for having more children than officially permitted. Other, more drastic measures include compulsory sterilization of people with a certain number of children. A policy of active or passive sanctioning of infectious diseases and famines to decimate whole populations is an even more drastic measure. The same can be said of what the science fiction literature terms "depopulation without discrimination," as "the fairest way to do what is necessary."[40] Not everyone, however, would agree that random extermination is the "fairest" policy. Now and again, the Chinese refer to selective human breeding as a "quality of life" policy. However drastic this may seem, it can be argued that this would be less devastating than all-out war between population groups — or, even worse, a war between the human species and the rest of the ecosystems.

Shutting our eyes to the harmful impact of good intentions will not increase the likelihood that these intentions will lead to a better world. Those who, in the name of morality, are determined just to hope for the best, can reap a selfish benefit by simply living their lives with a good conscience while in reality living a lie. But they may only be postponing the day of reckoning, leaving future generations ill-equipped, ideologically, to cope with the shock of reality.

In a culture dominated by hedonism and a self-centered here-and-now ethics, it will nevertheless be difficult to discuss the dilemma mentioned by Herbert Spencer in the 19th century. Spencer claimed that a misguided kindheartedness in one generation could lead to brutality in the next.

Many anti-racist viewpoints are defended on the premise that they are merely showing consideration for the victims of racism, whether in practical politics or through the self-perception of individuals in vulnerable groups. This argument does have merit — for example, as a reminder to exercise caution when interpreting aptitude tests that have produced different results for disparate groups. However, group distributions do not justify the categorization of specific individuals. Even after the American tests, which were the least favorable to African Americans with average IQ scores of 80, compared with Caucasian Americans' 100, a typical distribution would suggest that approximately 15% of colored test-takers would score higher than the average for Caucasians, and half the Caucasians would score lower than the same average. In practical terms, this means that we cannot judge any given person's capacity for achievement solely on the basis of his or her skin color.

The liberals' ideal of non-discrimination between individuals in a society under the rule of law doesn't necessarily clash with contemporary research in ethnic differences. After all, such research does not contradict the principle of evaluating individuals according to their own qualifications and not according to statistical features of the ethnic categories to which they belong. Unlike a lot of earlier racial research, contemporary research on the subject supports the principle that equality will initially benefit competent individuals in all population groups. But it is not certain that all ethnic groups will end up percentage-wise with equal numbers of representatives in every occupation, if qualifications alone are the selection criterion.

And so we have reached the last criterion of ideologies: the self-immunizing techniques. The simplest technique for immunizing a liberal immigration standpoint is to brand all opponents as racists, or as dangerous people set on legitimizing racism, and use this as justification for categorically dismissing their arguments without putting them to the test.

A more subtle form of self-immunization is to use research to safeguard completely against the risk of having to explain conflicts between ethnic groups in non-racial terms. In a book on race-related violence used by many European governments, we find the following definition of racial violence: "Any violence in which victims are selected because of their ethnic, 'racial,' religious, cultural or national origin. The victims are attacked not as individuals, but as representatives of groups that are normally minorities in terms of power. Buildings, properties and institutions may also be attacked, because they represent these same groups or their interests."

Since these authors give such a broad definition of racist violence, they are "immunized" from criticism by colleagues, who say that anti-racists are attacking social discrimination in general, which is a different matter altogether from traditional racism. On the other hand, if discrimination and violence linked to ethnicity, religion and nationality are interpreted as racism, we have a radical, expanded definition as opposed to the traditional one. The concoction of a cultural and a biological racial philosophy may not spring solely from confusion; it may also constitute a deliberate immunization against analytical criticism.

ANTI-RACISM AS MYTH

Many anti-racist arguments fit the criteria of an ideology. We could even say that what we are dealing with here is an issue-oriented, restricted ideology to match the more extensive new liberal ideology. All the same, not all anti-racial statements can be attributed to research-based interpretations or to an interest-governed ideology. An ideology can have a mobilizing effect on people with common interests, encouraging joint initiatives. Nevertheless, the ideology does not gain universal credibility without a safety net to fall back on, which causes a specific perception of reality to appear both right and reasonable.

This is where myths enter the picture. Central to myths, in contrast to ideologies, is the story; and not just *any* story, but one that binds together five identifiable hallmarks: Myths are intended to communicate something important about our lives, something that gives substance to a general theme by reducing it to a struggle between two forces, something that sees this struggle as a manifestation of good and evil locked in an archetypal battle that

must be re-fought and re-won. Thus the guardians of the myth are charged
with getting people to recognize the drama in their lives every time they are
faced with moral dilemmas in critical situations.[41]

As for the immigration debate, this story is not about people moving beyond the limitations of nature with anthropocentric pride in their own rights,
nor about those leaving overpopulated areas and crossing the borders of
civilization with no desire to adapt culturally. An in-depth review of media
coverage of the immigration issue indicates that the covert story repeatedly
being invoked is rooted in the events of the Second World War.

Admittedly, the time frame is occasionally expanded to include European
attitudes toward natives around the world in previous centuries. "The white
man's burden" is often depicted as a combination of racist arrogance, economic exploitation, and slave trading. Much could be said on all these subjects, but this would not necessarily portray liberal immigration policies as
moral penance.

Slavery, for example, is a far older phenomenon than modern racial theories, and the European form of slave trading cannot be viewed as unique.
Some historians estimate that Europeans were guilty of shipping around 10
million Africans slaves to America and the Caribbean over a period of three
hundred years. By comparison, 14 million Africans are estimated to have
been sold into slavery by the Moors in the Muslim world between the 7th and
the 20th centuries.[42] It is difficult to see how this story can furnish Asian Muslims with the unique moral right to residency in contemporary Europe.

The more recent variant of arrogant European racism, the source of our
long-term international guilt complex, was the persecution of the Jews by the
Nazis—German or otherwise—on racial grounds during the Second World
War. This story is often retold so stereotypically that it could almost be used
in a mythical context.

There are many ways to relate the events of World War II. Schools and the
media have certain established interpretations that have become the "correct"
version. These have many striking features in common with the five hallmarks of myths. The War is generally regarded as a battle between two forces:
Good and Evil, as embodied in anti-Nazism and Nazism. The former can be
expanded to include the western allied armies, in addition to Stalin's Red
Army and the many national resistance movements.

This may lead us to suspect that we are dealing with mythical stories rather
than historical factual accounts. The myth will have to assume that the decisive battle was between those fighting for democracy, liberation, and anti-
racism on the one hand, and those supporting dictatorship, repression, and
racism on the other. In view of estimates suggesting that Stalin's policies led
to a larger loss of civilian life than Hitler's Jewish crusade[43]—such a break-

down of warring parties seems artificial, at any rate from the vantage point of historical accounts of the War's atrocities.[44]

All the same, it must be said that all the allied forces during the Second World War were fighting a regime that was systematically exterminating Jews on racial grounds, even though this was not the key motive for their participation in the War itself. The fact that the five to six million civilian Jews who perished during the War enjoy a unique status compared to the 160 to 170 million civilian victims of an assortment of 20th century political regimes, based on R.J. Rummel's estimates, can be interpreted in a number of ways.

It can be claimed with good reason that the extermination of the Jews was more single-minded and organized—and thus more malevolent—than most other genocides, which were more indirect. Another noteworthy interpretation states that a number of Jews have been adept at exploiting historical research and focusing media attention on themselves.[45] But there is a third interpretation, which is also feasible. We could call this the mythical need: The reason why the genocide of the Jews figures so prominently in accounts of the Second World War is that this genocide can be linked so directly to racist and Nazi ideas, thus serving to unite the inhumane, the non-scientific and the politically authoritarian in one image. If this image can be made to represent the apex of evil, and even be portrayed as the opposite of new liberal ideals, then liberal interpretations have been handed a virtually impenetrable defense.

The relative aspect of the predominant myth becomes clearer when cast against the backdrop of an anti-myth. Instead of dichotomizing the fronts under the Second World War as an ideological conflict between Nazis and anti-Nazis, the basic contrast could be viewed as a conflict between people who were trying to defend their homeland on a nationalistic foundation on the one hand, and those who were willing to subjugate countries imperialistically on the other. The losers in this War were those who had not known the strength or necessity of a national policy. Alas, the Jews and Gypsies had to suffer because they had neither nation nor army to defend them. The Germans suffered defeat because they championed a supranational new order without first acquiring national and civilizational legitimacy for this new order.

To avoid misunderstanding, we should emphasize the following: When we call an account mythical, this does not mean that the basic subject to which the myth refers never took place, merely that the myth forces reality, which is multifarious, into the restrictive mold of a specific interpretation. When we say that the accounts of Jewish persecution are part of a contemporary myth, this in no way trivializes the historical consequences for the Jews. Attempts by so-called revisionists to cast doubt on the reliability or tenability of Holocaust studies are a derailment of the debate in this context. It is the validity, or the use of the accounts of the Holocaust, that should be questioned—that is, the relevance of certain historical events in an attempt to find answers to contemporary challenges relating to overpopulation and the relationship between different groups, societies and civilizations.

The spread of certain mythical interpretations of World War II suggests that we are dealing with interpretations that appeal to far more people than those who personally experienced this War. The link between the Holocaust and Fascism, and between Fascism and genetic explanations of differences between populations, has become an important reference for political spokesmen and for the media, in cultural life and research.[46] The reasons for this are manifold. Some have vested interests in promoting this type of reference to ethnic conflicts. Others might just be looking for a readily understandable and emotionally appealing explanation for threatening events. Mythical tales may indeed have a legitimate place in every culture; but it is important to be able to recognize a myth, even when it is presented as something else. A myth will seldom provide an exhaustive, well-rounded account of social reality, which is something complex.

ANTI-RACISM AS BELIEF

As we have previously pointed out, it is difficult to conceive of a culture based solely on logic and reliable empirical knowledge and which, on such a basis, laid claim to such a direct rendering of reality and morally-binding authority. In practice, all societies must institute certain forms of joint reality orientation and trust in the propitiousness of their interpretive cultures. We could imagine a functional culture as a collective interpretation of reality— based in part on belief and maintained by myths and ideologies, but where differing empirical derivations of collective understanding could be corrected as it became clear that adjustments had moved beyond functional limits.

We may be pitted against cultures with an explicit credo; and there are societies with no explicit foundation for any belief system. Where beliefs, myths and ideologies are not explicit, it may be necessary to approach these premises on the basis of hypothetical analyses of ideas that are taken for granted.

We have mentioned that concepts of human rights, and particularly the UN Declaration of Universal Human Rights of 1948, have become a widespread belief system for the intelligentsia in the West. One of the key dogmas has been the assumption that human beings have fundamental qualities independent of culture. Such a belief system may be well adapted to the premises of the new liberal ideology, as we suggested earlier.

The question should be asked as to the relevance of belief systems to the assumptions made by the forces of anti-racism in the debate on migration.

Why should key arguments in this debate be regarded simply as part of a belief system?

Let's be perfectly clear here: A system of beliefs does not consist merely of an emphasis on exalted ideals, the so-called "ultimate values" of what is "good." Such a system must also refer to an opposing force, to what is designated as "evil." This is where "racism" comes in as a means of understanding destructive existential forces. For historical reasons, racism has become associated with inequality and subjugation, as well as ignorance and arrogance— but first and foremost with Nazism and the Holocaust. Thus anti-racism can be made to serve as a bulwark against evil forces.

One hallmark of religious objects is that they exist in their own right; their authority does not stem from comparisons with anything else. Against this backdrop, we would do well to consider the cries of outrage that rise up whenever the Holocaust is compared with other types of genocide, or when racism is put on a par with alternative grounds for exclusion. There is a consensus that the Holocaust must retain a unique status—and, in a sense, it does.[47] Nonetheless, there is much insight to be gained by relativization. When this is perceived as a form of desecration, it means we are probably dealing with a cult centered on a belief system.

A number of researchers have come to see that antiracism is related to references that are most appropriately understood in a religious context. The Norwegian social anthropologist Inger Lise Lien has written that the word "racist" has come to denote the demons among us in the public immigration debate—the unclean, from which all decent people should remain aloof.[48] In fact, there is something to be said for this characterization. She could have gone even further and said that for many new liberal interpreters, Hitler, racists and the Holocaust have become secular mental images of Satan, demons and hell.

We could draw yet another religious parallel with the use of the term "racism": Let us consider the fear and foreboding that 17th century people faced when they could not combine an inherited tradition of theological interpretations, seen as the Divine Order, with certain mechanical theories of their day, seen as the explanation of Science. This foreboding was apparently allayed by defining scientists as "heretics," relegating them to a familiar, definable category. In the short term, when fear of one kind or another is associated with something familiar to us, something that can easily make us indignant, we may easily be lulled into a false sense of security. The need for such a sense of security can even cause us to provoke someone to assume the role of a heretic. But in the long run, security of this kind comes at a high price, since it insulates us from participating in the interpretation of ongoing research. We have reason to believe that the contemporary use of the term "racism" has much in common with the use of the word "heretic" three hundred years ago. Such labeling represents a facile—but in the long run, dysfunctional—response to cultural challenges.

The foregoing might seem like an all too cerebral discussion of the status and assumptions of "anti-racism." Most people tend to associate anti-racism with certain activist groups. These groups can come across as anything but subtle, but rather animated by apparently simple motives. Presumably it is possible to join an anti-racist movement with the sole motive of being identified with a force that appears to be politically accepted and yet legitimizes violence against groups that no one wants to defend.

All the same, it is an oversimplification to assume that we are merely dealing with people who seek legitimate outlets for aggression. Behind the slogan "crush the racists" lurks more than a primitive desire to exercise violence. The battle also involves the struggle of purity against impurity. Since racism is something murky, anti-racism, and the colorful community it purportedly represents, wraps itself in the mantle of purity.[49]

There is a universally human quality about all this. To be able to live in a sinful world, we all need—at least, now and then—to distance ourselves mentally from sin by balancing impurity against purity. We may become addicted to a "mental image" of purity. For those unable to associate purity with something that surpasses conventional social life, there is a tendency to look for it in versatile political categories, which totalitarian regimes have always been adept at exploiting. The image of purity can also assume the shape of a utopian world in which everybody loves everybody else, a world free from conflict and war. The struggle against impure racists is construed by anti-racists as a struggle for purity, just as opposing groups might think of their struggle against immigration from foreign countries in similar terms, and as other groups once construed the campaign against the Jews as a form of cleansing.

Perhaps we have found the key to the third shrine here—which hides the mystery that can explain why racism and Nazism have been daily fare in the immigration debate for decades, whereas ecological, demographical and civilizational issues have been conspicuous by their absence. If anti-racism is an element in the mobilization of a collective ideology—a myth that provides moral security and a faith that ensures purity—it will be extremely hard for the interpreters of anti-racism to relinquish their situational understanding in favor of weighty analyses that concede only morally relative dilemmas.

IDEOLOGY, MYTHS AND BELIEFS AS FORMS OF LEGITIMATION

The above-mentioned criticism of the form of argumentation employed by the anti-racist front should not be taken as a defense of the anti-racists' claims—for "racism" and against "anti-racism." What we have tried to show is that many anti-racists are operating under false pretenses. They purport to champion universal morality and claim to have modern research on their side, which—if true—would automatically give them a higher status and thus absolve them of having to take their critics seriously. But, in fact, such is not the case. Much of what purports to be research-based falls short of rigorous scientific standards. The strength and intensity of the anti-racism racist front is essentially based on ideology, myths and beliefs.

This fact needs to be driven home—not only because some debaters deserve to be set straight, but also to demonstrate how specific categories in cultural analysis should be applied. If the direction of a culturally-determined course needs to be corrected—and there is indeed much that needs correcting with respect to popular notions on migration—then it behoves us to familiarize ourselves with the phenomena we are dealing with. A biased focus on unsound scientific conclusions derived from certain anti-racist arguments will prove ineffectual in coping with attitudes steeped in ideology, myths and beliefs.

With anti-racism reflected in ideologies, myths and systems of belief, the new liberal culture has become the main point of reference. A philosophy of the individual and of human rights makes people prone to adopt the kind of anti-racist views discussed here. One thing all these views share is the exaltation of the individual, regardless of cultural background. When anti-racists link a non-liberal concept about immigration to totalitarian movements, and go on to invoke the specter of Nazism and the Holocaust in their defense, new liberalism is made to appear even more unassailable.

Even so, such a strong linkage should not impede a critical analysis of hidden elements within a legitimization system. A culture adapted to new liberal categories for understanding the relationship between the individual and society is not only narrow-minded, but also prone to several forms of dysfunctional orientation and adjustment.

An ideology that puts the individual in an external relationship with society and culture might at first glance appear to be liberating for individuals seeking to maximize their happiness in terms of objective potential, whether such happiness is measured in terms of bodies, money, technology or cultural stimuli. But this kind of culture will be of little consequence in the face of many of life's challenges. We have pointed out that new liberalism promotes an unsatisfactory moral philosophy, e.g. in the area of family structure. A strong individual quest for happiness, coupled with a weak family structure, does not bode well for sustainable reproduction. This is, in fact, the current state of affairs throughout most of Europe.

However, even though winning support for indisputable moral principles as a correction to new liberalism may prove difficult in pluralistic societies, we can assume that most Europeans would respond to consequence analyses showing how far they actually fall below the requisite reproduction level regarding numbers of children, whereas neighboring civilizations are producing more children than can be readily absorbed. Only if immigration is perceived in a basically positive light—as an aid to self-help—will the reproductive gloom in new liberal societies escape serious system criticism.

Thus it is claimed that much of the anti-racist mobilization in the West is not merely—and perhaps not even primarily—an expression of involvement on behalf of those immigrating to Europe. This mobilization is also an element in the self-defense of people who have benefited from ways of living that are adapted to new liberalism. Such people may not be very eager to draw attention to the dysfunctional processes that ensued.

NOTES

1. Jean-Pierre Gonot, Christopher Prinz and Nico Keilman: "Adjustment of Public pensions Schemes in Twelve Industrial Countries: possible Answers to Population Ageing," *European Journal of Population*, 11, 1995:371–398.

2. Though figures are not conclusive, we could point out that the UN's *Population Information Network* (POPIN) gives the following years for the passing of each billion: 1804, 1927, 1960, 1974, 1987. In 1993, The same population agency gave this estimate of milestones for future increases from 6 to 11 billion people: 1998, 2009, 2021, 2035, 2054, 2093.

3. Massimo Livi Bacci, *A Concise History of World Population.* (London: Blackwell, 1992): 147.

4. Department of Economic and Social Affairs / Population Division, United Nations Secretariat, *"World Population Projections to 2150," http://ww.undp.org/popin/popin.html* (Feb. 1, 1998).

5. UN's population division: *Department for Economic and Social Information and Policy Analysis.* (Nov. 13, 1996).

6. Paul Kennedy, *Preparing for the twenty-first century* (New York: Harper, 1993): 52.

7. *UN World Population Projections to 2150,* New York. 1998, Tab. 2.

8. Gustav Feichtinger and Gunther Steinmann, *Immigration into Population with Below Replacement Level. The Case of Germany* (Vienna: Springer, 1992)—Cf. also G. Feichtinger, *Demographische Analyse und populationsdynamische Modele: Grundzuge der Bevölkerungs-mathematik* (Vienna: Springer, 1979).

9. Cf. Encyclopedia Britannica, "Nations of the World, Statistics 1995" and UN 1998 revision of the World Population estimates *<http://www.popin.org/pop1998/1.html>* (1998).

10. Lincoln Quillian, "Prejudice as a Response to Perceived Group Threat: Population Composition and Anti-Immigrant and Racial Prejudice in Europe," *American*

Sociological Review, Vol. 60 (Aug. 1995): 586–611.—Lincoln Quillian, "Group Threat and Regional Change in Attitudes toward African-Americans," *American Journal of Sociology,* Vol. 102, (Nov 1996): 816–860.

11. Peter M. Vitousek's article in: *State of the World, ed.* Leister Brown (London: World Watch Institute, 1994).

12. The Research Group "Redefining Progress," Canada 2002.

13. Joel E. Cohen, *How many people can the earth support?* (New York: Norton, 1995).

14. *Focus,* Berlin 6, 1994: 73.—Cf. also international references to opinion polls on immigration in Anthony H. Birch, *Nationalism and National Integration.* (London: Unwin & Hyman, 1989) and in Peter Brimelow: *Alien Nation. Common Sense about America's Immigration Disaster.* (New York: Random House, 1995)

15. *MMI,* Oslo, April 18, 1987.

16. *TEMO,* Stockholm—March 18, 1991.

17. *Berlingske Tidende,* Copenhagen, August 12, 1990.

18. Virginia Abernethy, *Population Politics. The Choices that Shape Our Future* (London and New York: Plenum Press, 1995): chps. 16, 17 and 21.

19. *Encyclopedia Britannica,* Vol. 9, 1994.

20. John Solomos, *Race and racism in Britain.* (London: MacMillan, 1993).— Maxim Silverman, *Deconstructing the Nation: immigration, racism and citizenship in modern France.* (New York: Routledge, 1992).—David D. Anderson and Robert L. Wright: *The Dark and Tangled Path: Race in America.* (Boston: Houghton Mifflin, 1971).—Benjamin P. Browser, *Racism and Anti-racism in World Perspective.* (London: Sage, 1995).

21. Eliot White, ed. *Intelligence, political inequality and public policy* (Westpoint, CN: Praeger, 1997).

22. Helmuth Nyborg, ed., *The Scientific Study of Human Nature* (Oxford: Pergamon, 1997)—Bernard D. Davis: *The Genetic revolution.* (Baltimore: John Hopkins University Press 1991).

23. A. H. Halsey, ed., *Heredity and Environment.* (London: Methuen, 1977)—Carl N. Degeler, *In Search of Human Nature. The Decline and Revival of Darwinism in American Social Thought* (Oxford University Press, 1991).

24. Luigi Luca and Francesco Cavalli-Sforza, *The Great Human Diasporas* (Readings, Mass: Addison-Wesley, 1995): 123—Merritt Ruhlen: *The Origin of Language. Tracing the Evolution of Mother Tongue* (New York: Wiley, 1994): 150.

25. Neil Risch et. al.: "Categorization of humans in biomedical research; genes, race and disease," *Genome Biology* (Stanford University: School of Medicine/Dept. of Genetics, 1 July, 2002).

26. The following is essentially based on accounts given by professor William B. Provine of Cornell University at a seminar on scientific theory at the University of Oslo on May 27, 1994.

27. Asley. Montagu, *Man's Most Dangerous Myth. The Fallacy of Race.* (New York: Alta Mira, 6th ed. 1997).

28. L. C. Dunn, *Race and Biology. The Race Question in Modern Science* (Paris: UNESCO, 1951).

29. Mark Snyderman and Stanley Rothman, *The IQ Controversy, the Media and Public Polit.* (New Brunswik: Transaction Books, 1988).

30. Ronald Fletcher, *Science, ideology and the media. The Cyril Burt Scandal.* (New Brunswick: Transaction Books 1991)—N.J. Mackintosh, ed., *Cyril Burt: fraud or framed?* (Oxford University Press, 1995).

31. Martin Barker, *The new racism.* (Frederics, Md: University Publications of America/Aletheia, 1982).—Robert Miles, *Racism.* (London: Routledge, 1998).

32. Michael Banton, "The Nature and Causes of Racism and Racial Discrimination," *International Sociology*, Vol. 7, no. 1 1992: 69.

33. This study, carried out by Gallup, was reprinted in the November/December 1995 issue of *The American Enterprise.* It was also mentioned in *USA Today,* May 2, 1995.

34. Richard J. Herrnstein and Charles Murray, *The Bell Curve. Intelligence and Class Structure in American Life.* (New York: Free Press, 1994).

35. Claude S. Fischer et al., *Inequality by Design. Breaking the Bell Curve Myth.* (Princeton University Press, 1996).

36. Stephen Jay Gould, *The Mismeasure of Man. The Definite Refutation to the Argument of the Bell Curve.* (New York: W. W. Norton, 1996).

37. Cf. the problem statement and literature references in Robert Plomin, *Genetics and Experience. The Interplay Between Nature and Nurture.* (London: Sage, 1994).

38. Katharine Betts: *The Great Divide. Immigrant Politics in Australia.* (Sidney: Duff & Snellgrove, 1999)—Peter Brimelow, *Alien Nation: Common sense about America's immigration disaster* (New York: Random House, 1995)—John E. Rielly, "Leaders vs. the Public: Foreign Policy Preferences, *The Polling Report* , (No. 6:2. 1995)—Jeoffrey C. Goldfarb, *Civility and Subversion. The Intellectuals in Democratic Society* (New York: New School of Social Research, 1998).

39. Lincoln Quillian, "Prejudice as a Response to Perceived Group Threat," *American Sociological Review,* Vol. 60 (August 1995): 586–611—Cp. also Tatu Vanhanen: Ethnic conflicts explained by ethnic nepotism (Stamford, Con: Jai Press, 1999).

40. Quoted from Alice Glaser, *The Tunnel Ahead.* (New York: F&SF, Nov 1961).

41. Where a myth is predominant in the immigration debate, we can expect strong cultural pressure, not only on those who are politically active, but on the entire collective memory of a people.—Cf. Jeffrey K. Olick and Daniel Levy, "Collective Memory and Cultural Constraint: Holocaust Myth and Rationality in German Politics," *American Sociological Review*, Vol. 62 (Dec 1997): 921–936.

42. Raymond Mauny, *Les siècles obscures de l'Afrique noir: histoire et archéologie* (The obscure centuries of Black Africa. History and Archeology), (Paris: Société Française d'Histoire d'Outre-Mer, 1970).

43. R. J. Rummel, *Death by Government.* (New Brunswick: Transaction Publications. 1995), Tab. 1.6.

44. Pavel and Anatoli Sudoplatov, *Special tasks: the memoirs of an unwanted witness*, (Boston: Little Brown, 1994).—J. Arch Getty and Roberta T. Manning ed., *Stalinist terror, New Perspectives* (Cambridge University Press, 1994).—Sterphane Courtois and Mark Kramer, *The Black book of communism: crimes. Terror, repression* (Harvard University Press, 1999).

45. Peter Novick, *The Holocaust in American Life* (Boston: Houghton Mifflin Company, 1999)—Norman G. Finkelstein, *The Holocaust Industry: reflections on the exploitation of Jewish suffering* (London: Verso Books, 2000).

46. An article by J. P. Rushton, concerning reactions in a number of university environments to attempts to dispel the mythical taboos in this field, may be found in the periodical *Liberty*, Vol. II, No. 4 (March 1998): 31–35.

47. Alan S. Rosenbaumed., *Is the Holocaust unique? Perspectives on comparative genocide* (Boulder, Col: Westview Press, 2001).

48. Inger-Lise Lien, *Ordet som stempler djevlene (A word labeling the devils).* (Oslo: Aventura, 1997): 41f.

49. May Douglas, *Purity and Danger* (London: Routledge, 2002).

Chapter Eight

The Cultural Challenge

IN SUMMARY

We began this book by highlighting some events that have recently raised the specter of fear and uncertainty and have caused us to question the real strength of our western culture. This is quite a different mood from the hubris that predominated in interpretive environments in the aftermath of 1989, after western democracies had definitively won out over the eastern forms of socialism.

With the possible exception of certain minorities in former East Block countries, few regard Marxist social philosophy as a viable alternative to today's western course. Nor do Muslim social principles appeal to western societies, apart from specific groups of immigrants. Still, there is considerable skepticism not only of a number of western regimes, but also of the view that the West has discovered the ultimate culture to help us meet present and future challenges with confidence. Such skepticism only partly overlaps with a belief that non-western societies have hit on the answer.

Several events during the 1990s have fueled this skepticism. But it was only after the unexpected terrorist attack on financial and military centers in the United States on September 11, 2001 that doubt turned to outright fear. This fear has not only been directed against potential terrorist cells; it has also become a manifestation of our insecurity about the West's preparedness for terrorist emergencies. The US can certainly point to military and technological superiority over most potential attackers, but this fact alone is not enough to reinstate the confidence in cultural superiority that Francis Fukyama spoke about when he interpreted the victory of the West in 1989 as "the end point of mankind's ideological evolution."

At the start of the new millennium, there are widespread reservations about whether any society thus far has developed an ideology that, at the same time, can appeal to ones own population and lead to an adequate understanding of and communication with others. When groups of foreign antagonists display aggressive attitudes and threatening behavior toward the West, they are challenging more than the police and the military. They have also thrown down the gauntlet to those who were supposed to help politicians and the public to better understand current events. Potential terrorism poses a cultural challenge as well.

We began by saying that culture represents an important framework for collective forms of orientation and a set of premises for the way in which we adapt. Yet it is clear that culture is a word with many meanings, and not all forms of cultural interpretation will serve us equally well. The way that natural science divides the world into culture and nature is too generalized. The humanistic subjects, on the other hand, based on hermeneutic methods, can focus too narrowly on the work of certain thinkers and artists. We were originally in search of a way to comprehend recurring patterns in a collective orientation. An understanding of culture within the framework of the social sciences might well give us the broadest range of options.

We discussed cultural philosophy in the tradition of Edward B. Tylor, shared by social anthropologists and sociologists alike. But whereas social anthropologists have attempted to regard various societies as cultural units and have concentrated their study on specific societies, sociologists have preferred to look for different cultural systems within complex societies. To describe culture merely as "patterns" of attitudes and behavior does not necessarily help us understand culture as an explanatory variable in a given society's development. Culture commands influence through collective interpretations, leading to meaning and motivation. In the social sciences we will depend on hallmarks that make it possible to describe culture, or subculture, as "systems" that can be analyzed as an explanatory element in social development.

In the chapter entitled "Culture and Functionality," we examined how culture could be used as a bona fide explanatory principle for human actions, as opposed to other explanatory principles. No modern, differentiated society can be analyzed as a single cultural system, but it is possible to identify a variety of cultural systems—each with a potential explanatory force. We argued that ideologies have encompassed cultural systems that have profoundly affected the development of modern societies. Myths and belief systems can also be identified by specific hallmarks in the patterns of collective interpretations.

Understanding ideologies as systems involves recognizing their potential influence over and above the interests and intentions of those who apply them. Both as a system of thought and as an economically and politically institutionalized apparatus, an ideology can have a dynamic of its own, one favoring specific interpretations and reaction patterns while downplaying others. This means that even advocates of a given ideology can end up as its victims. In discussing ideologies that determined how previous generations interpreted society, we showed how their fall was largely due to political miscalculations derived from immanent thought systems.

As systems of thought, ideologies can be appealing, particularly when a directed self-interest is promoted as the common good. Well-developed ideologies can look like a safe bet with their immanent explanations, which immunize them against system-threatening criticism. This immunization against criticism, which at first glance might look like a hallmark of strength, has over time proven to be a devious aspect of former predominant ideologies, since this hindered the correction of lobbyists' orientation. This applies equally to conservative ideologies, old *laissez faire* liberalism, radical left-wing socialism, and radical right-wing Fascism.

The question was whether the prevailing views of our time should be analyzed as systems of thought linked to an overarching ideology. If so, even contemporary liberalism's claim of a new transparency might largely be regarded as a self-immunizing feature of this ideology. We concluded that the new form of liberal orientation met the criteria for an ideology. This means that several examples of political self-deception in our time, including the western hybris after 11/9, could be analyzed in relation to a dominant ideology. What has recently been called "new liberalism" is not merely a renaissance of old *laissez faire* liberalism. It is characterized by the passing of legislation granting rights to citizens, guaranteed by a State founded on the principle of public welfare. Still, it is fair to regard the ideology legitimizing this policy as part and parcel of the liberal tradition.

In contrast to other ideologies, liberalism is characterized not only by a high regard for individual freedom; the liberal notion of freedom is seen as the individual's liberation *from* social bonds and *from* cultural constraints. This implies that culture, and also social processes, will be seen in "external" relations to the individual. Such notions affect our general understanding of cultural as an institution, as well as our understanding of correct political priorities.

Many have pointed out the unexpected repercussions of an economy governed by a liberal market. It could very well lead to greater social and regional differences. Another dubious aspect of a market-based economy is the kind of detrimental impact on the environment and eco-systems that is typical of this type of economy.

In our socio-cultural analysis, we chose to focus on issues largely overlooked in the political debate—namely, the connection between a culture dominated by new liberal principles and the failure to maintain adequate integral morality, and a family institution necessary for an adequate reproduction.

CONDITIONS FOR MORALITY

In the second part of the book, we traced the inability of liberalism to justify and remain integrated with social morality—a favorite subject of sociologists. The sociological criticism of the liberal perception of morality has traditionally struggled with the difficulty of uniting differentiation with integration, as well as explaining the propensity of particularistic interests in terms of universal morality.

A society can continue to function even when its citizens exhibit varying levels of moral behavior. Still, there is a limit to the extent of moral deviation that any one society can endure without a serious loss of mutual trust, which in turn adversely affects people's willingness to put themselves out on behalf of their community.

The spread of violence and crime, along with political confusion about how to deal with it, can be seen as a manifestation of societies in moral decline. The long-term consequences could involve severe civilian unrest and mounting difficulties in winning political acceptance for necessary reforms. As a form of government, democracy requires a high degree of morality.

In a social context, morality occupies several dimensions, one of which relates to norms limiting individual impulses. Another dimension of morality involves people's motives for going the extra mile in their quest to improve society, including its norms. In both cases, morals are part of culture and not only an expression of personal attitudes. Belief systems, myths and ideologies are all morally significant. A morality adapted to a liberal philosophy about the individual as the ultimate goal and society will easily fall short in several areas, even if it can be seen as a counterbalance to totalitarian political threats. A tribute to individual rights, without an emphasis on concomitant obligations, could prove dysfunctional in cultures that are threatened by social anomie and cynical self-interest.

Emile Durkheim believed that the challenge of anomie was determined by a change in principles of integration, from a traditional solidarity based on equality and identification to a new kind of solidarity based on insight into the advantages of increased differentiation and dependency. Developments have not entirely borne out Durkheim's expectations. It was not primarily the generation growing up in the 1870s that experienced anomic conditions or witnessed the dramatic break-up of moral norms. Several studies in western countries actually showed a drop in crime, violence, illegitimacy, and alcoholism during the latter half of the 19th century, but a sharp rise in the latter part of the 20th century. Rather than a U-shaped model for integration, recent events have given the trend the form of a J-shape for anomie.

These trends follow a pattern that cannot be explained solely in terms of economic variables such as standards of living or welfare programs. Nor do these trends automatically accompany political circumstances, such as war and peace, or the shift between radical and conservative governments. Rather, the weakening of civil morality can be seen in the context of a rise in the veneration of the individual, which has not been counterbalanced by supraindividual morality. The development of dysfunctions stems from cultural changes.

This moral challenge cannot be met merely by political programs that bandy about terms like solidarity as slogans, often backed up by promises of larger welfare budgets. The awarding of new political rights does not compensate for the flaws in civil morality. Moreover, there is a limit as to how much backing politicians can expect from voters in championing little known causes unless these voters already have a strong sense of social loyalty. The development of individual rights with respect to public service and private consumption is not likely to provide a functional alternative to a decline in supraindividual morality—a morality which, over time, has been shored up by loyalty to religion, civilization, the State, the local community, social class and family.

A weakening of moral solidarity can lower our chances of reintroducing politico-economic reforms. People may simply be unwilling to pay high taxes to clients who, thanks to their asocial lifestyle, have run up enormous public bills. But it is not just in relation to crime and the willingness to pay taxes that a liberal culture may fall short. One area of life on which liberal morality has had a profound effect is gender relations and family formation. At least for the time being, the individual-oriented rights morality has to a large extent divorced sexual morality from conditions for stable family formation.

THE FAMILY AND REPRODUCTION

A lot of data highlights destabilized family morality in societies considered modern in the western sense. Statistics show that fewer couples are getting married and more are getting divorced. Quantitatively, fewer children are being born in western countries than are required for maintaining population replacement. On average, only two-thirds as many children required for maintaining population levels in the EU countries are being born as at the turn of the century. In addition, the data on the spread of mental illness, social maladjustment and cultural disorientation suggests that contemporary forms of culture and socialization are not working well either.

A liberal orientation implies that a given culture is selectable with respect to the needs and wishes of individuals. This, in turn, tends to cast the choice of partners and family formation in the light of what best serves the interests of the individual. For individuals with no supraindividual orientation, a fixation on one's body and well-being can easily be construed as key elements of success.

In the first place, liberal ideology has interpreted historical development as a process by which individuals free themselves from the Church, from traditions, and from the control of the family and the local community. Attempts to counterbalance the idealization of the self-realizing, autonomous individual has thus been neutralized.

In the second place, liberal ideology has provided people with premises for understanding themselves as individuals with natural needs and rights. Sex, perceived as an object of pleasure or as a means of relieving pent-up frustration and achieving happiness, becomes a coherent aspect of this perception. This is in stark contrast to an understanding of man as an intentional being with spiritual goals and to an understanding of man as a socio-cultural being. According to the latter perspective, sexual prerogatives could be regarded as a reward for commitment to family and society.

In a certain phase, romantic stories about love could be seen as an ideological crowbar against the arguments for the necessity of institutionalized marriage. Since the doctrine of progress has gradually come to be interpreted as an ongoing process of liberation, release from stressful emotional ties could also be viewed as progress. The pharmaceutical and adult entertainment industries have developed a variety of methods for stimulating and arousing people sexually, without commitment to or dependence on others, and by means that do not involve any significant risk of unwanted pregnancies and diseases.

In the family arena we have witnessed a parallel development toward more cohabitation and fewer children. The typical liberal response to this unpredicted and unintended development has not been one of self-criticism, but rather a program for increased immigration, in order to secure manpower in care-providing occupations!

These days, a number of major European cities can expect a predominantly non-European population within one or two generations. In the wake of popular protests against this policy, the western elite has denounced this reaction as a manifestation of prejudice and xenophobia, which in turn has been seen as a manifestation of a dangerous form of racism. Here too, the liberal's premises for argumentation have been on full display.

Several studies show that immigrants from Muslim countries, in particular, are not inclined to identify with European culture. The conflict in their encounter with the West does not primarily involve religious differences, such as seeing Jesus as God's son and not merely as a prophet before the time of Mohammed. Nor does racial prejudice appear to be an everyday experience for Asian immigrants. They react most frequently to what they refer to as the West's egotism and materialism and to what they consider to be a lack of morality and spirituality as exemplified by religion and the family unit. This means that it is the manifestations of a liberal culture that generate conflict.

The conflict between Muslim and western culture cannot be reduced to a mere difference in development and modernity. Western reproductive patterns, which do not ensure long-term survival for its populations, do not represent a functional modernity. Muslim family traditions, on the other hand, do ensure reproduction even if they do not correspond to new liberal ideals for equality and liberation. In 1996, the research center IIASA published figures showing that Europe's share of world population will decline this century, whatever the circumstances. The center calculated that this proportion would stand at around 7–8% by the middle of the 21st century. The original EU countries' share, which in 1950 had stood at 12%, is for the same countries estimated to be about 4% by the middle of this century. Based on demographic goals, Muslim populations, in short, are poised to gain, whereas the western liberals are poised to lose.

Normally, the prospect of such a development would provoke anything from moral panic to demands for cultural reorientation and a new policy. The fact that such reactions have not been approved, can tell us something about a dominant ideology. When someone says that we are losing, the response has been: "Who are we?" Furthermore, it has been said that all divisions of humanity into "us" and "them" are conventional. This had led to assumptions that it is only a matter of psychology and fantasy to replace one type of conventional identity with another. According to this reasoning, no matter which population groups happen to constitute a majority in future western societies, they will all be an integral part of the human race, with most people sharing our dreams and values.

What happened on 9/11, 2001 was in America an assassination—of this idea, that is. What happened in Amsterdam 11/2, 2004, when Theo van Gogh was stabbed to death in plain daylight, had a similar effect in several European countries. These events dealt a cruel blow to the notion of human oneness in cultural orientation. It also underminded the assumption that reproduction patterns are of no consequence, since it doesn't much matter who will take over in future generations. No matter how the West defines unity and diversity, other players will make our mutual diversity an issue, as this diversity is perceived not only as a variation in lifestyle and identity, but as a disparity between believers and non-believers, allies and enemies.

There are several reasons why western analysts and leaders should allow this conflict to stimulate a deeper cultural analysis, not least on a civilizational level. First of all, this would make it easier to understand the contemporary Muslim frame of mind—which is a factor significant enough in itself in a world in which civilizations interact ever more closely

Secondly, such analyses can help us cope more successfully with contemporary civil conflicts. Simply put, we can draw certain conclusions from cultural analyses—from the European experience with Muslim integration to the American experience with terrorists from abroad. This means that we can return full circle to the questions we posed at the beginning of this book: the cultural prerequisites for understanding the events of 9/11.

Moreover, a theoretical cultural analysis, with functional rules of thumb, can help us better understand the strengths and weaknesses of contemporary western culture and the ideology which, in 1989, was heralded as a historical winner. To grasp the limitations of the new liberal culture, we must look at its inadvertent consequences as well as its alluring presentation. This requires concepts for cultural comparisons.

CAN WE SURVIVE WITHOUT IDEOLOGIES?

In the foregoing, we have argued that ideologies have had a limiting and misleading effect on providing adequate reality orientation. This is true not least with regard to forms of orientation compatible with the new form of liberalism. It is necessary to understand ideologies in terms of certain analytical hallmarks, in order to recognize them, even when they are presented as something else.

The question then arises: Is it realistic to envision a predictable future in which we are free of all ideologies? The answer to this question will likely be "no," at least when asked in modern differentiated societies.

Despite their limitations, ideologies serve a number of key political functions in modern societies, based on guided change and on harmonious relationships between peoples that don't know one another personally. Ideologies simplify reality, and do so in such a way that the majority can view their self-interests in a broad political context. In politics, the alternative to ideologies that have a unifying effect will often be myopic egoism rather than a broad globalization.

Given that modern societies are reliant on ideologies, we could ask whether it is best to adopt one or several ideologies, and whether those that were once predominant should be considered outmoded or still relevant.

We hasten to add that there are very good reasons for why these once predominant ideologies have lost their status as the "last word" on the challenges of the modern world. We should also regard the new liberal ideology as just the latest stop along mankind's ideological evolutionary trail.

From a sociological point of view, all functional social systems consist of a combination of stability and change, of hierarchy and egalitarianism. Ideologies that predominated at certain times in western history over the past 200 years have prioritized these values differently. Conservative ideologies have favored hierarchies designed to ensure stability. Liberal ideologies have campaigned for free competition in an egalitarian market as the best way to ensure development without revolutionary upheaval. Radical left-wing ideologies have regarded equality as a goal that calls for radical change in inherited social systems. Radical right-wing ideologies claim that healthy social change calls for hierarchical policies and institutions that empower those groups deemed best qualified.

We will surely encounter new forms of these ideologies. The most we can hope for, perhaps, is that they will have in impact, in tandem with shifting challenges. But ideologies, on their own terms, are seldom open to pointed correction or in-depth dialogue. Self-immunization ensures that corrective interpretations are explained away. Dialogue assumes that we can get our bearings based on non-ideological categories.

This speaks for an important status of analytical science in modern culture. But it is unrealistic to believe that some future culture will invoke science as its sole basis for authority. And it isn't just the pervasiveness of human prejudice that militates against such an assumption. Objective science, as already mentioned, is based on the objectification of measurable data. This does not provide us with building blocks for meaningful attitudes, with incentives for displacing egoistic interests. Nor do the cultural and scientific ideals of making allowances for all perspectives that can contribute to a conclusion provide a satisfactory answer. In practice, it would appear that no culture is capable of being reconciled with every kind of perspective.

Based on Edward Tylor's definition, even future forms of functional cultures can be expected to rely on ideologies, myths and common belief systems. But living in dynamic societies makes it necessary to constantly adjust these systems, which means acknowledging that they are relative. The ideology of new liberalism, mythical notions of history as a victorious battle of freedom over supression, the belief system related to the UN declaration of human rights—these are all historically relative ideas.

This relativity, however, does not mean that they are altogether outmoded or that important elements could not be transformed to new cultural frames. Nor should the principle of cultural relativity be understood as a reason for reducing culture to a matter of personal taste or to regard cynicism as a sign of maturity. Egotism cannot compensate for the devotion to common tasks that may be a spin-off of collective ideologies. Individual moral considerations cannot completely exclude the necessity of moral simplifications with emotional appeal, deriving from certain myths.

While a society may depend upon culture in the form of ideologies and myths, it may depend even more on common belief forms. It is not just individual quests for meaning—particularly the meaning of suffering—which suggest that religious faith can be expected to remain an important aspect of human culture. Functional considerations about societies' premises, and the necessity of sacrosanct principles to protect a common ethic, all point in the same direction. Again, however, we do well to recognize faith as faith. Cultures that do not allow any critical correction of belief systems tend to slip into fundamentalism with rigid interpretations that block an acknowledgment of reality. On the other hand, cultures that are unrestrained in their criticism of beliefs might easily sink into a quagmire of cynicism, which is inconsistent with a binding morality.

It is easy to say that our ideal should be the ability to believe and yet realize at the same time that our conceptions of reality depend on a culture partly based on faith. It may be far more difficult to keep our feet on the ground, so to speak, when we recognize the cultural relativity of our orientation. This dilemma can only be overcome by including culture in our identification and by understanding the relationship between cultural forms and social functionality, as well as acknowledging our moral responsibility for correcting dysfunctional cultural forms.

Index

anomie/anomic conditions, 75–77, 82, 105, 175–76

authoritarianism/anti-authoritarianism: personalities, types of, 45, 66–67; societies, types of, 45, 51, 53, 65, 84, 97, 153, 163; other references to, 3, 11, 26, 33, 37–38, 45, 50–53, 63–67, 83, 88, 121, 153, 163–65, 180

belief/belief systems: commentary on terms, 10, 16, 24–25, 27–28, 30, 68, 72, 164–65; functional perspectives on beliefs, 2, 27–28, 30, 43, 51, 68, 135, 180–81; belief systems in new liberal thinking, 27, 30, 58, 68, 72, 164, 167, 180; other references to beliefs, 2, 27–30, 43, 50, 58, 63, 66, 69, 72, 110, 135, 164–67, 175, 181

civilization: commentary on term, 6–8, 10, 14, 42–44, 72, 88, 179; western civilization, 3, 6–8, 13, 40, 72–75, 108, 118, 120, 147; other references to, 3, 6–8, 10, 13–14, 23–24, 27, 29, 40, 51, 72–75, 82, 87–91, 100, 118, 120, 147, 154, 162–66, 168, 176, 179

conservatism: commentary on term, 36, 38, 42–46, 58, 180; conservative

interpretations, 6, 9, 27, 38, 43, 64, 85, 137; other perspectives on, 3, 9, 11, 27, 33, 36–39, 42–47, 51–52, 59–60, 62, 95, 137, 174, 176, 180

culture: commentary on term, 7–8, 14–15, 17–18, 32, 59, 72, 88–89, 173; sociological approaches to, 7–12, 14–18, 29, 33, 43, 60–62, 77, 92, 139, 172–73, 180–81; cultural comparisons, 2–3, 7, 18, 28, 65, 72, 89, 100, 110, 121, 159, 178

family/marriage: definition of family, 118–19; family formation, 7, 12, 83–87, 90, 104, 106, 119, 176; dissolution of families, 12, 77, 92–93, 97, 104–5, 107, 118, 120, 122, 124, 129–33; family functions, 83, 88, 90, 97, 107, 111, 118–19, 125–27, 138–42, 168, 175–78; differences between marriage and cohabitation, 90–94, 102, 106–8, 118, 122–24, 127, 134

Fascism (Nazism/National Socialism): commentary on terms, 49–52; Fascist interpretations, 39, 50–51; other references to, 2, 11, 33, 36, 38–39, 49–51, 53–54, 64–65, 103, 164–67, 174